THE GENERAL TO HIS LADY

THE GENERAL
TO HIS LADY

The Civil War Letters
of William Dorsey Pender to Fanny Pender

Edited by
William W. Hassler

The University of North Carolina Press · Chapel Hill

Copyright © 1962, 1963, 1964, 1965 by
The University of North Carolina Press
Manufactured in the United States of America
Library of Congress Catalog Card Number 65-19388
Printed by The Seeman Printery, Durham, N. C.

While visiting Richmond one summer day in 1935, William C. Pender, a rising young Norfolk attorney and grandson of General William Dorsey Pender, decided on the spur of the moment to pay an introductory call on Dr. Douglas Southall Freeman at the latter's office in the Richmond *News Leader* on North Fourth Street. Upon being informed by the receptionist that Dr. Freeman was busily engaged in writing editorials, Mr. Pender begged her not to disturb him and quickly excused himself after depositing his calling card.

Leaving the building and proceeding north on Fourth Street, Mr. Pender suddenly heard his name being called by a gentleman who was straining to catch up to him. This man, of course, was Dr. Freeman who warmly clasped Mr. Pender's hand and escorted him back to the office, apologetically commenting that "any relative of General Pender is always welcome in my office."

During the course of the ensuing conversation that morning, Dr. Freeman inquired whether Mr. Pender knew of the existence of any papers or diary that had belonged to the General. The youthful attorney replied that he knew of none but would inquire and be on the lookout for any. Four years later, quite unexpectedly, he discovered a cache of the General's correspondence in the cellar trunk of his deceased aunt (General Pender's daughter-in-law) whose effects he was perusing. This dusty repository held about two hundred faded but still decipherable letters which General Pender had written to his wife, Fanny, in the years between their marriage in 1859 and the fateful battle of Gettysburg in which he was mortally wounded.

Mr. Pender generously made this collection available to Civil War scholars including Dr. Freeman and Clifford Dowdey. The latter expressed the feeling of all who have read the General's letters when he said, "I was deeply moved by them." Mr. Pender subsequently donated the bulk of his grandfather's papers to the Southern Historical Collection of The University of North Carolina at Chapel Hill.

I first encountered the Pender papers in the course of researching my biography of A. P. Hill, the Confederate commander under whom Pender served during most of his wartime career. My reaction on reading these letters was that those which dealt with the Civil War period provide many refreshing and poignant insights into "the real war" which Walt Whitman prophesied "will never get in the books." With this in mind I undertook the transcription and editing of the General's papers for publication.

Unlike the stereotyped humdrum letters of most soldiers and officers, the vivid personal details of General Pender's animated correspondence sketch an intimate unvarnished portrait of the real man inside the formal gray uniform. His privy day-to-day comments about his personal problems, aspirations, colleagues and military doings, coupled with his husbandly advice and affections, depict an underlying humanity which characterized the truly great leaders on both sides.

In reading the General's frequent missives to "My dearest Wife," one shares the young officer-husband's emotions, struggles, and ambitions as he progresses from Captain of artillery in the Provisional Army to Major General, C.S.A., in command of the famed Light Division. As a regimental commander he confides to Fanny, "I fear I love too much the applause of men," and then rationalizes, "I would like to be a great man for your sake." Further up the ladder he touchingly notes, "This is a most lonely life." By the time he leads a division toward Gettysburg he candidly observes, "Responsibility is a load that is anything but pleasant."

Early in the war the budding officer, self-conscious of his rank and attractiveness to women, engaged in a harmless flirtation with an admirer at Suffolk. When he injudiciously related the epsiode in a letter to his hyperjealous wife she keeps him in suspense awhile before bringing him about with a searing letter (happily preserved and included in the text) which reduces him to a contrite penitent who begs forgiveness.

As Pender matures, his commentaries become increasingly

penetrating and perceptive. Thus he informs Fanny, "What we do not understand we cannot fully explain." He reassures her that "Danger always looks more dangerous in the imagination than in reality." He shrewdly observes that "Men are in some measure ranked in proportion as they rank themselves." His concern for their children's future evokes this notation: "Education is far more precious . . . than money. I want to educate my children if nothing else."

Many of the General's comments on the passing scene are significant and intriguing. Although he respects Jackson's fighting qualities, he has no affection for him and vows, "I never will vote for his being President." On the other hand he shares the army's universal admiration for Lee about whom he writes, "I do not know what we should do if he were taken from us." Pender's letters also afford a new view of Stuart and provide grist for the Hill-Jackson controversy.

This compilation of General Pender's correspondence to his wife comprises the wartime letters that are of greatest interest and relevancy; only a few letters have been omitted that would be of little interest to the general reader. To facilitate reading and comprehension I have paragraphed long uninterrupted letters, inserted punctuation and capitalization, and corrected confusing misspellings where necessary. Otherwise the original text has been preserved intact. Pender customarily addressed his salutation to "My dearest wife" and signed himself as "Your devoted husband." He addressed the envelopes to "Mrs. W. D. Pender." One envelope is especially interesting in that on the lower left hand corner is a notation: "Post-Master please charge W. D. Pender." Minutiae and passages that are boringly repetitious have been omitted. I have endeavored to supply the background requisite for continuity and the identification of the characters, events, and places mentioned. However, no attempt has been made to definitively chronicle or assess Pender's military career. My primary purpose is merely to have the General tell his own dramatic personal story.

In this labor of love I have enjoyed the able assistance of many new friends who ferreted out obscure information relating to the Pender and Shepperd families. My deepest debt is to William C. Pender, grandson of the General and senior partner of the law firm of Pender, Coward, McDuffie, and Addison in Norfolk. In addition to uncovering the Pender correspondence and presenting it to the Southern Historical Collection of The University of

North Carolina Library, he made available to me additional letters and clippings from his private collection, together with rare photographs and memorabilia. He also put me in contact with relatives and friends who were able to supply information about various items mentioned in the letters. Among these were S. Lee Pender, John R. Pender, Katharine M. Pender, J. N. Van Ness, Fenwick Shepperd, Colonel Worth Wicker, the Reverend John S. Spong, Rector of Calvary Church, Tarboro, N.C., Janie F. Allsbrook, Librarian of the Edgecombe Memorial Library, Eliza B. Gray, Mrs. J. Rodes Goodrich, Mrs. Edward Dillon, Jr., and Mrs. T. T. Gilmour. I also am indebted to my daughter, Ginny, for helping with the tedious chore of transcribing the letters, and to Joseph M. O'Donnell, Chief, Archives and History Division at the U.S. Military Academy, who provided me with the West Point records of Cadet Pender. Particular thanks are due the Research Council of Indiana State College for a generous grant which helped make possible the successful completion of this project. A special expression of gratitude and appreciation is due my dear wife, Mary, who patiently read and reread this manuscript and offered many constructive suggestions for its improvement.

CONTENTS

ILLUSTRATIONS

❧

The title page illustration of General W. Dorsey Pender,
C.S.A., is used by courtesy of Kean Archives, Philadelphia.

THE GENERAL TO HIS LADY

INTRODUCTION

Upon receiving a report, which subsequently proved false, that General John B. Hood had been killed at the battle of Chickamauga, General Robert E. Lee ruefully wrote Jefferson Davis: "I am gradually losing my best men—Jackson, Pender, Hood."[1]

William Dorsey Pender, whom Lee thus ranked with the legendary Confederate heroes, was born in Edgecombe County, North Carolina, on February 6, 1834, the son of an "indulgent" father, James, and an "affectionate" mother, Sarah. Dorsey, as he preferred to be called, spent his boyhood attending school, performing chores on his father's farm, and enjoying outdoor recreational activities on the flatlands through which coursed the Tar River.

At the age of fifteen Dorsey began clerking in the store of his brother Robert, fourteen years his senior, who was a prominent merchant in Tarboro. Although he was a conscientious and able clerk, Dorsey soon realized that storekeeping was not his calling. Instead he succumbed to the lure of soldiering and persuaded his cousin, R. R. Bridges, to use his influence with Congressman Thomas Ruffin of the Sixth Congressional District of North Carolina to recommend him for appointment to West Point.

Upon receiving his appointment dated June 24, 1850, Pender left for the Academy where he commenced his training on July 1. Here he met seventy classmates that included "Beaut" Stuart,

1. *The War of the Rebellion: A Compilation of the Official Records of the Union and Confederate Armies* (Washington: Government Printing Office, 1880-1901), Series I (cited hereafter as *O.R.*), 29, pt. 2, 743.

Otis Howard, Stephen Lee, Custis Lee, John Pegram, and Samuel Turner Shepperd.

The "Post Orders" and *Official Register* of the U.S. Military Academy for the period 1850-54 afford little insight into Cadet Pender other than to indicate that he was an above average student who excelled in mathematics and cavalry tactics. His leadership potential was manifest in his progression to Lance Corporal, Corporal, Sergeant, and Lieutenant of the Battalion of Cadets. However, the last promotion subsequently was rescinded because of Pender's failure "to make to the Commandant the written statement on his guard report as Officer of the day. . . ."

Brevet Second Lieutenant Pender graduated on July 1, 1854, standing nineteenth in a class of forty-six. Before taking up his duties with the First Artillery, Pender accompanied Stuart and Shepperd to the latter's family home in Good Spring, North Carolina for a vacation. During this pleasant hiatus near Salem, the handsome olive-complexioned, dark-haired intense young soldier from Tarboro took a fancy to Sam's petite sister, Fanny, who, though only fourteen years old, possessed an "indescribable" fair complexion and lovely voice which enhanced her charms. The host during this visit was the Honorable Augustine H. Shepperd who had served in the U.S. House of Representatives longer than any congressman of his era. Although dutifully respectful, Pender could never feel a warm rapport with this diminutive, strong-willed patriarch.

Upon reporting for duty at the end of the summer, Pender was assigned to serve with the Second Artillery at Fort Meyer, Florida, and later with the First Regiment of Dragoons in New Mexico. Then when the Indian uprisings alarmed the West, Pender rushed to the coast where he experienced all phases of frontier service from scouting to fighting.

During the engagement with the Apaches at Spokane Plains on September 3, 1858, First Lieutenant Pender, according to fellow-officer Lieutenant Lawrence Kip, "was suddenly attacked by an Indian chief. To his dismay, the Lieutenant discovered that his sabre had become entangled in the scabbard and would not draw. Quick as thought one hand grabbed the savage's arm, the other his neck, and in this manner hugging him close and galloping into ranks, he lifted him from his horse and hurled him back among the men, who soon dispatched him."[2]

Returning to North Carolina on a furlough, Pender on March

2. W. A. Montgomery, "Life and Character of Major-General W. D. Pender," Memorial Address, May 10, 1894, p. 7.

3, 1859, married Fanny at Good Spring.[3] A guest at the wedding reception noted the groom's "very pleasant manners and his fine military bearing."[4] The couple honeymooned in Tarboro and Washington before traveling across the continent to the Washington Territory. There at the end of the year a son, Samuel Turner, named for Fanny's brother who had died at Fort Leavenworth, Kansas in 1855, was born.

Leaving his wife and infant son at Fort Vancouver, Pender resumed his scouting and Indian fighting in General Harney's command. During these prolonged absences Pender faithfully wrote lengthy letters to reassure and cheer his anxious and lonesome wife. After his expedition repulsed a surprise attack by 150 Indians on June 25, 1860, Pender wrote Fanny: "Darling do not trouble yourself about the Indians. Fighting is supposed to be my profession, and my wife must get used to the idea." And knowing his wife's ardent desire to convert her husband, who had been raised in an "infidel" home, Pender fostered her hopes by stating: "I wish I could be good enough to become a member of your church." But the frontiersman's tenderest passage was the following one penned on June 19, 1860: "Oh! at night how I would like to have you, even between my rough blankets and hug you to my heart. Always when I go to bed I think 'now my dear Fanny is thinking of me, yes at this moment.' "

Pender's letters to his wife at this time also reflect his healthy outlook. In allaying Fanny's fears for his safety, he confidently avers, "If I may be allowed to claim any merit it is prudence and coolness in an emergency." Again, in advising Fanny about a despondent friend, he exhorts: "The best thing for Marshall is to be kept busy for then he will not have time to be melancholy."

On November 8, 1860, Pender was appointed Adjutant of the First Dragoons and assigned to duty at San Francisco until January 31, when he was ordered to Carlisle, Pennsylvania for recruiting service. Taking a furlough shortly after assuming this new assignment, Pender and his family visited friends in Washington after which they proceeded to North Carolina. During his stay at Fanny's parental home national events rapidly approached a crisis, forcing Pender to wrestle with the question of divided loyalties which vexed all southerners in U.S. uniform. After due deliberation he decided to cast his lot with the Con-

3. The spring at this location now provides water for the R. J. Reynolds Tobacco Company, Winston-Salem, N.C.
4. Letter of W. G. Lewis to D. Gilliam, October 21st, 1893.

federacy and accordingly resigned his commission in the U.S. Army.

At this decisive juncture in his career, Dorsey Pender had just passed his twenty-seventh birthday. As he exchanged the U.S. Army blues for Confederate grays, he cut an imposing figure. About five feet ten in height, he possessed a trim, well-knit figure graced with a dignity and ease of manner. His countenance conveyed both determination and assurance.

Leaving his wife and toddling son at Good Spring, Pender hastened to Montgomery, Alabama for a commission and orders. En route he dashed off a brief note.

THE LETTERS

Wedding photograph of Lieutenant and Mrs. W. D. Pender
Courtesy of William C. Pender

Weldon N.C.
May 8th 1861

My dearest Wife

I received your note this evening but have not had time to open it but I will thank you before doing so. This of all places is the most disgusting I have ever seen. It is perfectly impossible to do any thing with the men here & I shall not try until I get them in Camp. Yesterday as soon as I got here I went and selected a site two miles off, on the opposite side of the river, so I shall be able to keep the men away from here & I hope away from liquor. I shall meet with good deal of opposition in moving off from the men & citizens but now I will. & I hope by the end of the week. I am building houses, and shall have a p.d assured place. Some nice people live near the Camp. It is Garysburg. N.C.

Letter of W. D. Pender to Fanny Pender, dated May 8th, 1861
Courtesy of Southern Historical Collection

High Point, N.C., March 4th, 1861

My dear Wife

Excuse my writing so soon, but I hurried off so unceremoniously that I feel as if I ought to write you. You must be cheerful, and try to make the best of our position. It is bad but might be worse. I did not tell Turner[5] good bye so you must kiss him and make my apology to him. Keep the little fellow in good health. You may not hear from me as soon as you expect for the mail may be stopped, but you shall hear as soon [as] possible. I will write as soon as I get to Montgomery. My love to all. Tell Pamela[6] she must take good care of you. God bless you, darling, and keep you in good spirits.

Your devoted husband
Dorsey

~☆~

Montgomery, Alabama, March 14th, 1861

My dear Wife

I reached here last night after a tedious journey.... I have been very successful so far as I can tell. I was told a few minutes since by Maj. Deas who is in the Sec. of War's office that I have been put down for a Captaincy of Infantry, but that I must not speak of it yet. The pay will be $1350. I shall be pretty well up the list of captains. I applied for the Artillery, not wanting to go in the mounted service anymore.

My own darling be cheerful and believe that I have acted for the best. Col. S. Cooper, Adjt. General of the U.S. Army has resigned.[7] He is a New Yorker, but can not go [for] Lincoln and his Republican friends.... I shall never regret resigning, whatever may turn up. I feel now as I felt then, that I could not serve in the U.S.A.

This place is rather pretty but dull for one who has nothing to do. I shall leave here as soon as possible.... Please be contented at the turn things have taken in our affairs. I have been told I deserve the more credit for anticipating my state.[8]

5. Samuel Turner Pender, eldest son of W. Dorsey and Fanny Pender, was born November 28, 1859. He was named for Fanny's brother and Pender's West Point classmate who died on duty at Fort Leavenworth, Kansas, in 1855.
6. Pamela Martha Shepperd, Fanny's younger sister, was born in 1844.
7. Samuel Cooper subsequently became Adjutant and Inspector General of the Confederacy.
8. North Carolina did not secede from the Union until May 20, 1861.

You will have seen it rumored that Mr. Lincoln has determined to give [up] Fort Sumter, but how true remains to be seen, and if he does it remains to be seen what his real object is, peace or time. God bless you.

Your devoted husband
Dorsey

ϾϿ

Montgomery, Ala., March 16th, 1861

My dearest wife

I have at last received marching orders. I am off for Pensacola, Fla. tomorrow morning at 6 a.m. and without having heard from you. I confidently expected to hear this morning.... I am delighted to leave this place for it is not pleasant to loaf in a large city much less in a small one. General Braxton Bragg is in command at Pensacola.

Things are progressing very rapidly and smoothly. You have no idea how smoothly everything works, that is so far as one can judge. Col. Cooper arrived here last night and has been made Brig. General. When such men as Col. Cooper gives up such a position as Adjutant General of an Army to join us, it looks like earnest. I have heard but one wish about the reconstruction of the Government and that is that it may never take place. The people seem to be perfectly cool and deliberate in all their actions....

I suppose my present destination is only temporary as I have no Company there. I told the Secretary that when my company was enlisted I should like to do it myself and he gave me to understand that just now they had no time [to] recruit but in the course of a few weeks they would probably do so. I have been treated with great politeness by every one. I rather put a feather in my cap by resigning so promptly. They have at least given me a good position. Captain of Artillery, pay $1689.00 per annum. Little better just in these hard times than commencing on a small scale raising stock. I think with the chances of being on the sea coast all the time we will be pretty well off. As soon as I can draw any money I will send you some, in the mean time I hope you will have enough....

You must write to me often.... You shall hear from me soon as I can write after getting there. Darling try and be cheerful.

Believe in predestination so far as I am concerned. In the first place we have no war as yet, and if we do I should have been in it whether I had come here or not. Bred to the profession I could not have had the courage to have stood by without taking a hand. . . .

Now may the Lord protect you and our dear boy. Take good care of yourself. Take plenty of exercize, and visit enough to keep up your spirits. Honey if I knew you were tolerably contented and happy I should feel satisfied. Good bye and write often.

Your devoted Husband

~❧~

Montgomery, Ala., March 16th, 9. P.M.

My darling

The Sec.-of-War has just informed me that he does not want me to go to Pensacola, but remain here for the present, I suppose to work in the office, so you can address your letters here until you hear to the contrary.

Your Husband

~❧~

After receiving his captaincy in the artillery of the provisional army, Pender was sent to Baltimore to take charge of the Confederate security depot. Here he found the state seething with tension as agents from the North and South strove to tug Maryland into their respective orbits.

~❧~

Baltimore, Maryland, March 26th, 1861

My dearest wife

I am longing for a letter from you. Just think I have not heard from you since the second day after leaving you. It would be some consolation to know you had received all my letters. . . . I reached here Sunday night, returned to Washington last night, and came back this morning. Sen. [Louis T.] Wigfall of Tex. telegraphed for me. . . . They all seemed much troubled about the future. . . .

Mr. Wigfall treated me with great kindness, following me to the omnibus, saying that if there was anything he could get for me to write him; he has great influence in the South. . . .

I have no doubt that I shall be as well off here as anywhere else, but darling—I can not feel contented, quiet, or happy away from you. You have become necessary to make me feel all was right. I feel exactly as if some part of me was absent. You ought to be delighted at my occasionally leaving you for it shows me more plainly than anything else that you are my wife indeed. I see women who I can acknowledge are more beautiful than you, but I always say to myself, she is not as pure and good as Fanny. Darling you will appreciate my good opinion of you more by knowing that I am not blinded as to your merits or demerits. Honey, I try very hard to be worthy of you both in act and thought, but I am very bad in some things.

I have not yet told you my business here. I am sending men South to be enlisted in the Southern Army. I merely inspect and ship them. I do nothing that the law could take hold of if they wish to trouble me, but Baltimore is strong for secession, and I am backed up by the sympathy of the first men here. The police, Marshall, and nearly all are with us. . . . Do not fear for me whatever you may see in the papers, for rest assured that in the first place I shall be prudent and in the second I am well backed. I do not want my official capacity to be known except by a few who are with us. You can tell your father, but it probably would only worry him.

My darling how is Turner? Excuse my putting you second in my inquiry—and how are you getting on? Are you cheerful? Try and be so if you are not. . . . Good night.

Your devoted Husband

⚬⚜⚬

Baltimore, Md., April 3rd, 1861

My dear Wife

Your letter dated March 31st has just been received very much to my delight, for several reasons. One that it gave me news from you, and another, that it gives me a chance to burn a complaining letter I had written and to substitute this. In your last you did not tell me a word about yourself and I was fearful that you were not well and would say nothing of your health because you could not say you were well. As to your toe that is a small matter. I sympathize with you but being a soldier can not cry.

I am glad you have whipt Laura[9] and you may tell her for me that if she does not mind she will get a good one from me when I get there. And Turner it gives me so much pleasure to hear all about him, tell me what he can say, and what he does. Every word about yourself or him is of interest to me. It is those little everyday occurences that I like best to hear about.

Honey you asked me in what I am so bad about. You know I conceal nothing from you. You have liberality enough not to blame one for his thoughts if he tries to root them out. You know darling, one of my ruling passions, it possessed me like a devil for a few days, but I tried hard and conquered it. I felt that I would not only be sinning myself, but it would be doing you a grievous wrong, and I felt that I could never meet you again with that confidence that should exist between us. Honey do not think that I am worse than other men, or that I am trying to make myself out better than others. I felt that your letters would be an assistance [to] me, and I told you so. You have asked me a question and I have answered you as I always hope to be able to answer you, and I shall be, as long as I try to be worthy of you. I felt ashamed of myself but could not help it. Darling do not think the less of me, but think what my love and respect for you has saved me from, and treat my faults leniently. . . .

I send you a check payable to your father for $25 on New York. It might be worth at least 7 per cent premium in Salem. If you need more before I see you please let me know. It would be unjust to me not to let me know when you need anything. . . .

As to danger, I am not in the least, for not only are the best and larger number of the people with us, but the police is all right. They have been at the boat each time I have sent off men. I sent off sixty-one in less than a week. Sixty four had been sent a few days before I arrived. . . .

Honey are you satisfied that I love you as I ought, or shall I say and do more, or say less and do more? I feel proud that your family should think so well of me, and complimented at your father's forbearance. I certainly try to be worthy of it, and love them all as much as my own family. . . .

I will write you again soon. Please write me often. You do not know how much pleasure it gives me. I spent a very pleasant day Sunday. Went to church, dined out rode out and visited one

9. Laura Smith was a young Negro servant girl who attended Fanny.

or two nice gentlemen. I went to Bishop Atkinson's[10] old church to hear Dr. Con. He was delightful.

My love to all. Tell Pamela that her good opinion of me is ten fold returned. I think her the prettiest woman I have yet seen, and the most lovable one. It is very evident to every one that Jake[11] is a fine young man.

Enclosed I send you the Flag of the Confederate States. That is our Flag, for it is yours as much as mine and by it you must stick. Own to me Darling that you are a Democrat. You have no idea what satisfaction it would be to have you say. Good bye. I shall try to shop and I think there will be difficulty.

Your devoted Husband

∾⚜∾

The day before the outbreak of hostilities at Fort Sumter, Pender discreetly left Baltimore and sailed down the Chesapeake on a steamer.

∾⚜∾

On board of Norfolk Steamer, April 11th, 1861

My dear Wife

I received today a telegram from Montgomery to go there at once, and after that positive summons, I still determined to go by Good Spring for a day, but after getting on board, Mr. Forsythe one of the Southern Commissioners in Washington told me he had just received a dispatch to the effect that Fort Sumter would be attacked tonight and one of his colleagues told me I had better go as direct as possible, so my darling I shall have to disappoint you.

You must not be troubled at the news, but like a brave woman as you are bear up, reflect that you are not the only wife whose husband will likely be in the trouble. For we can not close our eyes to the fact any longer—war exists. May the God of us all defend the just.

I have not had a letter from you since the one you wrote Sunday last nearly two weeks. Is it just to write to me so seldom. You shall hear from me as often as I can write. I bought you a

10. The Right Reverend Thomas Atkinson, Bishop of North Carolina.

11. Jacob Shepperd was Fanny's younger brother. Only sixteen at the outbreak of the war, he became Pender's aide and was killed at Fredericksburg.

dress today but I fear it shows but bad taste. I had put it off until I had no time to choose. There is enough for dress and duster. If the dress does not suit, think of the intent. It was to please. Write me directed—War Dept., Montgomery—for I go there, but where to from there I do not know. . . .

I am glad to get away from Balto. I will write you as soon as I get to Montgomery and you write as soon as you get this. My own dear wife don't trouble yourself. Recollect that those who do not go into this are the exceptions. It is a good cause. Pray that I may do my duty and be spared. Kiss Turner. I assure you I am delighted to go south, for if we are to have war, I want to be in it. My love to every one.

Write me how you like the dress. I had not time to get any trimming. . . . God bless and protect you my own.

Your devoted Husband

❧

Following the Confederate capture of Fort Sumter on April 13, Lincoln issued a call for 75,000 troops to suppress the "insurrection." When Governor John W. Ellis in Raleigh received a request to furnish the Union with two militia regiments for this purpose, he replied, "You can get no troops from North Carolina." Instead, Ellis proceeded to order North Carolina troops to take possession of coastal fortifications as the state girded itself to enter the war on the side of the Confederacy.

Throughout the latter part of April and May local groups of Tarheels formed companies, each comprised of 109 men, to fill the ten regiments authorized by the state legislature. Soon 30,000 zealous volunteers were swarming into training camps at Raleigh, Garysburg, Weldon, and other concentration centers.[12]

Needing West Pointers to train both officers and raw recruits, Governor Ellis appointed Pender to the rank of Lieutenant Colonel and assigned him to instruct the First (later "Bethel") Regiment encamped at Camp Mangum on the Old Fair Grounds just outside Raleigh. From his new post Pender wrote Fanny on April 28.

❧

12. John G. Barrett, *The Civil War in North Carolina* (Chapel Hill: The University of North Carolina Press, 1963), p. 10; *O.R.* 1, 486; *Histories of the Several Regiments and Battalions from North Carolina in the Great War 1861-'65. Written by the Members of the Respective Commands,* ed. Walter Clark (Goldsboro: Nash Brothers, 1901), I, 3, 75.

My dear Wife

Your letter was received last night—also the letters enclosed by Mr. Shepperd. . . . Your cousin's letter is certainly a fine one and evidently written with the true spirit, and if some of our boasted volunteers had a little more of the same feelings it would be better for us all. The fact is Fanny we shall never be able to do anything until our Southern troops get two or three sound whippings. I firmly believe it would be the best thing for the South. The Southern people—as a class—think our southern man equal to ten Yankees. The idea of their being brought together and having to submit to inconvenience to prepare them for service is something they cannot see the use of. A part of the boasted Edgecombe Company have left, and more speak of leaving. The fact is we shall have a grand bust-up unless things are changed and that soon. I shall not be surprised at any time to find our Camp deserted. I . . . would resign my high rank for something more lowly if I could do so; but I am ordered to remain on duty in the State and have to do what the Governor orders.

. . . Cousin John Bridges has the right notions about soldiering and will be a fine officer. He ought to be something higher than Captain, but he says he is not fit whenever I insist on his getting something higher. Would that all of our big men—and small ones too—could be brought to understand themselves better; for we have several politicians here who are aspirants for military honors, and who imagine that because they know how to inveigle the people to elect them to the Senate, etc. they are capable to perform the most difficult military duties. N.C.'s first appearance as a seceded state will not, I fear, be very creditable.

I hope that if you make a flag for the Salem Company it will be a nice one, but it will be a work of love and entirely useless, for any number could be supplied here as every Company it seems bring us two or three. I am sick of flags as well as other things.

We have all the discomforts here that I ever had in the moutain [during his service in the Western Territory]. It is true Col. [D. H.] Hill and myself have a room together about 8 by 10 feet, a mattress and three blankets apiece, but we have not, either from laziness or something else, got anything to wash our face in. Our breakfast consisted of tolerable coffee, fried ham, and cold bread . . . what our dinner will be it is difficult to say.

But our physical troubles are nothing; I feel just as well and am as well satisfied as if we were at the Metropolitan, it is the worry of mind at hearing so much complaining. However I can stand it all without losing much weight. The men do not complain of hard fare, but restrictions upon their liberty. The old thing for Americans. Tell Willie[13] if he joins a Company for Heaven's sake never utter a complaint at anything. I think he ought to join.

I am delighted at your report of Turner.

Tell Jake I want him to go without loss of time to the Salem Band to see if they will come down here, and to find out the very least compensations they are willing to come for, and let me know as soon as possible. We want to get a Band here if we can get one reasonably; we, the officers, are willing to pay for it out of our own pockets. It would be of immense service.

Darling if you could send me a box of eatables it would be of more service than anything I know of. Substantials not fancies. And if you send, direct to me, Col. ———, Camp of Instruction, Raleigh. If it will be of any trouble don't send it for we can arrange to live here very well.

. . . Col. Hill who had charge of the Military School at Charlotte has command here. He is an able officer of the Army and a very fine man. [Stephen D.] Ramseur is also here. I met him in the cars the night I came down.

It is well you did not come for no good place could be found for you to board and I could have seen but very little of you, it being necessary for me to be in camp at all times, night as well as day. I hope to be able to see you again, but fear not as I dislike to be asking for leave while here, and when I get orders it will be necessary to obey them at once. If I can go to see you without any neglect of duty, I will. I am glad you got Kitty to be with you.

Honey, you must excuse this short and disconnected letter, for I cannot collect my thoughts. Do not trouble yourself about me, imagining that I am dissatisfied, etc., etc. I am well off as any one these times. We all have our troubles and annoyances, every one of us. My love to you all, to Pamela, your father, Jake and W—— [Willie] and you and Turner accept my whole heart. Write me often. I will write every two or three days if only to sign my name.

Your devoted Husband

ᏒᏬᏉᎦ

13. William Henry Shepperd, born 1830, was one of Fanny's older brothers.

My dear Wife

You will excuse my short letters, and the repetition of Volunteer affairs, but really I see no papers nor hear any news. The members of the Legislature come into camp every day which are about the only chance for knowing any news. Mr. Gaston Means of New York—Dr. [A. S.] Ashe's friend—reached here yesterday and said he had difficulty in getting out of the city. Every Southern man who leaves the North now has to do so by stealth. He says there is the greatest enthusiasm amongst all classes. All say we must and shall be conquered. They are taking the lowest scum of society and feting them on all occasions.... They say Richmond must be taken as a military necessity and held. They have soldiers quartered in the Capitol cooking and eating in these fine halls, hanging their muskets on chandeliers, etc.

Persons who have just returned from Washington say they never heard of such desecration in their lives. They are represented as being more like barbarians in their ruinous occupation of all public buildings. It would seem that they do not expect to be allowed to retain possession of Washington or they certainly would not allow the fine rooms of the Capitol greased and injured as it is said they do.

The [North Carolina] legislature I am afraid are not going to better our condition much, they cannot forget that they might want to come again and must act accordingly, that is some of them. If they do not act and that soon, N.C. is a doomed state—either to subjection or eternal disgrace. The Governor calls for ten Regiments of Regulars, some of the Members speak of three thousand. Every one nearly admits that we are totally deficient in military progress, and that volunteers are bad enough at the best. Still they talk of leaving the defence of the state to them, allowing them to elect all their officers. I am disgusted with North Carolina and am convinced that nothing can be done until we are badly whipt.

Governor [John W.] Ellis got $300,000 appropriated last session to buy munitions of war, and after getting it has only spent $27,000, leaving the state without powder enough to fight half of one battle, and if we did not have the arms that have been taken, hardly enough arms to arm a Company. I have told you often that we as a people—and in many cases as individuals are too mean to spend money. The Governor is very much blamed for not having spent the money in arming. I have never seen a public officer as mean in money matters. Even now any proposition that is made that involves the outlay of a few dollars, is answered by the reply, "it will cost too much."

The Regiment elects a colonel today at one o'clock, and if they elect one of the men spoken of, I shall ask to be relieved from duty here, and try to get permission to establish a camp near Salem, provided I am to remain on duty with raw troops.

I hope Turner has gotten over his indisposition and [is] not so cross. I have received in the last few days all your letters that have been following me round as well as your father's. My love to all. Now my darling write to me all about yourself and Turner and what you and Pamela do etc., etc.

Your devoted Husband

ᴥ❦ᴦ

Among the officers of the First North Carolina who subsequently achieved distinction in the Confederate service were Daniel H. Hill, James H. Lane, Robert F. Hoke, and William G. Lewis. The last recalled that instructor Pender "was firm, very courteous, and took extreme care to give these officers the very best advice and instruction. He drilled them as soldiers as well as officers; they all formed a very strong attachment to him and were all sorry to part with him when they were ordered to Virginia. The battle of 'Big Bethel' soon afterward proved unquestionably the excellent results of his training, teaching and advice."[14]

After the First Regiment was dispatched to Virginia, where veteran soldier Gabriel Rains pronounced it "the best regiment" he had ever seen, Pender continued his instructional duties as Commandant of the Camp of Instruction with the Third North Carolina Infantry at Garysburg.[15] *On May 8, he posted a letter to Fanny from nearby Weldon.*

ᴥ❦ᴦ

Raleigh, N.C., May 4th, 1861

My dearest Wife

I received your box this evening but have [not] had time to open it, but I will thank you before doing so. This of all places

14. Letter of W. G. Lewis to D. Gilliam, October 21, 1893.
15. *N.C. Regts.*, I, 76.

is the most disgusting I have ever seen. It is perfectly impossible to do anything with the men here and I shall not try until I get them in camp. Yesterday as soon as I got here I went and selected a site two miles off on the opposite side of the river so I shall be able to keep the men away from here and I hope away from liquor. I shall meet with good deal of opposition in moving both from the men and citizens but move I will, and I hope by the end of the week. I am building houses and shall have a pleasant place. Some nice people live near the camp. It is Garysburg, N.C.

Cousin Robert wrote to me today on his own account and in behalf of Cousin John, persuading me to accept the colonelcy of the 1st Regiment of Volunteers. By a special act of the Legislature it is put upon the same footing as the Regular State Troops and of course the Col. will be the senior Colonel of the State. The Governor has determined not to appoint any Generals, so the Colonel will be the Senior officer of the state. The Gen. will be appointed when wanted and from those who distinguish themselves. The companies have been picked and are in a pretty good way toward discipline—Volunteer—with all these considerations I have determined to accept it if I can get it. John Bridges will probably be Lt. Colonel. We shall be the first in the field—the Gov. intending to send it to Richmond within the next ten days. I shall not be much disturbed whether I get it or [not]. It is for one year and in that time I might be a General who knows! Under all circumstances I shall hold on to my poor little Captaincy.

I had a fine horse presented me today to serve during the war, by Joseph Hyman of [Company C] Edgecombe. If I have to go to Richmond I should be delighted if it were possible for you to come to Raleigh to see me, but you would not be able....

Hope you got the little dresses and were pleased with them, I know you were however. Honey I am very much grieved to hear you are getting so helpless. Pray do not let Turner worry you so much, for certainly where there are so many willing, they could take care of him for you. Try and not have to give up your walk. Have you consulted with Dr. Wharton.[16] If not please do so at once. I would write to Pamela and your father both, but I really have [not] been able to find time....

My own wife try to keep your health and spirits, for we all have enough to contend with these days. Sometimes I feel as if I

16. Dr. Wharton was the Shepperds' family physician.

would give up completely . . . but we all must strive these times. God bless you and our boys.

Your devoted Husband

~�֎~

Garysburg, N.C., May 14th, 1861

My dear Wife

Would that I were with you a few days to rest myself and get a little quiet nap, and then a talk. Honey my previous life has been easy compared to my present. I can hardly believe it, but nevertheless it is a fact, I frequently have not time to think of you. I found myself riding slowly along the road the other day thinking of you and it came to my mind that it had been some time since I had had such a chance. I never forget you at night. Darling it is not because I love you less. Just think I have to play Comdg. officer, Adjt., partly Commissary, and chiefly Q[uarter] M[aster] and head carpenter, besides drill master and general depository of military information. I walk from five in the morning till seven in the evening, but all this I am willing to do, but I can not bear to hear some complain whatever I do. An Angel could not please some of them. They have to be watch[ed] and prevented from doing every thing they ought not to do. If possible they have less forethought or dignity than *our* old soldiers. . . .

Enough of the soldiers. If possible I shall get rid of them. I have been very much flattered not only by the Governor, but by others, but as the effects of that soon wear off, I have nothing but a sense of duty to sustain me and that is growing weak. . . . I have writen to [J. F.] Hoke [State Adjutant General] to relieve me from duty here as soon as he can send one of them in my place. I think I shall write again to Montgomery, to be allowed to recruit my comp'y and if they will permit, I will go in your section of the country for awhile.

Darling your judgment is always good. I had not more than sent the letter saying I would accept the Colonelcy of the 1st Regiment, before I regretted and I made up my mind nothing should tempt me again to commit myself. I received a letter today from Cousin John advising me not to accept any position in our State Army, which advice was useless as I had declined the Governor to accept. I could get most any thing if I chose. I pressed David's[17] and Jake's claims the other day when the Governor passed here on his way to Richmond, and I have sufficient reason to believe they will both be appointed, if the Governor in his great press of business does not forget, which I think not probable. I come out square to any of them when I have anything to say.

It will be rather a fall to go back to Captain in the Confederate Army, for here in the state I am treated with the greatest deference. You would be amused to see how high I carry it, and I find it to be the best way. Men are in some measure ranked in proportion as they rank themselves. If I am to judge from what some of the young gentlemen who have been to Montgomery say, it is well I went before resigned officers became so common, for I became better acquainted and saw more of the big ones than they. Excuse all this self praise, but you see I can not stand praise. As Dr. Hitchcock said I like the approbation of others, and let it affect me. However much I write of self to you, I have enough good sense to not show to[o] much vanity to others.

Honey, your letter was received today, and my own precious wife how I do feel for you, in this time of suspense and suffering, and how sincerely darling, do I hope you may have a long time before you shall have to pass through the same again. I would give anything to be with you, even for twenty four hours about the time of your greatest suffering. Honey submit to anything that may be directed for your good. Take particular pains and not do anything to injure your womb, or injure your figure. Do not worry yourself about Turner during the time, but let others take care of him. You must restrain any desire to do anything that will strain you. . . .

Darling why should Jake make you stop writing, are you so feeble? Please tell me exactly how you are, do not keep anything back, for I had much rather know the exact state of your health than to be left to imagine how you are. . . .

Darling I write you as often as I can. I still enjoy your cake, etc. A Mrs. Moody sent me some nice cake and excellent strawberries today, and has asked me several times to call out to see her. She has invited me to dinner twice, but I have not had time to go. Her carriage will be sent for me whenever I can go. You see I am not suffering. I sleep at Dr. Johnston's who also is very kind and always has a plate for me. He only lives two hundred yards from my tent.

17. David Pender, W. Dorsey Pender's favorite brother, born 1831.

Good night precious and the good Lord watch over you and
our children.

Your devoted Husband

᭗᭝᭗

Garysburg, N.C., May 18th, 1861

My dear wife
Your letter of the 16th was received yesterday. It gave me
great pleasure to see you in such good spirits, and I am also
happy to feel in a better mood myself. . . .
I am tired of working for other people. I want to go and get
my own Company and commence with it. I was telegraphed
yesterday by Judge Howard if I would take the Colonelcy of one
of the Regular State Regiments. You see I am having office seek
me and through a judge at that, besides that I am approached
for letters of recommendation to the Governor. I have heard that
I stand very high with his excellency, and very direct too. Honey,
you will not think me conceited writing you about myself in this
way. I do not speak to others of myself. You know that I did
not in former times put on airs, and I believe I do not now, but
it makes one proud to think that my wife's husband is of enough
consequence to be asked to take a Colonelcy when so many older
ones are seeking it. The idea that Mrs. W. D. Pender's husband,
altho' poor is considered a man of some merit. I always thought
that you deserved something better than a poor insignificant
Lieutenant. I am no more than I used to be but others think I
am and that is more than half. I would like to be a great man for
your sake but I have not the confidence to try. Even if I could
I would be afraid to try a Regiment. . . .
Matters it would appear are coming to a crisis. Troops are
being concentrated very rapidly by both sides at Harpers Ferry
and at Old Point and Norfolk. It is hard to say which would be
better for us, delay or immediate action, for there is no doubt
that they are making tremendous efforts and are organizing much
more rapidly than we. They imagine we are much better prepared than we are. The fact is, our people imagine the only thing
to do to whip the Yankees is to form a few volunteer companies
and go to Richmond and the thing is done. Do not imagine I
fear for the cause. We fight for protection, they for revenge and
stubbornness. I have thought for some time that a little whipping

23

would be of immense benefit to us, not that I wish anything of the sort.

Sunday, 19th
[Same letter]
My own wife, today is Sunday and how it carries me back to those pleasant times at Vancouver when we used to walk to church together, I feeling so proud of my wife, and to hear [you] sing even with that old melodion. Honey, those were pleasant days—especially those spring days of '60. The pleasure of going out and then pleasant anticipation of seeing the baby when we got back. You will say I am getting sentimental; I own up; I do feel so this morning. Not sadly so but thinking of the happiness I have had in the world, and which we may enjoy for many a day. Darling, I am not that cold and matter-of-fact individual always that you seem to think. As soon as I begin to think of Good Spring I go back under *that* shade tree as the most perfectly happy time I ever spent—Oh! how I should like to be with you even this short day, but as it is otherwise, we will not complain. . . .

I shall go to church today if it does not rain too hard. . . . My love to all.

Your devoted Husband

ᘉᘉ

Goldsboro, N.C., May 26th, 1861

My dear wife
I was glad to hear through Jake last night, that you were still well and that Turner was improving. I am on my way to Raleigh where I shall probably be for several days, and I shall try to see you before I return to Garysburg if possible.

Honey after all I have said I have consented to take a Volunteer Regiment, and it is on business connected with the [Third] Regt. that I am going to Raleigh. [Thomas] Ruffin, [Alfred] Scales, [Thomas] Setter, [J. H.] Hyman, [John] Graves, etc. are in it. [Alfred M.] Scales was sent to Raleigh to get [T. L.] Clingman to request the permission of the President for me to take it.

They did it without my consent and concocted it without my knowledge. But when the consent was obtained I felt bound to go. It is the best Regt. yet formed. The election comes off tomorrow, but I was unanimously nominated last night. I know you will hate to hear this but I could not help it.

Jake has been appointed 2nd Lt. in [G. B.] Anderson's Regt. . . .
David . . . will go with me as Commissary of the Regt. . . . Love to
all.

Your Husband

აჭა

*At the end of May, Colonel Pender moved his regiment of
Third North Carolina Volunteers north to Suffolk, Virginia.
Here on May 30, he wrote Fanny, who just two days before at
Good Spring had delivered a second son, William Dorsey, Jr.*

აჭა

My dear wife
We reached here this morning about daylight and got into
camp soon thereafter. There were three other Companies here.
Gen. [Benjamin] Huger came up to look round, besides several
Colonels. The fact is the nearer to the scene of active operations
we get the less my importance grows. My dear wife I hope you
are getting on well. The Lord has been such a good Lord to us
that I can scarcely let myself think that anything seriously amiss
can befall us. Tell Jake that I was hurried while in Raleigh—
having not quite an hour—that I did not have time to see any one
about his commission or orders.
. . . I believe I am getting used to going without sleep for I
slept but little the night I left you and still less [last] night, as we
were packing cases and getting ready to leave which we did about
twelve, and now 8½ P.M. I do not feel sleepy.
Honey you must name our second whatever you please.
Dorsey if you like, anything you wish will be agreeable to me. I
was sorry you were disappointed in it. It was perfectly indifferent
to me. A boy will be better able to take care of himself in the
future. I pray that you will soon be well and strong, and that our
dear Turner is well. You must have little Dorsey for your favorite
for I feel that none can ever be so dear to me as that incomparable boy, Turner; the greatest boy in the world. You have no
idea how I love that "man"; he is of my own raising and training.
There are lots of beautiful girls here, and good many fine
horses, so when I have nothing else to do, I can look at something
beautiful or fine. . . .
Honey I have again to apologize for a short letter, but it is

now tattoo and I must go to sleep. I am well and in good spirits. My Regiment is keeping up its reputation thus far and I only hope it will continue to do so.

God bless you darling. Have your letters addressed to this place until you hear further from me. My love to Pamela. Kiss the children.

Your devoted Husband

ᗯᗲᗩ

Suffolk, Va., May 31st, 1861

My dear wife

I have only time to say I am well and getting on finely. The people are very kind and the Regt. doing well; so all my anxiety is concerning you. My dear wife may the Lord give you a speedy recovery. You must make Pamela write for you until you get strong. Do not attempt to write until you are perfectly able. Oh! how I should like to see you and the "little angel stranger," and dear Turner how I hope he is perfectly restored to health if not thought....

Honey I know you will feel disappointed when you see how short this letter is, but really I can not write more as it is now tattoo, and I have some tactics to study before going to sleep. But I will make up by writing often. You shall receive a good long letter before long.

God bless my dear wife
Your devoted Husband

ᗯᗲᗩ

Suffolk, Va., June 2nd, 1861

My dear wife

I hope you have not been as unfortunate as I have, for not a word have I heard from you since leaving. I do not blame any one, for if your letters got to Garysburg I expect they detained them. But I fear some derangement has taken place in the mail. You must recollect that now five cents in money must be paid, the U.S. postage stamp being of no value now.

We are getting on very well. No sickness of any importance, and no complaining among the men of importance. Some say I am too "damned strict" and others that I am just right. The people are as kind as they can be. We have a delightful camp; fine shade, fine spring water, and good drill ground. I do not wish anything better than to be allowed to remain here long enough to get the Regt. a little in condition. They begin to make quite a presentable appearance, much better than you would suppose. I am now in command of the troops at this place —one cavalry camp, besides our own, and if I chose several post[s] besides this. Four thousand troops are to be ordered to this place, but my own Regt. is as much as I want, and as I can take care of. Altho so near the enemy we are about as ignorant of their movements as you are in N.C. It is said we have a very large force at Norfolk, how many but few know.

I am treated with the greatest kindness by the people. Several invitations to dine today, as well as Sunday invitations to tea. Dined today with the most beautiful girl in Suffolk—and it has [a] great many very pretty ones. . . .

My horse came last night—the one given me by messers Davey and Norfleet. He is really a very fine horse—goes well under the saddle and splendidly in harness. . . . They paid $200. Mr. Davey in addition sent me a nice Dragoon saddle and bridle. It is a fine present and one I very much appreciate. Very few will be able to get a better mount than *your Colonel*. He is a large "bay"— magnificent you might say on his carriage—named "Jim."

My rich relatives—and those only who are supposed to know my inability to buy a fine horse—allow those who are not expected to have any particular interest in me, to present me with a horse. They are willing enough for me to work for the reputation of the family but that is all. Put not your trust in relatives.

Honey I flatter myself that thus far no one need be ashamed of me. I occupy a high position for one so young and have been able to sustain myself so far. I do not feel elated or conceited for the future is before me and I feel the terrible responsibility, and the many chances for me to ruin myself in a military sense.

Darling I have said nothing of you and dear Turner and Little Dorsey, but not because I have not thought of you. I am very anxious to hear from you all and look forward to each mail with hopes which have thus far been sadly disappointed. One consolation and a great one it is I feel that when I do hear you will have gone through the worst and almost ready to be up. I will not allow myself to think but that you are doing well. It is the best way. Honey why should I not be satisfied in this world.

Let me enumerate the reason[s] why I should. A fine **Regt,** nice gentlemen who treat me with the greatest deference—you have no idea how much an affectionate brother, a fine horse, a good mount, the good opinion of the world, and Oh! the best wife in the world. Honey every woman I see has to undergo a comparison with you and none will stand the test, none, none; Oh! my dear wife your husband loves you and appreciates you more than tongue or pen can tell; and to proceed, the finest boy in the world, for I think none can compare with Turner. And last, but I assure you I do not consider it the least, the affectionate love of one such as Pamela. Assure the dear creature that next to your love I appreciate hers next. She is not expected or required to give it and for that reason it is valued the more.

I should be much obliged to anyone who can get your brother's [Samuel's] sword from Willie without hurting his feelings and send it to me by express at once. Tell Jake if I apparently neglect him he must not think hard of me for I have more than I can do. I have not as yet been able to organize my staff and consequently have more than my share of work. I will keep you posted as to my movements.

Your devoted Husband

⁓⋇⋇⁓

Suffolk, Va., June 3rd, 1861

My dear wife

You must expect only a short note tonight. I wrote you a good long letter yesterday, giving you all the news I have to write. I do not know what the papers say as I have no time to read news papers.

My own wife may you soon be well, and I can not but feel that Turner is already restored to his normal good spirits and appetite. My labors are not so laborious as at Raleigh and Garysburg but involve more writing and thinking. I had my first Regimental drill today and progressed very well.

Poor David is the most miserable man you ever saw. He broods over the future all the time. Oh! how blest I am, he who deserves so much happiness should have so much misery and I who am less deserving should be so blest.

Honey you cannot, it seems, believe how much I think of you. I see none who seems to me to be so refined, intelligent or good as you are. Do not trouble yourself if you should miss a day or two in getting letters, thinking I may be ordered from here, for you shall hear of it at once. We are getting on charmingly. I have not yet had time to see my relatives. They [are] plain people but very respectable.

Honey I have not heard from you, so you can imagine how I feel. If it were not for the constant occupation of mind I should [not] be able to remain away any longer. God bless you and the boys. My most affectionate love to all. Get some one to write me often. Good night.

Your devoted Husband

ᔕᔕ

Suffolk, Va., June 6th, 1861

My dear Wife

I have just received Jake's letter dated June 3rd and was very happy that you are getting on so well. According to his account you are doing much better than with Turner. I was glad also to hear that Turner is getting better, but I fear he does not progress as fast as he might. I hope tonight's letter will give you as good an account of you and a better one of Turner.

I stayed with your Cousin Bruce last night at his farm. He has a nice farm and comfortable house. If we had such an one I think I should be content to live on it and work hard for a competency. He treated us with the greatest hospitality, as much so as I ever experienced from anyone. He is all the time alluding to you and seems to think you about the greatest girl he ever saw. . . .

I went down to one of our batteries this morning, and had the pleasure of seeing the tents of the enemy at Newport News, and also one of their steamers. I am in command about here but attend to my Regt. and let other people attend to theirs. I drove my horse back 20 miles in two hours and half—pretty good driving over a wet sandy road.

I am in a terrible mood this evening, so you must excuse me if this letter is not particularly interesting. Tell Jake I am under a thousand obligations to him for writing to me so punctually, and as a reward I will write to the Adjt. Gen. [R. H.] Riddick about his commission, etc. this evening. I have written to have him ordered on duty. That is to say, I have requested it to be done.

By the time you get this I hope you will be thinking of walking about your room. Jake says you look prettier than he ever saw you. He also says the baby is the prettiest baby he ever saw of his age, and that he is the longest one. You must love Dorsey as I said before, for Turner is mine. I raised him and must love him without any rival. The Mother always takes to the younger and the father the oldest.

I have just had the misfortune to lose all the money I had— $25 or $30. But the state owes me forty dollars for money spent for it the last few days. The Confederate states owes me $115.30 which I shall write for at once.

It is a great pleasure to have David with me, for besides his being my brother he is very efficient. Enclosed I send you a news paper article. Some other time I will try to tell you who wrote [it]. I was told today by Maj. [W. G.] Lewis, who lives in Raleigh, that I had a very high reputation there. But here I am writing of myself again. You know however that I like approbation, but more particularly that you should know that I am doing credit to Fanny Shepperd.

Why does not Pamela write to me, or would it be improper? I think she could write to me merely telling how you and Turner are. But for Jake I suppose I should have to remain in ignorance as to how those most dear to me were. Jake said in his letter of the 3rd that you wrote me the next day. I am anxiously looking for the mail. I received Pamela's letter this afternoon so you need not tell her what I said about her not writing. Her description of your state delighted me very much.

I have just returned from an elegant supper where we were handsomely regaled. As it is past 10 o'clock and I get up at five I must close. God bless you and the boys. Good night.

Your devoted Husband

❧

Suffolk, Va., June 9th, 1861

My dear Wife

I was very happy when I received your letter, and instead of scolding, I blessed you. You have been blessed honey in your confinement most assuredly, at least up to last dates. It came on earlier, before the hot part of June and July and then you could not have been better than you have. I wish you were perfectly recovered, I should be tempted to have you come down to see me. This is the most pleasant little town I ever saw. The kindest and most hospitable people I ever saw anywhere. The ladies keep my table covered with flowers and smile on me in the most bewitching manner and some of them are certainly like pinks. The colonel is quite a lion. Do not be jealous for none of them have the attractiveness of Mrs. W. D. Pender. I have not failed to let them know that I am married for *poor creatures I do not wish to destroy their rest.*

We have had various rumors in the last few days, but as long as we remain here we shall not be hurt unless accidentally. They have enough to do on the North side of the James River. It is supposed here that Gen. [J. B.] Magruder made an attack on their camp at a place called Newport News about 25 miles from here across the James River yesterday for both musket and cannon firing was heard and seen from this side of the river, and four steamers soon thereafter took more troops to them. Newport News is an encampment they have back of Old Point and on the James River.

General Magruder is stationed at Yorktown 7 or 8 miles from them. The impression is gaining ground that they have not as many men in and around Old Point as was supposed. We have at least 25000 to 30000 men within 7 or 8 miles of Norfolk, and no doubt could attack their camp if necessary. The troops here are intended I suppose as a reserve for Norfolk or Richmond, and also to prevent their getting possession of the Petersburg and Seaboard roads which cross near here; and which if in their possession would completely cut Norfolk off from speedy succor, and therefore important even if fighting should not take place here. To get here they would either have to march twenty miles or come up a small and difficult river, in [the] latter case their approach would be known.

They had a little affair at Yorktown two days ago, in which their steamer Yankee was badly handled. Our first Regt. is there. Our 2nd at Norfolk in a swamp. So far as location is concerned we have the best of any troops in this section of the state. We are at the head of several springs, where we have plenty of good spring water and shade, and in the way of eating everything that we could wish. We could not be more comfortably situated.

As to the war I know but little—having to get nearly all our information from the papers. Eighteen miles below us at the mouth of this river—the Nansemond—at what is called Pig Point Battery they had a little firing three or four days ago dismounting two of our guns, but hurting no one. The steamer was supposed to have received several shots. We are drilling four times a day having Regimental drill once each day. In two or three months we shall make quite a presentable appearance. I will send you a piece from the "Christian Sun" printed here, which had a word concerning us. I told you I intended to get dignified when I was made Colonel—recollect when we first came home.

Mary[18] gave me a good scolding for giving David a position, but has since relented and sent her love. David says he shall make Mary go with you and Pamela this summer. Do not fail to go. By the way let me give you the fashion here in summer dresses. Cape something like you have seen on the old fashioned overcoats or rather more like the one on your cloak. I have seen several and they wear no shawl, etc. and it looks very pretty, particularly for good and small figures. Material on the same style as yours. Honey I hope they have not let your figure be spoilt by not keeping your bandage sufficiently tight. Anything, but do not lose your figure.

I am troubled to know when I shall be able to get any uniform, for [I do not know] where the money is to come from. . . . I have money due but do not know how to get it. North Carolina owes me $40 which I get tomorrow.

Someone told your father that he had offended me by the way he spoke to me the day you were sick, for he spoke to me about it and said he was excited, but did not intend to hurt my feelings. I accepted his apology and allowed him to keep his hat on. I hope he has not worried you much during your sickness.

We had service in camp twice today. Our Chaplin is a Methodist but a very sensible man. Brother of Major Andrews of Vancouver. Great many of the ladies came out this after[noon] to hear our service and remained over to dress parade. They are getting to come out in numbers every evening and bring us bouquets, etc. etc. dish like apple dumpling. We have dress parade without the music. I would [pay] $25 per month out of my own pocket for a band. . . .

We had a grand time Thursday—the day appointed by Mr. Davis for fasting and prayer. Honey write me as often as you feel like it. I will write you again tomorrow. We had a false alarm last night and the men altho excited showed fight. It was nothing but some one deviling the sentinel and he hollered for the Guard.

Tell Pamela I again take back anything I had said about her not writing. She is a dear creature and it makes me feel proud to

18. Mary Pender was the wife of David Pender.

have her say she loves me so well. I should like so much if you both could be here.

Your devoted Husband

~❦~

My dear wife

I received a letter from Jake tonight without any date, but he stated you had written, I know it is of late date. By the time I get a letter dated as late as today saying you are still doing well I shall feel that you are again beyond trouble. I was sorry to see by Jake's letter—at least I imagine—that Turner is not recovering as fast as he might. I wrote Brother Robert that we were disappointed in the baby and had to change the name from Ruth to Dorsey, and that I had hoped that it might be like you. We must hope that if you have to undergo the same thing again— which God forbid—it may result more to our wishes than this time.

I rode my horse to drill this evening, and cut up considerably at first but tamed down before the drill was over. . . . We shall soon be worth seeing. Whenever [a] good many people are about looking at us, I always wish you could be by. People take me to be over thirty, because as they [think] I have such a high office. I am probably the next to the youngest Colonel in the service. But I would willingly give it up for my own proper Compy.

It is generally believed here that our troops have given the Federal forces a good whipping at Newport News on the opposite side of the James River. They have apparently been fighting two days and the firing recedes towards Old Point, and they have certainly had to break up their camp. I have no doubt but they have been whipt after continued and hard fighting for many hours. If the state of affairs should be as we suppose from all the indications, it will be glorious news to the world. The only trouble with us here is that we are as secure here as you are at Salem, at least while we stay here. The people here seem to feel perfect security from attack or interference.

Honey I am in as perfect health as I ever was and as well satisfied as I could be away from you. I should like to see you, but there is no chance. I have to refuse others and of course could not take a leave myself; besides I would not be willing to leave the Regt. in the hands of anyone else. Not vanity, but things would not go on as I would have them. I think every one has confidence in me and the men rather fear me I think. I sometimes hear the men question an order, and when told it is the Colonel's directive they say no more.

Now my dear wife I must close. My love to all. Kiss Pamela and the children for me, and may Our Father in Heaven protect and bless you and the little ones. Try to get some good grown nurse to remain with you, so that you will not have to worry too much with the children. Write me whenever you feel like it. Tell Pamela and Jake I feel very grateful for their kindness in keeping me infomed as to your condition.

Your devoted Husband

꙳

Suffolk, Va., June 12th, 1861

My dear wife

I was a little disappointed this evening in not hearing from you, but hope it is not a relapse that has again prevented anyone from writing. It was nothing more than I expected for you to have a fever, and my mind was very much relieved when I heard you had passed that ordeal. I sincerely hope you may soon be well, but let me beg you darling not to exert yourself too soon or too much; recollect honey how any indiscretion will trouble you for life. . . .

We got news today confirming what I wrote you as to our surmises about the fight. The 1st N.C. Volunteers with some companies of Virginia troops making about 1000 were attacked the 10th by between 4000 and 5000 Yankees and after a hard fight the Yankees fled in great confusion, being pursued four or five miles. We lost one man, they several hundred. Their Colonel was killed while trying to rally his men. Our men were apprised of their approach by one of our men who had deserted and returned in time to give the alarm. Our men [were] behind intrenchments. The Yankees intended to surprise our men but were foiled by the timely repentance of the deserter. Does it not seem that The Lord of Hosts is on our side. It certainly [is] a glorious thought that the troops of the old North State should win the first pitched battle, and so gloriously. The fighting continues near Hampton. We can hear the guns all day and all the reports say that they are being driven back on Old Point. The only thing

I have to regret is that we are on this side of the James River. I know our boys would give a good account of themselves. I am proud of my Regt.

I started to Raleigh this morning, and got off the train after it started in consequence of reports in the papers. I started to have a row with the Governor and get what we need and have been promised or give up my command in the service. I have been fooled with long enough and am determined not to stand it any longer. We are not yet fully equipped and have not been treated as well as the others. I send Capts. [Thomas] Ruffin and [Alfred] Scales tomorrow to raise a row in Raleigh or get the things. I am not Lt. Pender any longer but Col. Pender knowing my position and worth. As an officer I know thay have none who stand higher with the people, and if they force me out of the service it will be their look out.

We keep tomorrow holy as a day of fasting and Prayer, set aside by President Davis. I never looked upon any fast day before as I do tomorrow. I feel that we certainly have cause to thank God for the many instances of his goodness and Divine Protection. We have service in camp as well. I was invited this morning by the Rev. Mr. Hayne to make a few remarks to the citizens of Suffolk in church assembled, which I had to decline.

Now Darling I must close. Do you want me to write you the war news from time to time or not. I know you are woman enough not to be troubled as much by the true statement of facts as you would by the various rumors you will hear. Honey when you get well enough write me often. Now, Darling, my own Darling may God bless you and the children and preserve us to a good old age for each. My love to Pamela and the rest of the family.

Your devoted Husband

❧

Suffolk, Va., June 13th, 1861

My own dear wife
I sincerely hope you are not worse, but as I have not heard from you for two days I fear and cannot help it, that you are worse. God grant that my fears are without any ground. As long as I know you are doing well I feel quite contented, for I have not time to trouble myself unnecessarily, but when my fears are

aroused I get low spirited. Oh! darling I would give anything to see you tonight, if only for a few hours. . . .

It is late honey and I had but little sleep last night so I must close. We had a fine sermon today and I enjoyed it very much. God bless you darling and give you a speedy recovery.

Your devoted Husband

Suffolk, Va., June 13th, 1861

My dear wife

I was delighted this evening by the receipt of two letters, one from my dear wife and one from Pamela. . . .

Honey you have no idea how delighted I was to hear that you were walking about the room, and the next thing I want to hear is that you are completely restored. Poor little Turner, how much he must have been reduced. Do you not think that the less flesh he has while cutting his teeth the better it will be for him.

Honey you say it is not fair that I should give all my love to Turner instead of dividing it with Dorse. I have no doubt but that after I become well acquainted with the latter I shall love him as well as Turner, but Turner is such a dear boy, and the other I have had such a short acquaintance with. In the meantime I know your heart is large enough to give him plenty to exist on. . . .

Good night my own precious darling. My love to all.

Your devoted Husband

Suffolk, Va., June 18, 1861

My dear Wife

I was delighted this evening by receiving a long letter from you dated 16th. You are a brave woman and one worthy of a braver husband. Jake's note was received also, and the result of his visit was as I feared it might be. As to what advice to give him I am at a loss. Going in the ranks would go hard with him, and every position in my regiment is filled. If he wants to see some of the war the only thing I know for him to do, is either to volunteer in some company that has already been ordered out of the state, or come and stay with me. I will be very glad to have him come and stay with me as long as he chooses. If he were to go without volunteering, I would have him live with me. But if he were to volunteer he would have to take his chances with the others, and could not expect to see much of me except officially.... Tell Jake that anything I can do for him will be done with great pleasure.

It is generally rumored and believed here that Harpers Ferry has been evacuated and from necessity, and that is about the only military news that I have heard that I have not written you.

Some of my men caught three men from Old Point yesterday. They are Virginians, and to my mind are clearly traitors, and I accordingly sent them to Gen. Huger at Norfolk to be dealt with as he might think proper. Two deserters from our troops at Norfolk were also taken up by my men, who have also been sent back. One of the men who had come from Old Point says they have about twenty thousand men as well as he could judge. Whether it be the truth or not, I do not know.

Mary wrote me a letter the other day begging me to let David go home for a day, but I had to write her tonight saying I could not as I had determined to let no one go unless absolutely necessary. David would not go if I were willing for he sees what a position it would put me in. He says if necessary he will have to resign. Mary has been sick abed, but is better.

David is a very efficient man and I should dislike to lose him, and besides he has gone too far to turn back and I shall try to prevent him from resigning. I beseeched Mary not to force him to resign, by her continual repetition of her sorrow. I sent her your letter, under pretext that she probably had not heard from you lately, but in reality to show her how a brave and good woman could resign herself to the necessities of the times.

How much better honey, for you to do as you do, than as she does. I could not go to you anyhow, and you make me much better satisfied with the separation. Oh! darling you are a brave and good wife and the Lord will reward you. You have not been blessed beyond your desserts, and the Lord will certainly reward you still further.

I wrote you I had sent Capts. Ruffin and Scales to Raleigh after some things for the Regt. They were completely successful, and the Regt. is now as well equipped as any in the field.... I was not light upon the Governor, for the way we had been sent off with promises, all of which had been broken. In reply he wrote the kindest letter you ever saw, saying to let him know what I wanted and he would attend to it in person.

I find I am not capable of getting on with politicians who do not mind breaking their word. I believe them and they deceive me. Tell Jake if he wants to go with volunteers to come to us. Now my darling I must close as it is late. I wrote to pappa tonight.

I write to you nearly every night. My love to all. Try to have sufficient nerve to bring Dorsey into subjection.

Your loving Husband

෴

Suffolk, Va., June 23rd, 1861

My dear Wife

I was doomed to disappointment last night for I had expected a nice letter from you, but instead I received a short note from Jake merely saying that Fanny had been sick but was better and was supposed to have caught cold. My dear wife it pained me to hear that you had had a relapse, and darling, how homesick it made me. Oh! how much I would give if this war was at an end and we could be allowed to live happily together as we have always done. I sometimes feel that if it were manly and honorable I would be willing to give up all hopes of distinction and military ambition, to live quietly with my wife and children. But anyone with a military education is in honor bound to come forth these times and defend his country against the countless thousands of the unprincipled villians.

It is no use for me to dream of home and quiet as long as the war lasts. But that shade tree will rear itself in my memory and oh! that happy day. Darling, I should like to know that you were well enough to enjoy it in my absence. It was the happiest moment of my life. You may think it foolish to always be talking about the tree near the garden gate.[19]

Darling, I pray that nothing serious is the matter with you, that you have not caught cold in your breast; and if you have, it

19. Pender also refers to this tree in his letter of May 19, 1861. His allusion is to the tree at the gate to the Shepperd home in Good Spring. Lying on the grass beneath this tree one summer day, surrounded by his loved ones, he experienced what he later described as "the happiest day of my life." Samuel Turner Pender, the General's eldest son, described this incident in a sketch of his father published in the *South Atlantic Magazine,* 1877 (cited hereafter as S. T. Pender's account).

will produce no serious inconvience. You have not told me how you got on with it this time. And Turner, notwithstanding all your reports to the effect that he is getting well, I fear he is not all right. Why should he be so long in getting well. Here it has been nearly four weeks and still the report is he is not well but improving rapidly. Honey please let me know precisely how you both are. I had rather know the whole truth than be left in suspense. . . .

I wish it could be so you could come down to see me, but it is too hot for you and the baby and again I might leave here while you might be on the road. I think the best thing is not to give the notion a thought, for it is impracticable.

We hear various war rumors but they nearly all turn out to be either totally false or very much exaggerated. It is expected every day that they will have a big battle at Manassas Gap. I sincerely hope they may, for it may tend to a settlement of this question. The evacuation of Harpers Ferry is considered a fine move, for all the machinery had been moved and it was no more than any other small town in the mountains, whereas Winchester, the present position of Johnston's command, holds in check two large bodies of the enemy and protects the entrance to the great Valley of Virginia. Nothing but the above move and one or two little skirmishes have taken place since the battle at Bethel. . . .[20]

A lady offered to make me a cap the other day; I told her if she would make a net for a lady I would take great pleasure in sending it to you, whereupon she said she was not going to make anything for my wife. I think she goes on the principle of your Mobile acquaintance, that she had rather gain the attention of a married man than a single one. She can try on me, and see who is the loser. She has intimated once or twice that she had fallen in love with me. My servant says that when he takes my horse through town they all ask whose horse it is and winds up by saying that they know it is Col. Pender's.

Now my own dear wife, let me know when you are sick. Make some of them write to me when you are not able. You may judge how much I like to hear from you by your own feelings. My love to all.

20. On June 10, 1861, Union troops under Major General Benjamin F. Butler were repulsed at Big Bethel, Virginia, by a small Confederate force under Colonel John B. Magruder. The only Confederate casualty was Private H. L. Wyatt of Colonel D. H. Hill's First North Carolina Regiment. J. G. Barrett, *The Civil War in North Carolina*, p. 30.

May the Great God protect us all and bring us together for a long and happy life.

Your devoted Husband

ᨏᨏᨏ

Suffolk, Va., June 26th, 1861

My dear Wife

Let me state my grievances in the beginning and I shall be in a better mood to finish up. Have you not neglected me in your pleasure at Spring House. You say you were well when Dr. Wharton got to see you Thursday, and altho' you had not written for several days, still you put off writing until the next Monday. . . . Was such delay justified by my treatment of you. . . .

You say you are going to have the baby christened, but do not tell me who is to be the God father or to represent me. I would not deprive you of the pleasure of having it done by the Bishop, but do you not suppose these little questions of any interest to me, or have you taken me literally when I say I love Turner and you will have to love this baby. As to the reason, I have nothing more to say than I have already said.

I was at a little gathering two nights ago, and had a very nice time dancing and flirting with a very nice girl. I am trying to get her to knit you a sac for the hair, but she said that she is not going to work for my wife, but will do anything for me. . . .

ᨏᨏᨏ

Suffolk, Va., June 28th, 1861

My dear Wife

. . . I received a letter from Custis Lee tonight. He is in Richmond engaged upon the defences around the City. He is Major of Engineers in the Va. Army. Beaut Stuart is Colonel and also John Pegram. They have gone to the Western part of Va. with General [R. S.] Garnett. I should like to be with them. I am getting tired of staying here doing nothing but drill in the dust. Everyone is getting tired of loafing, and if we stay here much longer, my troubles will increase, for some of the Regt. are getting to behave differently from what I could wish. Still they are the best set of men I ever saw, and I would not leave them for anything in the world, except my dear wife and children.

I would indeed like to see Turner. If you could hear me brag on my wife and child you would suppose no one ever had a wife or child before. Custis wishes to be remembered to you particularly. He mentioned my desire to leave here to join his father [R. E. Lee]—who is Commander-in-Chief and he said he would move me as soon as he could. . . .

Honey, I had determined to write for you but our stay here is so uncertain that I think it would be wrong to let you come down. I should be more than happy to see you, but I do not want to stay here two weeks longer.

Do not make flags for we can get along very well without. If you have time and want to do something don't let what I say prevent you, for I only do not want to put you to any unnecessary labor, when you have so much to do. . . .

Your devoted Husband

ঙ✿চ

Suffolk, Va., June 30th, 1861

My dear Wife

You see I am still constant in my correspondence, and so I intend to continue. We have nothing under the sun new. The only change from the monotony was the death of one of our men today. Poor fellow, he had been sick for over a month with various diseases: diarrhea, measles, and finally typhoid fever, brought on by his own imprudence. Fortunately, he has neither mother nor wife to mourn his loss. We intend to send his remains home if I can get permission for two men to take them. We have [a] great many cases of measles but very mild, for out of two hundred and sixty none have died.

Mary has been in bed nearly all the time since her arrival and I have not seen her since the first evening she got here. I went twice and failed; tonight she was better but I could not go down. She will go home in a few days, as we have the measles and the town people have the diphtheria. Even if you were able you could not come under these circumstances.

I received a very affectionate note from Ham[21] yesterday which I shall answer as soon as I get the chance. Honey I know you would fully appreciate my letters if you knew how I have to steal the time to write them. Scarcely a night that I do not have to write from two to six letters. During the day I have to be on the go or studying tactics.

21. Hamilton Shepperd was Fanny's elder brother, born in 1836.

To show you what a favorite I am with some of the ladies, yesterday one of them had two peaches—all the way from Georgia—given her, she ate the small one and kept the large one for me with the request that I should eat it all. You see I have good friends. They say if I get sick I shall be taken care of. They all manifest the greatest curiosity to see you. I tell them you are great on talent and music and pretty considerable on looks. If you should ever get this way you would have to exert yourself to sustain the reputation you have. David says everything I do is complimented. They certainly treat me very politely. Everyone bows and says "how are you Colonel." I know but few but speak to all.

I shall write to Dr. Wharton tonight for his mare. He wrote me I could have her for $200 credit. I may or may not need two horses, but if I should not, I can sell her for at least as much as she will cost; and if I should need her, it would be bad to be without her.

The Doctor wrote a very nice note in answer to mine. I thanked him for his kindness to you and Turner.

Mary complains very bitterly of you for not writing her. She said she wrote you as soon as she received the news of the birth of the baby, but had not heard a word from you. I told her you had not been able.

I received a very nice pair of shoulder straps yesterday.

Good night, Darling, and may you continue in good health and spirits. I have been hard at work today mustering the troops.

Your devoted Husband

≈❧≈

Pender's frequent allusions to his harmless flirtation eventually evoked the following letter from Fanny which she significantly prefaced by admonishing her husband to "Read to end."

≈❧≈

Read to end

Good Spring, June 30th/61

My dear Husband

I will try to answer your letter fully and definitely, and hope it will give satisfaction. It is true I was well when the Doctor arrived, but I was not out of bed. I had been keeping very quiet for fear of a return of the chill—I sat up for a little while on Friday, but the fever had left me as weak as a baby—I gained strength very rapidly, however, and would have written to you on Saturday, but there was no mail until Monday, so I deferred writing until Sunday—I wrote as well as I knew how, little thinking that the letter which gave me so much pleasure in writing should be the cause of so much complaint.

As to christening the baby, I had just heard that the Bishop was to be here and thought it would be the only opportunity I should have for some time. I should, of course, much prefer your being with me on such an interesting and solemn occasion, but would I be justified in postponing it? I intend to have no God-parents—Father will of course represent you. I did not know, before, that you attached so much importance to the rite of infant baptism, or I should have written more at length about it. The name I only proposed as a joke—no, Mr. Pender, I have ever had too much respect for your opinions—or fancies even—than to wish to act in opposition to them.

You could not expect Jake to write as definitely as I could have done. I have tried ever since you left to have you informed as to mine and Turner's health, and if the letters were not written exactly as you wished, I could not help it—remember, Mr. Pender, that I am not quite as strong as I might be, and I have a good many duties to attend to that distract my attention from the sheet before me. I never sit down to write a letter that I do not have to get up half a dozen times to perform some little service either for the baby or someone else. And often, I attempt to write with both children screaming in my ears and indeed, indeed I never intended to neglect you. It was but natural that I should be glad to see my favorite brother from whom I had been separated three years.

I have never in the whole course of my married [life] done anything deliberately that I knew would pain you—your will has always been my law—and I have ever tried to *obey* to the very letter the commands of my Lord and master. You have indeed fulfilled your duty in writing to me, and I have blest you a thousand times for it. . . .

You say that the ladies seem to think I am a very *superior woman*—it would be a great pity to [undeceive] them, and might detract somewhat from your distinction—so I had better remain, for a great many reasons, where I am. . . .

"I was at a little gathering two nights ago, and had a very nice time dancing and flirting with a very nice girl. I am trying to get her to knit you a sack, but she says she is not going to work for my wife, *but will do anything for me.*" Now, I ask you candidly, in your sober senses, why you wrote me such a thing as that? Was it to gratify your vanity by making me jealous, or to make me appreciate your love still more? You are very much mistaken. I feel indignant that any woman should have dared to make such loose speeches to my husband and that he should have encouraged it by his attentions, for you must have gone pretty far for a woman to attempt such a liberty.

My dear, ever dear Husband, do not think this is only a little jealous feeling—I know it will amuse you now, but the time will come when you will remember it. I never thought to hear that he, whom I loved above all the world, whom I respected and esteemed till now, would stoop to listen to such improper language —do you think the lady would have made such a remark in my presence? Then it was not proper for you to hear. I never expected to hear you admit that you had been *flirting*. What would you think to hear me use such an expression? And would it be more immoral in me than in you? I did not think you would trifle with my feelings in that way in the future. I had rather not hear these things. You cannot, of course, intend to give me pleasure by mentioning them.

I know you love me, my dear Husband. I have had too many sweet and precious proofs of it to doubt it now. You have ever been the kindest and best of husbands, and I have loved the very ground you trod upon—the very air you breathed. I have tried to please you. God knows I have—I have tried to consult your wishes in everything—and do you think even if I did not write exactly when you expected it, that I deserved such a letter? I cannot think what reason you could have had for it, you ask me to look over and forget it—I have forgotten all the anger I felt at first—but I can never forget that letter—nothing you have ever said —nothing you have ever done, nothing you have ever written in this whole of our married life—ever pained me so acutely or grieved me so deeply. I know you are sorry for it now, for you must feel it to be unjust, but it is enough to know that you could, in any mood say so much to pain me. . . .

Turner is the dearest little fellow. I know you would love him more than ever if you saw him. He is getting right fat again.

Little Dorsey is a beautiful child for his age—I am really getting to love him a good deal. . . .

All send love to you. God bless you!

Your faithful Wife

Pender returned Fanny's letter of the 30th with this notation.

❧

Suffolk, Va., July 2nd, 1861

Fanny—

If you wrote the foregoing deliberately and premeditatedly please retain this letter as evidence in the future, that you have torn my heart, that you have brought tears, bitter tears [to] the eyes of one who has loved you and tried to honor you. Oh! Fanny my letter was cruel, but you have surpassed me. The imputations are certainly hard to bear. Vanity is one of my weaknesses, but God knows not to such an extent as you charge. Let me not believe that this letter is a forerunner to such misery as it might indicate. I have loved life dearly, but tonight I feel that this war had no terrors to me. I at first thought that I would read part of it to David, but I could not bear that anyone should know that I had ever received such a letter from my wife. I felt the want of support under this the greatest blow I had ever received. Not only a Tyrant but a vain unprincipled wretch.

Your Husband

❧

Three days later a hurt and remorseful husband unburdened his feelings in a letter postmarked Old Town, Virginia.

❧

My dear Wife

To my great surprise I received a letter from you today which I assure you afforded me the most sincere pleasure. You will excuse me for alluding to the subject, but really I should not have been surprised if I had not received any more letters from you. I had about made up my mind that we were henceforth to be as strangers. You will be surprised at this confession, but Honey I could not see how you would ever write me such an affectionate letter again, and darling, if you knew what I have suffered since receiving this letter you would believe that I was not putting on.

Oh! Fanny, Fanny, how could you suppose a dishonorable act, for if as you say *"the young lady* acted dishonorably and I must have encouraged her," I was acting in bad faith and again darling you accuse me of prevaricating when I said I wanted to see you but that you had better not come down, which would have been prevaricating if my intentions had been as you intimated.

That letter was in my mind awake and sleeping, and again and again would my grief have to be relieved by tears. If you had simply said I do not love you I could have stood it, for I should have known that you did not mean it, but to accuse me of dishonorable acts. But honey let it pass with the last remark that if you knew how much I suffered you would believe me sincere [in] what I've said.

. . . It is certainly lonely enough [here] to satisfy a monk. I feel as if we had been laid on the shelf for the war. No chance for us having a fight I fear. . . . God bless you.

Your husband

෴

Early in July Pender moved his regiment to Camp Ruffin at Ben's Church near Smithfield on the James River. On July 9, he wrote:

෴

My dear Wife

Anxiously do I look forward for tomorrow as I expect your Sunday letter. It takes one day longer for us to get our mail than at Suffolk which is quite a deprivation. Our mail today fail[ed] [to arrive] from some cause or other.

You will see that I call this place Camp Ruffin. It is in honor of Judge Ruffin. I did not know anyone whose name would confer more honor than his. The location and appearance of the camp is anything but agreeable in looks or in comfort. We had to clear out an immense thicket, dead vegetable matter of which now smells terribly in my tent. Speaking of my tent, it is a very nice and large one, and I have it all to myself. It is nearly large [enough] for a family. . . .

We have three camps stretching over about 3½ miles. Four cos. at two of the camps and two at the third. We can see all the movements of the enemy by water, at Newport News. It would amuse you to see the curiosity evinced by our men at every movement of theirs. I suppose you will have seen Lincoln's message.

He calls for 400,000 men and $400,000,000 to make quick work for our subjection.

I hope the work will be done quickly for we are more able to cope with them now than we shall be after they have drilled more. Undrilled we have all the advantage. I look forward to a large engagement near Martinsburg with great interest. It will test our relative strength. With anything like even numbers the thing would be certain, but looks as if they were to precipitate two armies upon Gen. Johnston either of which is larger than his. Let it come and may God defend and strengthen the just. If we are worsted then we can try it again and again and the result will be the same. They cannot conquer us.

I wrote Ham the other day I believe and ought to have an answer soon. What is Jake going to do. I see that the Regt. that Ham and William are with has been accepted into the service of the Confederacy. Who are their field officers? I hope they may get good ones. But I wish still more that we all could go home and have peace and quiet.

Honey this is a poor letter, from necessity not for the want of inclination. My love to all. I would write to some others of the family, but I am on the go all day between the camps and when night comes I feel but little like writing. My own dear wife, may you have good health and strength, and may the children keep well. How I should like to see you all. Darling how are you off for money. Let me know, for I have plenty to send you. I have near $100 in cash and $200 due me.

Good night and may God bless you.

Your devoted Husband

🙙🙙

Camp Ruffin, Va., July 11th, 1861

My dearest Wife

Your letters dated July 5th and 7th were received night before last and read with the most profound pleasure. I felt darling as if I had given you unnecessary pain in returning your letter, but I felt it would be better than writing you an unkind one myself. Darling rest assured that as soon as your next letter was received my heart melted. I did not love you the less at any time but felt miserable at the insane notion that I might be losing you. Honey say nothing more about [it], and rest assured I do not know in feeling that it was ever written except by the increased love I bear you. You may think that I surely say this to please you, but in reality if the thing be possible—it is undoubtedly true. Think no more of it.

I received Pamela's letter and the slippers this evening, and you may rest assured they came in good time, for I have nothing but boots and they are disagreeable. Kiss her for me and tell her how delighted I am with them. I wrote her last night.

I am ordered to Portsmouth as a witness before a court martial Monday next. The change will be very agreeable for I am getting tired of this banishment. I did not believe such a lonely place could be found in Va. We have some few people to come out to us occasionally.

I am anxiously looking for the mare I bought from Dr. Wharton. I expect from what the Doctor writes that she will be quite a dasher. My horse is showy, etc., but I had rather have a smaller animal. . . .

. . . How I should like to see my little family. You all must not make Turner precocious for precocious children invariably turn out to be dull men. I will be satisfied with his being merely smart. . . .

I saw an extract from a New York paper yesterday that England [and] France are considered as certain to recognize our Confederacy. France is to lend money and England is sending troops to Canada. If it proves to be true we are certainly in luck and need not fear for the result. I hope sincerely that something may turn up to cause peace to be made and that speedily. I prefer quiet and my family to war and separation.

I will write you again before I go to Portsmouth. My love to all at Good Spring. Darling let me [urge] you to get a nurse at once for we are certainly not so poor but what we can afford to pay most any price for a nurse. Do not fail to get one if you can. It is too much for you to take entire care of the baby. Good night and may the all powerful creature watch over you all.

Your devoted Husband

෴

Camp Ruffin (near Smithfield), Va., July 20th, 1861

My dear Wife

. . . Honey I wrote to you I have been on thorns fearing you will not come. It will be a heavy disppointment to me. I am all the time thinking of what I shall do when Fanny gets here and

48

how happy I shall be. Oh! honey if you do not come. I am even thinking of keeping you here all the summer provided we stay as I think we may, unless the war breaks out here. . . .

We have no definite news of the Rich Mountain fight. Gen. [R. S.] Garnett is undoubtedly dead and [John] Pegram a prisoner. They took about seven hundred of our troops and killed about twenty. It was a sad day for the South. Two finer men and better officers are not to be found. The papers of yesterday and today contain news of a fight at Bull Run, a part of the defenses near Manassas in which 3000 of ours defeated 5000 of theirs with a large loss on their side and trifling on ours. They have [a] dispatch in Suffolk today to the effect that a big battle had been fought at Manassas between the whole of the forces on either side commanded respectively by [Winfield] Scott and [P. G. T.] Beauregard in which we were again victorious, with 13,000 on our part and 20,000 loss on theirs. This as to the loss is of course very much exaggerated. As to fact that a general engagement took place I have no doubt for the news for several days has gone to show that it could not be avoided.

. . . Good bye until we meet.

Your loving husband Dorsey

Fanny apparently spent about three weeks with her husband for their is a gap in his correspondence from July 20 to mid-August.

Weldon, N.C., August 16th, 1861

My dear Wife

I merely have time to say that I am on my way to Raleigh to secure if possible the Colonelcy of the 6th. I shall probably leave Raleigh for Richmond tomorrow and then back to camp, where I shall try to make myself satisfied if I fail, and which place I shall [leave] for good, I hope, if I succeed. If I get the appointment I want to be at Manassas next week. We are all getting on well at Camp Ruffin. Very little sickness at present. David says if I leave he can't stand it with the 3rd and will give up his captaincy. Capts. Ruffin and Scales talked about resigning and going with me as privates. They talk very seriously of resigning if I leave. I am convinced that ⅘ of the Regt. will hate to see me leave. All say that it will go to rack.

I wish I knew whether you had started home or not. I shall write to you directing [the letter to] Salem. If I were certain that you were there I might possibly go to see you for a day. . . .

Your devoted Husband

~☙~

At Raleigh Governor Henry T. Clark fulfilled Pender's wish to be appointed commander of the distinguished Sixth North Carolina Regiment. The officers of this regiment which had covered itself with glory at First Manassas had unanimously petitioned the Governor to name Pender to the colonelcy left vacant by the death of the gallant Charles F. Fisher who was killed during the action of Beauregard's left at Manassas.

Pender joined the Sixth, encamped at Bristol, near Manassas, late in August to find its fitness and morale deteriorating under Lieutenant Colonel Charles E. Lightfoot whose conduct, according to Captain B. F. White of Company F, "had been such as to create an estrangement" with Pender's predecessor, Colonel Fisher.[22]

~☙~

Camp Jones—near Manassas, August 27th, 1861

My beloved Wife

I have to announce to you that I reached here yesterday and am regularly in harness I suppose for the war. My presence was hailed with joy, but for some reason the Lt. Col. is very unpopular. I find the health of the Regt. terrible. Only about two hundred and thirty fit for duty, and great many of the sick dangerously ill. I fear we shall [have] great many deaths before we get through. And the accommodations are almost worse than none. I shall do all in my power to relieve the poor fellows. I jumped into hard work and harrowing sights.

We are about four miles from the battle ground and twenty miles from the advance guard. Beaut Stuart who commands in advance has gained probably more reputation than any young

22. *N.C. Regts.*, V, 581; Montgomery, "Life and Character of Major-General W. D. Pender," p. 10.

man in the Army. It was talked in Richmond that he was to be made General. Every one speaks [of Stuart] in the highest terms.

I have had the satisfaction of meeting two old friends of the old Army who serve in the same Brigade which makes it much more pleasant. There is no telling when we shall commence our forward movement. We cannot take half the men if we should move.

I had the honor of taking tea with Gen. [Joseph E.] Johnston last night. Mrs. Johnston is with him and charming lady she is. They recollected me from Leavenworth and treated we very kindly. Old officer has an enormous advantage. What I have seen of [General W. H. C.] Whiting I like very much.

Darling if you could put me up some preserves, pickles, etc. ready to send it would be of great comfort. Butter and some lard also. I will let you know when to send them. I saw some ladies last [night] who ran away from Baltimore. They went to the lower Potomac [and] crossed where it was 8 miles wide. They left their own clothes and brought three trunks of soldier clothing.

I am very anxious to hear from you, as I have not since I left you.

. . . There is a 2nd vacancy in this Regt. which I have written to the Governor to give Jake. I hope he will for if Jake is to go soldiering I would like to have him with me where I can be of service to him. I would like very much to see Ham but fear I shall not. Darling you profess sometimes to think that I do not care anything about your brothers, but you are very much mistaken, for I really do take the greatest interest in them and love them. Write me often and direct to me in the 3rd Brigade.

Now my dear wife I must close. God bless you and the children. I know you pray for me and darling I need it for with all my efforts I am a great sinner. My love to all. . . .

Your devoted Husband

If you do not hear from [me] regularly you must not be uneasy, for when we move it will be difficult to keep up regular correspondence.

෴

Camp Jones, Va., August 29th, 1861

My dearest Wife

As we are ordered to hold ourselves in readiness to march at any moment I will write to say that if you do not hear from me in some days you must not feel uneasy. No one knows our destination, provided we move, which the General thinks doubtful. The General means our man, Gen. Whiting. It is very discouraging here. I should not be able to take more than three hundred men if we were to go.

I wrote to Ham yesterday to send me eatables if he could get them. Also telling him I would be glad to have him with me as my guest. That I could furnish him a tent I have. I should really be glad if he would come and stay with me. Warrenton is only about twenty miles from here.

In looking over my trunk I find that I left all my handkerchiefs, most of my drawers, and some socks and shirts at Camp Ruffin. But I still have enough to get along on until we get to Washington where we can get them provided we get there at all. Our progress however that way is very slow.

I hope you like your [sewing] machine for I really feel proud of that purchase. Let it keep you from such constant labor with the needle as you are in the habit of. Take plenty of exercise and prepare yourself for horseback. Please don't forget my injunction about the pills and reclining as much as possible. Please try and get well of that awful affliction. I would not have been so much shocked if I had heard of your being very ill. Oh! those wounds, why was woman so intricately formed, so much afflicted with disease and suffering. And honey I did it at Camp Ruffin. I who am the cause of most of your troubles. . . .

God bless you and the children and give you health and strength. I am getting very anxious to hear from you, for I have not received a letter since leaving you.

Your devoted Husband

Camp Jones, Va., Sept. 1st, 1861

My precious Wife

. . . David is making out his papers to resign. Thomas Bain is going to resign and come and stay with the 6th. I hope so for I long for the 3rd. Between us there is not such a Regt. in the service. This does not compare with it, and I fear never will. But still I can bring it out a great deal, and have already done something towards it. Gen. Pemberton told David that the 3rd had lost a Co. that was irreparable. I try hard enough to get some credit, but I fear I have lost some of my energy and zeal for I cannot work with that interest that I did.

What sad news from N.C. We all feel the deepest interest in her saftey and to think the rascals have landed [and] commenced their ravages. What a terrible state of excitement there must be in the eastern part of the state. Thank the Lord you are out of their reach.[23]

We are improving quite rapidly in health and if the weather continues good most of the men will soon be well. I found men when I got here going about in the rain barefooted, and [a] great many have no socks. I am going to write an appeal to the ladies of N.C. to send some socks and drawers to them. Speaking of drawers I find that old Allen managed to lose all my new ones but two, and all my handkerchiefs but three and the yellow ones. Just enough to get along with. I have plenty drawers—soldiers—that I used to wear.

I have the most terrific luck with my horses. Fan is now so lame that I cannot ride her, and the bay horse being in Richmond, I find myself afoot once more. . . .

I shall try to see Ham if possible. Has Jake received any appointment yet, and will he come if he does? If he gets the appointment and comes on, I have already a place for him. He must study hard and make himself efficient and then he may get to be Adjt. Do not tell him so however. But I wish Jake would give up all ideas of soldiering and stay at home. If he is to soldier I think he had better be with me, for I will and can do more towards bringing him up properly than any one he would probably get with. The place I am trying to get him would throw him with nice young men.

Now my Darling how is your health and affliction, and how are the children, and when will Pamela and Helen be back. And above all how do you get on with your [sewing] machine? You have no doubt found out by this time that I am exceedingly fond of that purchase and want you to be properly pleased. If it does not work you must let me know. How do you get along alone, and have you as yet been able to get a nurse? Do not cease to try. Tell Jake if he would spend some of the time he has been devoting to raising troops, to raising a nurse his good works would be more promptly appreciated.

Now my dear wife I must stop as it is late, and I still have my

23. Pender referred here to General B. F. Butler's amphibious operations against Fort Clark and Fort Hatteras which fell at the end of April, 1861. J. G. Barrett, *The Civil War in North Carolina*, pp. 36-47.

appeal to the patriotic, besides one or two letters to write tonight. I hope you are getting along well. I wrote to Gov. [H. T.] Clark[24] last night to send us a chaplain. Kiss the children and give my dutiful respects to your father. Write me whenever you have time. God bless you and the boys.

Your devoted Husband

✿

Camp Jones, Va., Sept. 5th, 1861

My dear Wife

Your letter was received day before yesterday. It was long looked for, and highly appreciated. You say you hope I am better satisfied here than at Camp Ruffin. I cannot say that I am. In fact I begin to think it impossible to be satisfied, but the nearest to it I could get would be out of the military and with you. But then I should feel as if I ought to be serving my country. This between us is not the Regt. that I had before. The men are not as good a class and the officers are nothing like as intelligent. This is strictly confidential. And the morale of the Regt. is bad. They had gotten despondent and truly they had enough to make them so. I find it hard to keep up my spirits with so much sickness and so many deaths. We have had six in the last week and several more will die. But the health of the Regt. is much improved. I feel that my presence has been beneficial to the feeling of officers and men. . . .

I received a short note from David the other day saying he was fixing up his papers preparatory to resigning. David did not speak very well of Hamilton [Ham]. He was seen talking very confidentially with some men that he would not have talked with in my presence. I fear he allows his ambition to get the better of him.

As to the clothes, it will be about the best way to send them, provided any one comes with the boxes for the 11th. If not, the time of their arrival will be doubtful. If you could send me ½ doz. handkerchiefs they would be quite acceptable, as I have only two white ones. Anything in the way of eatables will be thankfully received, but do not send anything that would spoil in two or three weeks, unless as I said before they are sent in care

24. Henry T. Clark succeeded John W. Ellis as governor upon the latter's death in office on July 7, 1861. J. H. Boykin, *North Carolina in 1861.* (New York: Bookman Associates, 1961), pp. 28, 32.

of someone who will bring them to me on the 11th. If any does come, tell them I will pay what expenses are incurred.... Eatables are very scarce here. Butter, hams, preserves, pickles, lard, and some candles, coffee or tea, matches and sugar, etc., etc. One large cake might be tried. I should almost despair of getting them, however, unless there were some one to look out for them. If you can, buy me some No. 8 cotton socks. Three or four shirts will be sufficient. The fact is my dear Child, I shall not reprove you for anything sent. . . .

I am so glad that you have consented to try horseback riding again. As to the machine, the money would have been spent in some other way.

I read the burial service over a [Gimpo?] yesterday, and to save me I could not help crying. Oh! darling how I do hope to be able to turn from my sinful ways. I think I feel more the weight of them than formerly and that I try harder. If the wish could make me good, I should certainly be so.

I am horrified to see how *white men* calling themselves gentlemen neglect their poor helpless negroes in this camp. They have free boys in most cases forced from home—and in several cases when they get sick they are allowed to die without any care on the part of those who are responsible for their well being. Two have died here in the last four days and one more will certainly die before many days.

I believe I wrote you how Burton Craig treated me—very rudely and ungentlemanly and was heard to say I should never command his son—well I have just received a letter from him asking favors for his son and asking me to write him, etc. Surely the great fall as well as the small. It made me mad and again I would not have missed such an exhibition of truckling for favors. I shall surely take my time in complying with his request if at all.

Just got another letter from Guy saying David had gone home on ten days leave, at the end of which time he would return to settle up and resign. He writes rather despondingly. We all have our troubles.

I think it time Pamela and Helen were returning. I cannot help from disliking the idea of Pamela being with him or Conally, who by the way I am told is not much of a Captain. I would hate to see the day that she should consent to have either of them. Now my dear wife, may our Lord Jesus Christ have mercy upon us and lead us in the right way, and give us health and strength. My love to all.

If Jake gets the appointment and decides to accept, tell him to come on at once. He will want [a] good many blankets. I have four and sleep cold every night. I wrote home for two more but fear they will not be enough as I shall have to take one for my horse.

Your devoted Husband

ᴧᴔᴑ

Camp Jones, Va., Sept. 8th, 1861

My dear Wife

I received your letter this evening dated Sept. 2nd and write especially to relieve your distress about Ham. I went to see him yesterday and found him much better. He had been very ill but his fever was broken and he seemed quite lively. I also received a note this evening from Mary[25] saying he was still improving and that she thought my visit had done him good. I had a pretty long ride of it; starting about 9 o'clock thinking it only about fifteen miles but by the time I got back I had ridden about forty five. I was with him only two hours. He seemed delighted to see me, and spoke affectionately of his dear sister. . . .

You need not trouble yourself about my health, for everyone is improving, but I have made up my mind not to stay in camp if I should get sick to speak of and moreover in case I get down, to write for you. I have no idea of being without you in case of need.

I hope your machine is all right. As to any danger to me from battle, you can rest easy, for the chances as I wrote you before, are that we will be in reserve.

I think Mary very pretty, and my dear they seem to be good people. I do not think you need trouble yourself about that point. If she herself is worthy of Ham, her family will be no drawback. Altho' living in a very small house, they show elegance and taste, signs of better times past.

As to Ham I felt very near to him, and think as much of and love him as much as you could wish. Darling I do not balk as I used to. I have no ill feeling for anyone, I desire to do good to all. Honey, I sincerely try to be a Christian. I have faith in Christ and hope for the best. But if the hope and belief in good works is wrong, I fear I am in the wrong way. I cannot help from believing that our acts *if* done from *fear* as well as *love* will help in the world to come. For without the desire to do good and the

25. Mary Fant Shepperd was the wife of Hamilton Shepperd.

practice of it, how are we to change? Miraculously; I fear not and hope not.

Honey do not believe that my efforts are fanciful, and hope that I may not fall back in despair as is too often the case. Honey I am troubled because I fear I do not take that interest in reading the Bible as I should, and studying its truths. I read it, however, every night and try to practice by day. But darling is it against me that under all this there is a desire to please you and go where you do in the world to come. Oh! honey the idea that when we go to our final rest you will go to everlasting life and bliss and I to everlasting damnation agonizes me. Let us go together....

Ham said you had brought on your nervousness by worrying about me before I came back in '58. That you loved me and allowed it to get the better of you. Darling, do not be ashamed if you did, for surely you have your reward if my love, my existence can reward you. If ever man loved and worshipped a wife, I do you. Your good opinion is worth all others to me; your judgement to me is superior to any others. But darling when I get with you I belie this ... [letter is torn here].

∾✿↝

Camp Jones, Va., Sept. 11th, 1861

My dear Wife

I returned today, having been absent since day before yesterday, and found your letter dated the 5th waiting me. We will move in a few days in a direction not at all agreeable to most of us, that is further from the present seat of interest—Arlington and Washington, but you need not change the address of your letters until you hear from me again.

Indeed darling you have my warmest approbation in your efforts to improve in your music, and if ever we get the chance you shall have all the advantages that can be had. You could not have pleased me better than by telling me of your new interest in it; and intention to practice for the future. Do not let that good resolve go, but hold fast to it.

Honey, altho' writing that you were in better health and spirits than for some time, your letter left me more sad and depressed than any you have written for a long time. The thought that you had been suffering as you must have been, made me feel very sad indeed. Oh! Darling, and I have to reproach myself for it. Honey, the same that causes you so much trouble is my stumbling block in this world. When I think I am getting better it rises up and stares me in the face to my great mortification, for I do feel humbled and mortified to think that the most dangerous of all our passions and the most sinful when indulged, should be the one that I cannot conquer. But I will toil on in the good road and see if it cannot be overcome in thought as well as act. It is the greatest curse it seems to me that could have been laid on man.

But darling I do not recollect when I ever got such ascendancy of it as now. I begin to hope, honey, that some day I may be able to go up and kneel with you and receive that, which I look upon with so much awe, and which must be the greatest comfort, of any of the visible acts of acknowledgements of the true Religion. Honey, write me and tell me how you felt when you joined the church, in comparison with your previous feelings. I am afraid I want encouragement.

I was talking last night with a young gentleman member of the church, telling him my great decision to conversion and he said I ought to do it, and not to resist it. I know that if I were once to impose upon myself that awful and sacred obligation, I should try harder to be worthy of it. Oh, darling, would it not be a happy day, if we could in the fulness of our hearts go up together. I think I am in earnest. Gen. Whiting and Col. [Benjamin] Alston are both communicants. You used to abstain from writing or talking about religion for fear of worrying me, but I would like to hear you in that subject. Your explanation of the Bishop's sermon was, I think, of great benefit to me. Write me honey how to do and what to read.

I heard some talk this morning of the mails being stopped, so if you do not hear from me when you might expect to do so, do not feel anxious. You may have this one consolation; I think where we are going, there is not much danger of the foot [soldiers] having any fighting to do. We go off the main road to danger and glory.

My quartermaster is the husband of Minnie Lord. She is expected here soon. His name is Scales, and very highly spoken of. I like him very well.

You must get someone to inquire at High Point for your machine, and if it is not there I will write to Richmond and see if I can get upon the track of it. As to clothes, honey, I have plenty to last me except shirts, and plenty of those for the present.

Our troops are very near Arlington, but it is not yet in our possession. There is good deal to be done by our Generals before

Washington is taken. I suppose you have seen the arrival of Gen. [A. S.] Johnston, Mallory, Dickson, Bower and others from Cal. daily.... Gen. [J. E.] Johnston and staff came over to see our Brigade drill today.

...Do not discontinue those pills, etc. until the Doctor tells you. You do not say whether you saw Dr. Wharton or not and if he carried you the instrument I wrote you about. I fear darling you were not as contented and in as good spirits as you tried to make me think you were. Darling, do everything in your power to get well. Have you succeeded in getting the money for your check. And have you yet got a nurse. I hope so sincerely. Write me often. God bless you and the children and bring us together again soon. My love to all.

Your devoted Husband

ᔕᶿᔓ

Camp Jones, Va., Sept. 14th, 1861

My dear Wife
Your letter dated the 8th reached me today, and I was delighted to hear thay you have so near gotten over your affliction. I hope ere long you will be able to report yourself entirely recovered. I agree with you that Pamela had better be at home. Aside from any other objections I cannot get over the idea that they [Pamela's admirers] are but little better than those who eighty six years ago were not considered as near all right as they should have been. It has worried me very much. If the worst should come to the worst I shall never get over it. If she ever marries either, I do not wish to see her any more. And take my word she will see the day when in her secret heart she will regret it. Mark my words. There is an unexplainable conviction in my mind, an unaccountable dislike to the thing. But I presume as I have no right to have a say, the best thing will be to hold my peace. One thing, she has no one who loves her better or takes more interest in her welfare than myself. ...

I am sorry about the machine. I wrote today to Sloat—the manufacturer—to see to it and if it had been lost that I should expect another put in its place. But I hope it was at High Point.

I am getting very anxious to hear that Jake has been appointed and wrote today again urging the Governor to have it done. If Jake should get it and could, it would be of immense benefit to the Regt. if he were to bring what few men he has enlisted. The Regt. is gradually diminishing.

We are to move tomorrow and will not be able to carry more than three and thirty or forty men fit for duty out of seven hundred and ninety eight. They average about one per day in deaths. But few new cases, but the old ones are hard to get up. Still I do not despair; the general health is much better, and the spirits of the men are getting more buoyant. I never saw such long faces as when I came here. Together with sickness and misdirected discipline one never heard a good laugh or an attempt at a song. If the men were heard to be at all noisy it was stopped at once. Strictly between us, if Col. [Charles E.] Lightfoot had remained much longer in command, the Regt. would have been lost beyond redemption. They were at that point where most anything would have caused a [mutiny?]. He ground them in some few of his military school notions,[26] but did not know how or would not alleviate the severity of discipline by a kind word or act. The sick were allowed to wallow in mud and to shift for themselves. They had an assistant surgeon who had never done anything but compound medicines, and Lightfoot seemed to make no effort to get any other. In fact, he seemed to be totally ignorant of their wants, or totally indifferent. He talked incessantly of disorganizations, etc. without one single effort—effectual at least—to remedy it. My dear, these conceited military school teachers are worse than good men ignorant of the first principles of drill.

The more I see the more I am disgusted with the idea that to know how to drill entitles a man to any position. If he has sense it helps him, but if not it were better for him and those who have the misfortune to be under him, that he did not know right-face from left. I have written more fully than I ever expect to speak to anyone on this subject. Lightfoot has some good points. He is a nice gentleman and will carry out orders, that is he is a good assistant. He says he goes by the book. I gave him a hauling over yesterday that will serve to teach him his place for the future. I am Colonel "de facto" as well as "de jure." He is hated, and I think I am beloved by most of them. Do not think I have had any trouble—not by any means. Our relations are the most amicable. The Major—[R. F.] Webb—is a fine man. The Adjt. [B. R.] Smith is a good boy who acts as if I were very dignified....

I am about at the end of my paper and what have I said?

26. Prior to the war Lightfoot had been a teacher at Tew's Military Academy in Hillsboro, North Carolina. *N.C. Regts.*, I, 338.

Nothing but to show that a little of the old vanity still remains. But not so much I hope as of old. Honey did I ever tell you the remark that Lt. Murray of Capt. Ruffin's Company was overheard to make. It gratified me more than anything I ever had said about me. I was glad that my motives were understood. He said he believed that if there was a good man, I was one.

I must say in connection with the sick that [a] great many go to private houses in the vicinity, particularly the officers.

I went out to see my old classmate Gracie today and met a relation of yours, a Dr. Aher, raised in Hillsboro. . . . He knows your father very well. I know darling you were gratified to hear that I had been to see Ham, and that I felt or he felt so near to me. Mr. Zant has since sent me a box of very nice vegetables. You seem to think that I am living very badly. Indeed I never lived better than I have for the last week. Harris is getting to be a good cook and tries very hard. I only wish I had someone that I desired to mess with me.

I shall be quite set up when Jake comes on. I wrote you I needed shirts. Now I had better tell you that I do not. I got three that I left behind and do not wish any more at present. You had better not send those you are making just now, but keep them until I wear out some I have on hand. I have the greatest quantity for present use, and [would] rather not have so much baggage. The only thing I need at present or for some time to come is socks and blankets. Drawers might come into play, but as you have none to make them by it would be difficult to have them fit, and unless they did I could not wear them. I wrote to brother Robert to send me a couple of blankets, but from some reason he did not do it. If you can find any in Salem you might send me two prs, ½ doz pr socks no. 2 if to be had, and if not 9's. Eatables will be received most thankfully.

I fear I shall have to close before I finish having my say, as it is getting very late. We have been expecting to move since last night, not much doubt but what we shall tomorrow. We go to the Potomac or near it, in the vicinity of Dumfries, about 24 mi. below Alexandria. Out of reach of much fighting. But I am content to abide my time for a fight. I have come to the conclusion that there is no use in wishing to place ourselves in danger; that it will come soon enough. I shall be content if it happens to be my luck not to be in a fight. If it comes I shall be ready and willing to meet it. And the chances are that if a fight was going on, I should elect to be in it. But I should much prefer this horrible war could end without any more bloodshed and misery. Oh! the terrible heartrending anxiety that the poor women must suffer for those whom they love. The anxiety of some poor fathers who come here to see their sick sons. I was going round the hospital this morning to see the sick, and I came upon one old man sitting by his son—spectacles on—with a brush keeping off the flies. The poor boy pale and emaciated looking as if he had one foot in the grave. I sat down and commenced talking to the old man; he finally remarked, but I am forced to leave him in the morning.

Honey, I try to cheer the poor fellows and do all I can to make them as comfortable as possible. They generally seem glad to see me. I go about every other day. I spoke to one fellow this morning who I have noticed in a very low condition when I came, but who is better now. I spoke to him, he asked if that was not his colonel and finding out it was, became quite garrulous, telling me how he was, how he had walked about the tent and how he wanted to try today again to walk. They are quite comfortable now. Fine tents and plenty of room, attention, Drs., etc. When I came they were crowded in little tents that leaked when raining and was like ovens when the sun shone. The Lord have mercy upon them. But you have no idea how little idea of prudence they have. Like children.

Sept. 15th—We do not leave today.

You can continue to direct your letters as heretofore until you hear to the contrary. We may not go. Your letters come very regularly now, thanks to the devotion of the best wife in the world. God bless my ever dear and good wife and may *we* live to a good old age to the honor and glory of our Heavenly Father is my nightly prayer. Oh! Darling if I could be worthy to number myself amongst the sheep of his fold; to feel that if there is such a thing in Heaven as marriage and giving in marriage, that we may enjoy everlasting bliss together. The idea that when we separate upon this earth we may never meet is awful. It stares me in the face all the time. Darling, the desire to have true faith in Christ and reap the blessings secured to us all by his crucifixion is constantly uppermost. Honey, I hope you have entirely recovered both in body and mind. Do not forget your good resolution about your music. Had you not better get you a nurse. It would be better if you were not so much confined, but had some time to read and exercize. Do not forget the latter, recollect your health depends upon it; and somewhat your enjoyment upon the former. Do not neglect your mind. You know I am so proud of

that, as I am fond of [your] whole self. I will write as soon
as we settle again. Now good night, and the Lord protect us.

Your devoted Husband

∽❧∾

Camp Hill, Va., Sept. 19th, 1861

My dear Wife
After marching—"slowly but surely"—about twenty miles
yesterday, we reached camp about five miles from the Potomac.
Again moved our camp today about one mile where we will
probably remain some time. We have infinitely better water and
camping grounds, and we ought to improve rapidly in health.
The Regt. as it marched was only about 350 officers and all.
Tomorrow we send for our sick. I met today Stephen Lee, one of
my classmates that I have not seen since '54. He was an intimate
friend and one that I have been very anxious to see. He will be
camped about three miles off.
My short note of two nights ago was but a poor return for your
long and nice letter, but I thought that night that my troubles
had come to a climax, but I have about overcome them, and
things work smoothly. I do not expect that we shall ever have
any fight—that is on land—down this way. The authorities are
becoming excited in this vicinity. Batteries which will cause the
enemy great inconvenience [are being emplaced]. In less than
ten days the navigation of the Potomac will be closed unless ships
can whip batteries. We have made one thing by coming here:
[we] can get out of reach of the continual shouting and whooping
of some of the volunteer Regts.
. . . I am anxious to have a description of your concert. I have
been perfectly surprised at the interest that you manifested in it,
and I suppose you surprised yourself. I want to know how you
sang and how you were dressed. I suppose those two trifling
young men are still dangling around Pamela. I must say if it is
so that she loves that fellow Conally, and persists in it, that she
will not come up to my expectations. She who has always expressed so much contempt for conceited coxcombs and men without manliness. But there is no accounting for taste. When she
takes him I'll bother myself no more about her.
Lightfoot was left in command of the sick and convalescent at
Camp Jones, and before we left he prepared a long letter about

drills, parades, etc. The Doctor suggested that he have the dead march practiced also—and [Lightfoot] wound up by signing himself Brig. General. At least an order was sent purporting to be from him so signed. Did you ever hear of such a thing? He is an ass and I shall be annoyed by him.

Honey, I wish I could follow your advice and do that which I know would afford you so much pleasure, but darling, I am afraid. I know I am unfit. Any excitement takes my mind from those things that I ought to be thinking about. I feel it and it worries me; I feel angry with myself, when I find myself, in thought neglecting to reflect and think constantly as I have for some weeks until the last two days, of my sinfulness and how much I need the help of our Savior. I want to keep him and his sufferings constantly in mind, but have failed lately. I read and pray but—oh! I fear to no use. I would like some religious books. I think if I had the life of Capt. Vicars it would be of benefit to me. As you say, darling, it is very hard to think that we, the images of God, are to pass away with this short and unhappy life, for we are all unhappy compared to the happiness of the blessed in Heaven. To think that two who love each other as I know we do, may be separated at any time for eternity. I have faith but not the right kind. I believe in all the attributes of our Saviour, but just as I have had no claim on him, that I had not interested him in me, and that I am bound to be saved. Believing as I say in all his attributes, still there is a hazy kind of understanding in my mind. I cannot bring myself to that thorough understanding of his care towards prisoners. Darling, you understand what I wish to say, but I cannot express myself, for what we do not completely understand we cannot fully explain. I feel that when I reach that understanding I shall have reached a point, from which I may claim to have started a Christian career. May the Lord bring me to that condition. I will read and pray and try to do good works. If I can do more tell me how that I could feel as you do. I never could see the use of reading what is called religious books, but now I think I understand how they are beneficial, and if I had them I would read them.

Now my precious wife I must close with the determination to do better in my next. Kiss the children, continue to take good care and not exert yourself too much. God bless you and the boys.

Your devoted Husband

My dear Wife

Your letter of the 15th reached me today, and you may rest assured it was gratifying to me in more ways than one. You anticipated my last letter for in that I asked you to write me how you were dressed. Oh! how proud I should have been to have seen you and heard you complimented. I love your beauty, but darling I love goodness and love better, and if you were not pretty I should not love you the less. You know we were married a long while before I began to think you pretty, and I know I loved you then. Honey your goodness and love for me is prettier than any beauty of form or face of the most faultless could be. Do not let your resolve to practice die out with the necessity. If you could get up a concert in behalf of this poor Regt. it would be a good work for those who need it. They are mostly poor men, some of them with starving wives at home. Wives and children crying to them for bread and they unable to help them. What agony they must suffer and most of them in this condition are Irish. . . . I sympathize with the poor fellows, but my purse is not heavy enough to help them.

My dear wife I sincerely join you in the wish that it could be so that you could start on your way to join me as Helen [Mrs. Francis Shepperd, Pender's sister-in-law.] has her husband. I do wish to see you more than ever, and if I were at or near Smithfield I would not hesitate one moment. And I most heartily join you in the wish that we had a home of our own. I begin to think that I could do something in civil life. The only thing I fear might stand in my way, is my loose way with money. I believe I could and would work hard enough and I think I have judgement enough. And I have not given up the idea of resigning at the end of the war.

Honey, the very thought that Pamela loves young Conally makes me feel as if I loved her less. I cannot help it, and I believe if I were to know it for certain I should cease to care for her, but I hope not. . . .

I am so glad you have got your machine. I wrote to Richmond the other day about it, and received a letter today saying it had been sent through mistake to Greensborough, but would be sent on. But in case it did not go right it should be replaced. When you have to sew I want to know how you like [it], for I feel proud of it. You must not let the box be destroyed for you will want it to carry the machine in when you move it. I rather think it a handsome piece of furniture, and you never asked what it cost.

Ham writes to me as dear brother all the time now and really seems to be fond of me. I love him very much considering the little I have seen of him. . . .

Honey, continue to write me how to do, and all about religious matters. I do not think that good works are enough, but I think if a man tries to do good he is more likely to try to love his Lord and Savior, for [if] he follows headlong the dictates of his sinful heart he will never give himself to think of anything but what is sinful. Now Darling, I try to bring myself to think of His goodness and Holiness and to love Him for his mercy to us sinners. I try to appreciate his sufferings for us and to reward him by devotion and faith. I want to be a Christian; I want to show some return for the agony he suffered for me, but oh! darling, it is a hard, I fear an impossible thing for me.

Don't let Turner forget me. Make him talk of papa some little, [even] if he is too little to know anything about [me]. It is a hard thing to think that our own child does not know anything about him; to feel that he may never. But darling when the thought enters my mind that it might be that I might have to leave you, it is terrible. I feel that it would be less painful to have you leave me, for Darling I could and would have it worse than you. Knowing you as I think I do, I tremble for you when the thought arises. You would not stand it. But let the evils of the day be sufficient thereof. One thing I think is certain, I am safe so long as I remain here, so far as the contingencies of war go. Nothing but a natural death can await me here.

Now my dear wife, May God in his infinite mercy and goodness bless us. Kiss the children. Tell Pamela I shall be delighted to get her letter. Give father my love.

Your devoted Husband

꠳꠲꠶

Camp Hill, Va., Sept. 26th, 1861

My dear Wife

I returned today from a little trip some five miles, where we went yesterday expecting that the Enemy would attempt a landing last night, but they were not so imprudent. We bivouacked last night, and spent a very pleasant time; making our tents and fixed camp a little more interesting however on our return. I have nothing to write you. I will not be surprised to hear of another descent upon our coast at any day as it is reported the Enemy have gone south on a grand expedition.

My horse is well and will be sent from Richmond in a day or so, so you will have the mare after all. David wrote me the other day that he was coming to see me in Oct., when I shall send him to Tarboro to have [the mare] in readiness for you. The winter here will kill her. My stallion is the finest horse I ever backed, and is the admiration of everyone.

I wish I had been at your house while that conceited fellow was there. I should have made an attempt at least to stop his condescension. I hope sincerely Pamela does not care for him, but in my mind it is unfortunately too evident. I tell you no woman with the spunk she has, never lets anyone to whom she is indifferent treat them as you say he treats her. The consummate puppy, Miss Child indeed and he the only one to call her so. I never want to lay eyes on him for I fear I should be unable to prevent myself from treating him rudely. You may tell her what an undying contempt I have for the fellow, if you please. Bragging of his exploits in the battle. If he was half a man he would not brag on himself even if he had done anything. It worried me to hear you say he had manners that you considered fascinating. One who is so quick to detect deceit, and dislike anything like it, in anyone, even your husband, to call that doughty soldier fascinating. She had to follow him to Salem did she. I will try never to write or say any more about him, to anyone. . . .

It makes me unhappy when I think of that man for I had thought there was no human being for whom I had any bad feeling. I know it is wrong and sinful and I try to have kind feelings for all. Really I try and have succeeded until I came across my future wishes for Pamela—for I want her to marry some manly fellow who will not forget her . . . in contemplating his grand self —in feeling as I ought towards all men. Every evening darling, darling, I ask myself what wrong in act or thought I have done during the day, and determine to do better the next. It is not only night but at all times of the day I ask myself this question.

Honey, my greatest trouble is that I know I do not love our Savior enough. I do not have the absorbing love for him that I ought, as evinced in the careless way I read my Bible. I cannot read it with that sole and concentrated attention that I ought. You ask me if I have seriously considered your advice about joining the church. If I were with you I feel as if I should without any doubt, but here alone and with my surroundings I am afraid in the first place, and have no chance in the second. Pray that it may come to pass at no distant day. I feel that it is our duty to Christ to be Christians, to subject ourselves to his rule after he has suffered as he has for us. I want to read some books upon religion but do not know what or where to get them. Could you send me any by the mail. My improvement, if any, I fear darling is in the weak desire, rather than in reality.

I received a letter from Raleigh saying the Governor would not consider my recommendations made of persons outside of my Regt. so mine as well as Jake's hopes are gone. I wrote Adjt. Gen. that I was disappointed as well as surprised as he had written that the Gov. said he would consider it favorably. Tell Jake not to be down in heart, that there will be more suffering than glory this winter, and that he can try again in the spring.

Honey, our surgeon says he would advise that you take some more of those pills. You cannot get too strong, and upon your strength he says your future escape from the return of your disease depends. Honey, don't scold me for asking him, for I feel so solicitous about you in that respect, knowing that so much depends upon your health.

Honey, you say you get perfectly desperate. I too get low in spirits and want to see my precious wife worse than ever—but we must fight against it. We are only in the same condition as others, and my wife to talk so unpatriotically, I am astonished, after your talking so bravely sometime since. Cheer up Honey, we will be happy together again some of these days with our two incomparable boys. We won't have any more. It is getting time for me to go to sleep as I slept but little last night. Write me often, cheer me darling, for you do not know how much I need it. Our separation is not all in my case. I did not fall upon a bed of roses when I came to this Regt. But things are getting better. The spirit is better and instead of 230 for duty we have 600. The officers are returning, etc. God protect us from all temptation and danger of body as well as soul. Kiss the boys and tell them about Papa. Good night.

Your devoted Husband

∾❦∾

Camp Hill, Va., Sept. 28th, 1861

My precious Wife

Do not let the size of my paper frighten you at the beginning. I was delighted last night by the reception of your letter of Sept.

19th and 21st. You can judge of the pleasure I enjoy in your letters by that you have in mine. They are the only bright spots in my existence. I look forward for them with feelings in accordance. You say you want me to be proud of your success with the machine and I am. I know you have only to try and you can accomplish as much where good sense has any play as any woman. You only did what I knew you could and consequently I was not surprised.

My dear you relieved my mind very much by what you say about Pamela. Before I felt uneasy, now it is only a little doubt. Oh! how I should like to see you all, to hear the dear prattle of that dear boy. Do not get him as Will Heger was, having attacks of the brain. Let his body develop more, and his mind less. Your patience will no doubt be tried, while in Edgecombe, both by the children in Tarboro, and the crossness of Papa and the childishness of Mamma at home, but you must remember their love for me, that I have always been indulged by the former and shown by the latter what a good and affectionate mother was. They are old and childish, both of them, and will ask you a thousand questions, but none will be more anxious to do everything in the world to please you than they will. They will spoil Turner more than your father, but you must incure the chances of being called stubborn, tell them that it is my direction and they will think it all right. They think there is no one like me.

We are in a distressing state of quietude here now, but look for something on the river soon. We play a secondary part here, the batteries being of the most important consideration. The health of the Regt. is very satisfactory indeed. There are two or three only who are at all dangerous; the others are improving rapidly. When I came to the Regt. there were only about 240 men fit for duty, now we have about 650, and others that soon will be all right. To Dr. [P. A.] Holt [Surgeon of the 6th N.C.] the most credit is due, but to myself is a little to come. We did all we could, he to administer and I to give all the assistance in fixing up and cheering them. I know that with both officers and men there is a strong feeling of gratitude and attachment towards me. They would not lose me, to fall again into the hands of Col. Lightfoot—for anything in the world.

Honey, you say right in so far as my trying to do right for others' sake, but I fear I love too much the applause of men; still I do not think the disdain for their good opinion could make me do what I knew to be wrong— (Should right be right or unright.)

This is a most lonely life, but honey I feel that it is the best. If I were in the midst of excitement or gaiety my mind would be taken from those things that it ought to dwell on. I hope in time to be strong enough to resist anything of the sort but now I think and feel that everything is for the best.

Darling, your letters are of great benefit to me. I cannot resist shedding tears when you write about our Savior and his goodness to us. I have come to the conclusion from reading Acts that I might become a member of the Church at once, for we cannot think that all those who repented and were baptized by Paul could have been as good as they should have been. In fact it seems to me that that act was about the commencement of their regeneration, for in many instances he did not perfect his work at once, but returned to them to complete it. Baptizing them first and showing them that their regeneration was complete afterwards. Was I right in this interpretation, or are we to suppose that they were perfected at once, and the descending of the Holy Ghost upon them was a perfection of Christianity that we need not look for in these days. Darling, I wish I could be convinced of the necessity of Christianity as you have in the Church, or is it the baptism. In confirmation is there any baptism or is the former act sufficient. If the one baptism is all, I feel sufficiently convinced, but if there are two I want to have it so explained that I can believe. One other matter, darling, is it necessary before joining a church to believe that is the one and only true church. I should prefer joining the Episcopal, but why—for I cannot see why— could I not be equally safe in some other Protestant Church. I want to be fixed upon these points. I want to become a member of some church for I do not feel safe, of retaining even what little progress I may have made without some external help. The open profession has, I should think, a tendency to do away with that fear of the laughter of the unworldly, which I believe all feel more or less at first. What you write me, honey is of great comfort.

Darling, I hope I am not conceited in believing that I feel some more hope than at first, but still I cannot concentrate my whole soul and mind when praying. Little externals will even in that solemn act, draw my attention. I feel that in as solemn an act that nothing ought to be able to attract my attention. I wrote to David to get me the books you wrote about when he comes through Richmond. I am very anxious to read them. Continue to write me how and what to do. I will try all in my power.

Honey, I know from the way you wrote about your health

being very good that you were not as well as you might be. Do not fail to take some more of those pills and if you have none and have lost the prescription, write to Dr. Wharton for them. Please tell me exactly how you are, particularly as regards that affliction you were suffering with.

I do not anticipate the stopping of the mail. My letters may be a little irregular in reaching you as we are twenty miles from the Office and may not always have an opportunity to mail them. Honey, do you have your monthly sickness or not. Tell me all about yourself, how you look, feel, act, and everything. Do you continue to have that interest in your music. Do you read or walk any, do not neglect these essentials. They are more important than your sewing. I have not time to read over this, so you must excuse any omissions. Do not get low spirited. We will try to see each other some time this winter. I want to see you worse than I ever did but I know that it is impossible so I try not to fret under it.

Is your concert again for the 11th. Do not worry yourself about the Regt. for I understand the ladies in the Western part of the state have all been working for it. You are properly called upon to do for those from your immediate neighborhod, but I think they might have the generosity to offer to help you after you do all that makes the concert at all interesting, for without you what would it be.

Put your arms around Pamela and kiss her for me and ask her when she is going to write me. And the boys, hug and kiss them a thousand times. Tell Pamela please write. She ought not to wait for me for I have more to do than she. My love to father and Jake. I never hear from Willie. May the good Lord have mercy upon our souls.

Your devoted Husband

᷈

Camp Jones, Va., Sept. 30th, 1861

My dear Wife

I write particularly to let you know of a determination I have come to, that I know will give you great happiness. I have determined to be baptized as soon as I can get an opportunity. If I can find no minister I shall try to go to Fredericksburg. I know honey that I am not worthy, but if I wait I may never be, even to take that first step. I feel sincerely desirous of doing what is pleasing in the sight of God. His image is continually in my mind, and wrongdoing grieves and worries me, and I sincerely try to do better. I love our Savior—not as I should, however. I desire to put away all covetousness and sin and I believe in the Apostles' Creed, and I feel that the connection with the church will be a great help to me. . . .

I pray that I am not taking this step too hurriedly or unworthily, but if I am it will be done with good intentions. Pray darling that I may instead of falling deeper into sin, grow in faith and grace and be worthy of the sacrament of confirmation. . . . I know that I am to some extent a changed man, but still honey I cannot have that absorbing feeling for Christ that I know a Christian ought to have. . . . When I first commenced thinking seriously on this subject the idea how it would please you was uppermost, but now it is different. I think of pleasing God and saving my soul and then that it will be a source of great happiness to you.

Oct. 1st, 1861. I put off finishing this letter last night thinking I might get one from you until it was too late, but as it was I would have had no chance of sending it. Yours of the 24th reached me tonight. You write darling in low spirits. You must cheer up. We will try to see each other this winter by some means. I feel quite reconciled now to the absence, for I believe that I have thought more of the future. If we had been together, my pleasure in being with you would have left but little chance of thinking of our Saviour. Your letters are tho' of great comfort. When we come together I hope I may be more worthy.

I talked with the Chaplain last night and told him as near as I could my feeling and the change that I thought had come over me. He, after talking a long while with me, said he thought I had good grounds for hope. Today I have not had such tumultuous feelings as for the last few days, but I think I feel more safety, more contentment. It may be more indifference for I am afraid to say to myself that I am this or so. Continue to write me and encourage. You know how susceptible I am to anything of that. Let me think I am doing well and I am the more likely to do so. . . .

How do you get on with your sewing machine. You must have been very low and feared you might write a gloomy letter. I am glad your health continues good. My health is as good as it could be. We are getting on very well now, and I have but little to worry me. Everything works smoothly and the health of the

Regt. is very good compared to what it was. We have not more than a dozen in hospital here now.

How about your concert. You seem to take no interest in it, or your music. The causes of my talking about resigning has passed over and I shall try to hold and do my best. I know I can do better for them than most anyone they will get. My inclination leads me to give up military life and return to North Carolina to live with my wife and children, but I know that it is the duty of all who have any experience in military to do other in these times. It is thought that a big fight will come off near Arlington to-morrow or next day, but it may turn out as all expectations of that sort have for more than two months.

You lament my moving here, that it takes me further from you, whereas in fact I [am] one hundred miles nearer. That is to say, we are only about twenty five miles from Aquia Creek, which is more than one hundred miles nearer Richmond than Manassas going by the railroads. And the mode of getting here is easier as far as the railroads are concerned. Honey, it distresses me that you should grieve and worry so. I know I want to see you worse than I ever did and as much as I could—in fact I would give any-thing in the world to see you—but I try to be content. Oh! you have no idea what a lovely trip I had. It is next thing to last summer's trip, but I am not half as miserable, in fact I am only a little homesick, the balance I can stand. I must close sooner than I intended. My love to all and particularly to Pamela. Kiss the boys. Write me often and give me all the news, all you do and everything about you. God bless and protect you all.

Your devoted Husband

෴

Pender's mention of moving referred to the regiment's trans-fer to Freestone Point on the Potomac above Dumfries. Here the men did picket duty along the Potomac and Occoquan and guard-ed the batteries which commanded the Potomac at Quantico and Evansport.[27] Early in October, Pender again writes Fanny about his plans to become baptized and join the church.

෴

27. *N.C. Regts.*, I, 300.

My precious Wife

I felt so disappointed last night when the mail came in without anything for me, altho I could not much expect a letter. I would not be satisfied if I got one every day. Darling, I hope you are in better spirits than when you wrote me. You will soon have to be thinking about your trip east to Edgecombe. Are you going to take your machine. Above all Honey do not neglect your music, because you are there. If brother Robert has no piano go to David's when in Tarboro and keep it up. I know you will want to astonish me when we meet and you will not know when I come....

It is supposed that they will have a big fight near Fairfax Court House soon. Our troops have fallen back to within the vicinity of that place, for what reason I cannot tell, but it is said that Falls Church and those hills we have been occupying are of no importance. That we weakened our position by holding them. I report only what I hear, for I know nothing of the positions or their relative advantages.

We hear here that Gen. [R. E.] Lee has defeated [William S.] Rosecrans, the latter being mortally wounded. It is to be hoped that Lee has gained a victory for two reasons: the safety of the country and his own reputation, which had begun to suffer somewhat. Custis, his son, is aide to the President.

Honey, I have become perfectly reconciled in my mind to being baptized. I thought at first that I could not be worthy, but now I feet perfectly easy on the subject. I look upon becoming a member of the Church as a matter of course. Since the first night I talked with the Chaplain I have imagined at least that I have felt a peace and contentment I never knew before. That night I was in great doubt as to whether my measure of faith was sufficient. Since, however, it does not trouble me much. It may be my own conceit, or it may be that I have relapsed into indifference, but I hope neither. If nothing happens I shall start to Fredericksburg tomorrow evening to be baptized the next day. And may our Father in Heaven prevent me from doing it unworthily.

I hope you have written me about when I may expect to look for the box your dear hands have worked so diligently at. Oh! my precious wife, I do love you so faithfully, and darling I feel that a new love will be added to the old—that of striving and hoping to be a Christian towards a Christian. I do so long to see you. Sometimes I think, what is this life when spent away from those so dear to us, and amongst those who care nothing for us. I know the people here care for me just in the proportion as I can be of service to them, but my dear wife, love is enough to make me happy.

You say, Honey, that you had two different lives, one when with me and one in my absence. I have frequently thought how different you are always in health in the two positions, and I never could understand how anything I did, could cause it, altho I always blamed myself for giving such rein to my inclination. I could not understand it. But I believe with you that it is more the continual and great excitement your mind is always in, which has an effect upon your nervous system. Next time we live together you must get over that. You must keep well and not get sick to have me nursing you. I know it is pleasant to both parties, but let us try the other awhile.

I have been very much disappointed and worried at Jake's not getting his appointment. I really felt as if it would be a little more like home if he could be with me. If he had come I would have done my best to make a good officer of him.

I wrote home last night, and I told them that they must not spoil Turner. I told Papa that he must not give him things to eat that you did not want him to have, so you may expect him to be a little stiff on that subject for a day or two, but it will soon wear off. I told them they must not interfere in your whipping affairs either. I fear they will spoil him for you have no idea how they love the very thought of him. He is mine and that is sufficient. But Dorsey will be Mamma's favorite.

Fanny, I did wrong in writing to you as I did about Dorsey [being] baptized. And now my dear wife I make all amends I can. I am sorry for it, and let me entreat you to forget that I ever wrote any of that letter. Have the child baptized as soon as you can and think fit. I have been thinking of my objections since last Sunday, and it has troubled me. If you do not have an opportunity before, you can in Tarboro. Let me beg you not to worry about shirts for me. I do not wear those white ones that I have. It costs too much to have them done up—10 cents apiece. It was never my luck to get into quite such a settlement as this. They have stopped making butter as milk is more profitable. They have doubled their milk as well as watered it. It is almost impossible to get anything but watered milk. Can you not send me occasionally a little silk and thread in your letters. One skein of silk and a little thread in two different letters and a few needles.

Now my dear wife I must close. I feel that this will be a very unsatisfactory letter to you, but it is the best I can do. I never like to miss an opportunity of sending you a letter and this morning the ambulance was going. My love to father, Pamela and Jake. Give my love to Mary Ripley and tell her I should be delighted to see her. God protect and bless us.

Your devoted Husband

❧

On October 7, Pender took the step he had been contemplating and preparing himself for—baptism. The evening following this momentous event he wrote Fanny the joyous news.

❧

Camp Hill, Va., Oct. 7th, 1861

My dear Wife

... Oh! Fanny I feel that I love you better and better every day; my guardian Angel. My existence. My only real pleasure is in reading your letters. Honey let us be together once more and you shall feel that I say is true. You, darling, who will be the success of my salvation if I ever reach it. For by your pen and Christian life you have shown we what I ought to be, and you have inspired such love in me as to cause me in the beginning to try to do something that would prevent our separation in the world to come. My darling, in the beginning my love was the cause of my trying to do what was pleasing in God's sight. Now, however, my own wife, I hope it is for our Saviour's.

I was baptized today in the presence of the Regt. by the Rev. Mr. Loomes Porter of Charleston. He is a good man and was very kind to me. He gave me my choice as to the place and I told him I had none, and he thought it might be beneficial to the Regt. I was willing to have it done in the sight of all, for with God's help I shall endeavor to live up to the vows I then took. I hope I have done right in taking this step. I tried to know what was the best, and let us pray that I may be worthy of the blessings offered to those who will accept them.

How I wish my Christian wife could have been present. I know it would have caused her great joy to see her husband overcome the fear of the scoffing of the unworldly, and then bow down and acknowledge his God and Saviour. Alston and Lee—Stephen D.—were my witnesses. I am not satisfied with myself, but I suppose that is the condition of all.

Honey, I know you pray for me, and I want you to write to me; help me my wife for you know how hard it is to do right and how many temptations surround me. God have mercy upon me a sinner.

Honey, you speak as if you thought I do not love Dorsey, but indeed you are mistaken. There is but little if any difference in my feelings for him and Turner. He is the image of me, the seed of my body, and the bearer of my name; how could I help loving him—and greater than all, the offspring of my faithful and loving wife. I hope with you that they may not be raised in ignorance of their father. Some day I hope to leave the army and we will all live together.

Your devoted Husband

~❧~

Camp Hill, Va., Oct. 9th, 1861

My dear Wife
Your letter dated Oct. 2nd and 3rd was received today, and I was grieved to see you write in such a gloomy humour. Darling, you must not let yourself get so depressed in spirits. We all have our troubles, worldly as well as spiritual. I have determined to try and be as well reconciled as possible to my condition. My worldly prospects are as good as I could expect. My spiritual prospects are gloomy. I want to do what is pleasing in the sight of our Lord but oh! it is hard. And Fanny, what can I expect when I see you so depressed as to your future. If you cannot be content as to the future, what can one so steeped in sin as myself expect. Do not say you are not a Christian, for Fanny, you are my earthly model, one who I most long to approach in Godliness, and if you say you are unworthy, what *can* I expect. But honey let us fight on in the good cause, let us sustain and encourage each other, let us not faint by the wayside, for certainly He will not desert those who sincerely try. My wife, despair not, grieve not, all things are for the best, and by His arrangement.

Do not let your father worry you. Try and put up with his whims. Think how much you have to be thankful for even around your small circle. What children you have. Having to have them, they are as good as you could wish, and what a sister and brother, plenty of everything. Some of the poor fellows under me have wives and children who are starving and who can have no hope of seeing each other until this war shall close. I promise you we shall meet, the Lord willing—before many months. Tell Pamela her letter was the greatest and most just rebuke I could have received. That I deserved it and take it, as one who knows he was in the wrong. It shows me how much better she is than I am. God bless her, she has taught me a lesson, and I think the more highly of her. I shall write her soon. Make her forgive me. I extracted an explanation which I had no right to.

...I never see a paper scarcely. I regret very much having written to you how we were living for in fact we live very well as to the material. You all worry and stint yourselves at home to send to us who need it less. Now do not think that I am not happy at the idea of getting the nice things you have sent me, but fear you put yourself to too much trouble for me, who ought to have been satisfied with what I have....

My dear wife, I will close for tonight, but add a little in the morning. You must not be disappointed when you do not hear from me for the chances of getting off mail is getting difficult. I received Pamela's letter. Good night and the Lord keep us.

You seem to think that I am playing a part all the time. If I praise your beauty I am laughing at you—for I was unfortunate once as to have said in joke that your looks were against you. Why can you not forget that, I think I have forgotten or cease to speak of things you have said or done nearly as bad. Again, you seem to think that all I have to do is to laugh at your brothers, particularly those you think most of. You know I think highly of Jake, or I should not have put myself to so much trouble to have gotten him with me. Banish those notions that I have nothing to do but make fun of you. I am President of a General Court Martial that will take us two or three weeks. Some of the charges involve death.

...Kiss the boys. The Lord watch over us.

Your devoted Husband

ᴄᴠᴥᴥ

Camp Hill, Va., Oct. 11th, 1861

My dear Wife

Your letter of Oct. 4th reached me this evening, and you rather took me by surprise in telling me of your near approaching visit. It was high time I think for you to visit some of your relations. I am glad you went to see Dr. Wharton's family, for we certainly owe him a great deal on the score of kindness if nothing else. But is it not strange that none of the ladies have shown you any attention?

Now Fanny to what is uppermost in my mind. What did Capt. Conally say to you, and why did you not tell me before. Oh! why did that man cross my path. I had hoped that such anger as I had in my heart this evening had passed from me forever. But I prayed in all earnestness for support against such feelings. Of all men in the world he was the last for my good, that should have inflicted such a blow. Fanny, why did you not tell me before. Why did you let him call you Miss Fanny. He had no right, and from that he was led to the other. He cannot and should not so address you in my presence. You know I am sensitive in these things, and why allow what you know I cannot bear—probably unjustly on my part—in my absence. I know it was your dislike to wound his feelings, but you know the man, and he could claim no right. Write me what it was I owe him for caring for the box and I will pay him.

Oh! Honey, I get desperate some times. Yesterday and today I have felt as if I wanted to run and hide myself, and remain alone. God in his mercy sustains me. My load in life in comparison with some but a little more would be too much sometimes. The court martial. Putting charges against many that involve death. And then the trying of those charges. The continued drag upon our tempers. Above all the absence from those that are all to me on this earth. . . .

I was amused last night by the firing of cannon which, however, turned out to be only the cursory [Confederate] firing upon a picket discovered to them by the flash of their muskets firing upon some of the enemy in small boats who had fixed a small schooner in the mouth of a creek. I have avoided giving you anything as to our strength or position and probably intentions for two reasons. First it would be imprudent as the letters might get lost or stolen and come to the eye of the Federals—they have gained a great deal of information from imprudent ones in our Army and through our papers—and secondly it is against orders. I should like to be able to give you some information upon these points. But even if allowed, we subalterns know but little. By the bye, did I write you that Beaut Stuart had been made Brig.

General and placed in command of all the cavalry in this Army of the Potomac. He has risen from Lt. Colonel by hard work. . . .

The Chaplain . . . is grand company to me. I like him very much and his society is more comfort to me than that of anyone in the Regt. . . .

Now my precious wife I must close. Kiss the boys and Pamela. My love to father and Jake. My wife I humbly pray for our salvation and that we may enjoy that "New Heaven on Earth" together. . . .

Your devoted Husband

ᘓᨛᓭ

Camp Hill, Va., Oct. 14th, 1861

My dear Wife

. . . You must be satisfied with a poor letter as I have to write in the Court. For fear that you did not receive my letter, let me tell you again that I was baptized—yesterday was a week. I hope sometime to be confirmed. I am not a Christian but do the best I can.

Let me know a week or ten days before you go to Edgecombe so I can direct my letters there. I fear David will not be able to come to see me as he is very sick. I fear he will die. Poor fellow and poor Mary. He is not dangerous that I know of, but I have feared some time that he could not live long. It is impossible to say what we will do or where we will be this winter. Now it is impossible almost to get permission for anyone except sick to go home. If I had a good case of sickness I might get to see you, but will not absence be preferable to that? . . . I got my big horse from Richmond a few days ago. He is not well and I fear will not be for some time to come. I have been fortunate in getting my horses but unfortunate afterward.

I hope you have made my peace with Pamela, for I feel that I acted and wrote with great injustice to her. I am very sorry that I cannot write a long letter now but will have to close. I am very well and getting along finely. Your box will reach me safely I feel certain, as Mr. Fant will look out for it. Do not forget to let me know beforehand when you will go to Edgecombe as I do not want you to be there without hearing from me. I write you regularly three times a week. . . . If you get a chance, have a likeness of yourself and the children together and send me. Tell

Pamela I will answer her letter as soon as I get the chance. May God bless you all.

Your devoted Husband

∾✢∽

Camp Hill, Va., Oct 17th, 1861

My precious Wife

Your letter containing the silk was received this evening. You are very good to write me so often and punctually. They come as regularly as clock-work. I should feel very lonely if I did not get so many nice letters. Honey, do not rejoice so much over my effort to do right for we know not how strong I may be. I fear falling by the wayside. I was guilty the other night of unclean conversation, but I suffered enough from it. My shame and mortification was real, and I made a new resolution not to fall again in the same sin. I also made a resolution not to despond but try to take everything as for the best. I hope what I did may be a lasting lesson. If we could be together it would be such a help to me.

Do not think I hold wrong notions as to the grounds of my salvation if I am saved. I do not trust in my own efforts of themselves but hope that God in his mercy, seeing that I desire and try to do right, will save me from everlasting damnation. I believe he will if I do as near what we are commanded as my weakness and sinfulness will permit. But I know I have not reached that point yet. I feel that my feeble and short effort is not sufficient to blot out the past. I pray God that I may live long enough to become stronger in faith and good works.

I received a letter from David two days since. He had been sick but was getting better. He did not say whether or no he would come to see me. Mary was well. I wrote to David this evening and told him of my baptism. I hope he will reflect and do the same. Not that he is not a better man than I am, but he might be better in the sight of God.

Tell Pamela if she never marries until I recommend her a husband she will get one worth having. He shall be the salt of the earth. I have one in mind now, but to bring them together is the trouble. He is a man that any woman could be proud of and happy with. Stephen Lee of my class. Tell her she is the dearest creature in the world except three—my wife and my children. I never saw anyone that I thought would have forgiven as much as she has in me. I should not in anyone. Fanny, I know you thought that it was not very Christian like in me, writing as I did about Capt. Conally the other day. But my dear wife, I was sorely tried. The temptation was strong, and it overcame me for awhile. I feel no hatred to the man, but you must let me know what he said. Nothing would teach man to let his wife be treated with insult or disrespect. The health of the 11th is much better, so Ham told me. He is with them by this time.

Do not trouble yourself about not being able to do anything for the Volunteers, for there are plenty who have more time than you to work for them, and [a] great deal of unnecessary work was and will be done for them. Some of them wait, because they believe that they will get more. My men all got good shoes yesterday and are now comfortable.

My dear wife if you think you will need your machine, why do you not take it with you. It would be but little trouble and less expense. Put it in the box. . . . I am glad you are going to get you a nurse. You will need one 'round Tarboro, but not on Town Creek.[28] I hope you will find it pleasant to stay with the old folks [a] good deal. It will be a great comfort to them.

Nothing new since my last, except the opening of two batteries on the River upon all Federal craft that go up or down the river. You will see by the papers that Frank[29] need not worry himself so much about the defence of New Orleans.

I was very sorry indeed that I had inadvertently been the cause of such disappointment to Jake. Now my precious wife, I must close. I forgot to say that I have received two letters since writing you. This is the first chance I have had of sending you a letter since my last, four days ago. Rest assured I shall not miss an opportunity. My best and greatest love to Pamela and the rest of the family. Poor boys, they will have to go without the worrying they would get if their papa was with them. May our merciful Father watch over us all. My dearest wife, my more than wife, God bless you.

Your devoted Husband

സ്മ

28. Town Creek was a hamlet located near Tarboro, North Carolina. Pender's father and mother lived in Town Creek while brother Robert resided in Tarboro.

29. Francis E. Shepperd, Fanny's older brother, was born in 1834. He was graduated from the U.S. Naval Academy and later served with the Confederate Navy.

My dear Wife

Your box came today and I assure you I was delighted. The blanket is beautiful. I have not had anything to please me so well in a long, long time. You could not have hit the thing better by any chance in the world. Everything is as nice as they could be, but I am sorry to say that one of the pots of jam was broken and the fluid out of the peaches, which got on my handkerchiefs and drawers and they were to some extent mildewed. But that is of minor importance. The box was shipped from Richmond by express to Warrenton, from whence it was sent to Bristoe. The blanket is very much admired as being the best thing of the sort in camp. I received a letter from Ham today. They were all well. Before I forget it, Mrs. Scales sends her love, in return to you.

We have nothing new here except our batteries caused two small schooners to haul to and they were captured today. I am about seven miles from the batteries and consequently only hear the guns. Our Court is not half through its labors. I am getting very tired of it, and hope some move may break it up.

Give my most sincere thanks to Pamela for the cake and tell her it is very nice indeed, as I can testify to by experience. Ham paid me the compliment to say that he would like to be with me [a] good deal as he thought we were congenial.

Do not let your desire to improve in music die out, nor your taste for reading. I am not a little proud of your musical qualities and intelligence. . . . My dear wife you must not rejoice too quickly for I have only commenced to try to do what is right, and am by no means so far advanced as to give you such lively hope, but let us hope. Indeed, I wish you were with me, not only for our present happiness but my future good. Your example as well as your unbounded influence over me, would all be for my good. Oh! darling I rejoice that I have love enough for you and sense enough to place unbounded confidence in your advice and wishes, as to what I ought to do and you desire. I think darling I have always tried to please you as far as it is possible for one to surrender his judgement and inclinations. But thank the Lord our views so much accord that we need never have any serious differences. My more than wife, my guardian Angel and companion, your superiority has, I feel, had its influence on me, instead of my dragging you down, you have, contrary to experience, drawn me up, at least a little. I am more of a man if not a better one than when you took me for better or worse. Your refinement is slowly but certainly wearing away some of my roughness. God bless you. Your mission in this world has not been a barren one, and may you long live to be blessed with earthly happiness as you surely will with Heavenly, in the world to come.

I suppose I shall soon have to direct [mail] to you at Tarboro. You will find more than a sister in my sister Patience,[30] and in my mother a childish but fond old mother. They will think nothing too much to do for you. Read the Bible to them and try to interest them in it. They, I hope, only want instruction. My father's condition troubles me, for I know he has been a great sinner, and it is time for him to repent. You know not what influence you will be able to have on them. They are fond parents, both fond and proud of me. I am the pride of Papa's life. You will be surprised to see how proud of me he is, although he says but little at home about me.

Gen. Whiting talks of sending Mrs. Whiting away, so you see even Generals cannot always have their wives with them.... My love to all.

Now my dear wife, I must close. May our Father in Heaven watch over us and bring us together again on this earth to live long to His glory.

Your devoted Husband

∾❧∾

Camp Hill, Va., Oct. 21st, 1861

My dear Wife

I received your two letters of the 12th and 15th last night. Your letters are to me like oases in the desert. They afford me the greatest pleasure, and serve to make me try to keep up my interest in religion, but oh! darling it is mighty hard in camp where one has so many crosses, to continue his interest, absorbing interest, in the welfare of his soul. I may say it is impossible for me. I never saw exactly such a set of envious, jealous, fault-finding officers in my life. Each one instead of watching to do his duty, watching to see if I allow one more than he gets. I do not mean to say they all do this, but enough to make my life anything but one of contentment. I can say heartily I wish I were back with the 3rd, and if I were to consult my own feelings I would leave them to their fate, and that would be the worst calamity I could visit upon

30. Patience Pender, born in 1828.

84

them. But one thing is certain, so long as I am here they shall know that I am Colonel.

Darling, do not let my complainings worry you: it will be over in a day or so and then I shall go on as usual, quiet and monotonous. Long before you get this letter, this mood will be over, so laugh at my childish complaints.

I think you have been very economical indeed, honey, and I hope you will not trouble yourself about getting out of money. I have $400 now ahead to send you, and at the end of the month will have $150 more, but the trouble, darling, is how to get it to you. I shall write Brother Robert tonight to let you have what you want, until I can get an opportunity to send you what I have on hand to Tarboro. Now Fanny, you surely cannot trouble yourself because you have to ask your husband, who is away and can know of your wants only by your writing him, for money. Who should you ask. Now do not let it worry you. Don't I know that you are economical. Have you not had to spend your money for things to send me?

I am so glad you have got you a nurse. But one thing I must differ with you in. As to exercize. You may not feel any better at first, but you could not help being bettered in the end, provided you did not overdo yourself in the beginning. You, it is true, ought to be able to judge better than I, what is best, or at least what life makes you best, and that you ought to follow, whatever I may say to the contrary. I should think that moderate exercize would make you stronger and thereby bear the destroying influences of married life better.

The drawers I have not yet tried on, but feel sure they will fit, for some of those I had the same patent fitted very well indeed. The blanket improves with acquaintance. My precious Angel, you could not have fitted up a nicer box and one more to my taste. I only wish I could send you something nice in return. I can only send you my sincere thanks and more love than I can express. My good wife, your letters are so consoling to me, continue to write such, for you have no idea how much they keep what little spark of Christianity I may have in me alive. If I shall ever live to arrive at the same degree of Christian perfection I feel that you possess, I shall know that my life has not been fruitless to myself. Oh! how thankful I am to God for giving me such a wife. How blest I am in worldly possessions. I have not half that desire to make money that I did. I only feel that I ought to pay what I justly owe and beyond that I feel content.

You ask me if I have no companions. Dr. Holt and the

Chaplain are both agreeable and are with me a great deal. I like them very much, particularly the latter, but you can feel the want of that old army association that we have been accustomed to.

... No one knows when we may be attacked.

The shyness of my people will wear off when they come to know you better. ... Do not think of such a thing as having your washing done out with any of my family. How would you have felt if I had when at your house sent my clothes to Salem to get them washed. They would not forgive such a thing, nor would I. If they cannot have that much done it would be time for you to go somewhere else. Now my darling, God in Heaven watch over you all and Oh! may He help me to a better appreciation of my duty to Him. My best love to them all. Kiss the children. Good night.

Your devoted Husband

ﻖﻮ

Camp Hill, Va., Oct. 26th

My dear Wife

I received your letter dated 16th instant. My dear wife, I am sorry I wrote you that letter. I did not doubt your ideas of propriety or that you would allow yourself to be insulted with impunity. Oh! darling, I did not for a moment intend to accuse you of such things, but you wrote that he had made the most impudent speech you had had made to you, and knowing that the man is famous for his impudence, how could I think otherwise than that he [Captain Conally] had said something that should be resented. My precious wife, believe me, I did not intend to say or insinuate anything which should cause you to suppose that I doubted your conduct. But Fanny, I cannot like the man and I do not want him to call you Miss Fanny. I cannot help it. I do not know why it is that I do not like him unless because he made a bad impression by refusing to come to my room at Raleigh, even when he expected to see you the next day. I thought he was disposed to try to slight me. My own darling, do not be troubled any more at my complaining, whining letter.

I have on a pr. of the drawers you made. They fit very well indeed with the exception of being a little tight about the calf of the leg. They wear very comfortably, and I should not have mentioned the tightness about the leg, but in case you should make any more, to guard against it. They are really very comfortable. The handkerchiefs are badly mildewed, but will do as well as any others. This is the last letter I shall direct to Salem.

I am so glad that your machine is such a help to you, but of course you do about twice as much sewing as you did before, it comes so handy to do this or that. You ladies get so in the habit of working that unless you have some in your hands you do not feel natural. I am glad you have come to the conclusion to let Turner run out, for I think it will be the best thing for him. Do you think hot water best to bathe children in now? See how healthy my boy [Turner] is and how puny yours [Dorsey]. Dorse is a good advocate for the cold water system. Turner must be improving very rapidly in talking. I hope the little fellow does have some idea of his papa's appearance. It is a right sad thought that one's own child does not know him.

Mr. Porter brought me some nice books. "The End of Controversy Controverted." "Double Witness of the Church." "Confession of Sins" by Dr. Lewis of Brooklyn, "Sacra Pravata" and two others, but I am sorry to say, no Prayer book. He has written in three of them, presenting to me. I have not seen him since he baptized me. He is always on the go for the benefit of the sick in his camp. He is such a good man. You have no idea how he is beloved and how much he does for them. He has quite a storeful of clothing for the sick, all gotten through his exertions. I wish I could see more of him, but I will try to read his books with all the attention in my power. Honey, did you not think when you got that letter that I had started badly, in my new life, but honey you must not judge me harshly, think how hard it is to conquer mischief so as to do right. With God's help I will continue to try.

There are two regiments camped with me now.... I am writing this in a big hurry as I expect the boy to come after it every moment. I hope you will get the money I sent you in time to relieve your necessities. Honey, take this letter for what it is intended, a kind of loving one, to remove all grief at my conduct from your mind and to show you my great affection for you and our children. Your last letter was a nice one. It was written in such Christian spirit and then you give me all the little gossip about the children which I like so much. If I cannot see you all I like to know how you are getting along. I sincerely hope your illness was nothing serious and that you have been over it long ago. My dear wife I must close, but if this does not go off this morning I will add more. I am happy to say our Court is over for the present. May our Lord Jesus intercede to our Lord in Heaven for us, and make us [as] he would have us. My love to all.

Your devoted Husband

ᶜᵛ⁕₎

Camp Fisher, Va., Oct. 29th, 1861

My dear Wife
... My darling. I hope you have not supposed that I have complained at you about writing, for surely I have had no reason. Your letters have been as regular as possible. I have all along been thanking you for being so prompt and regular.

Camp Fisher is the same Camp Hill that I have been at for the last month, changed as more troops have come near me. I have no idea when we shall move, it may be an hour or it may be weeks. We are holding ourselves in readiness for any emergency. You must not believe anything you see in the papers. I will tell you of what is going on as far as I can. Even through official sources it takes several days to sift down to get anything like correct reports. Our batteries a few miles below us have completely blockaded the Potomac. We have any number of reports as to the movements of the Federals, but they all or nearly all turn out to be nothing.

Ransom's cavalry passed near here this morning, and a finer body of cavalry I never saw. The horses are superb. The appearance of the Regt. will strike the attention of anyone. I saw him [Robert Ransom] and [Col. L. S.] Baker. They seem to be in fine spirits, and I think will not have much time to rest before they will have a chance to show of what stuff they are all made of. They have suffered dreadfully with measles since leaving North Carolina; having to leave about 150 men on the road, mostly at Richmond. Ransom will probably have to serve under Stewart[31] who graduated four years after him and who was far below him in the same Regt. in the U.S. Army. But we military men have to hold down our pride sometimes, when it is pretty hard.

Tell Pamela her beau [S. D. Lee] is about to be made Major

31. G. H. "Maryland" Steuart. Ransom graduated from West Point in 1850, Steuart in 1848. G. W. Cullum, *Biographical Register of the Officers and Graduates of the U.S. Military Academy from 1802 to 1867* (New York: Houghton, Mifflin and Company, 1891-1920), Nos. 1173 and 1405.

of two Light Batteries. She shall yet get a husband of rank and merit.

Honey, I think our chaplain will resign eventually. Do you know any Episcopal minister who would take the place. The Methodists have had nearly all the chaplains and have in nearly every instance resigned, and I think he will not be an exception. He has been a little unwell for a few days with cold and a tendency to jaundice. I have seldom seen anyone act so childish. He was frightened out of all reason, fearing an attack of fever in camp. He worried and fretted and finally went off to Petersburg this morning to get well of a cold and his little billiary derangement. Did you ever hear of such a thing. One walking about all the time to go several hundred miles to get well of what he was fearing only. I thought that one of the prettiest attributes of Christianity was fortitude and resignation. Sinner as I am, I can do better than that. I feel certain he will conclude his connection with us soon by resigning, and if he should I shall consult my inclinations next by recommending one of our persuasion.

I am reading Bishop Kipp's book. It seems to be conclusive and for one in my condition who wishes to believe it right, I think it be not very difficult to think that the Church is The Church. I read Dr. Lewis' book "Confession of Christ" which I think admirable. It was of great comfort to me. If you have never read it I will try to send it by some chance. Oh! darling that I may grow in grace and be worthy to call myself a follower of our Saviour. If an earnest and continued effort to please God will avail anything, I may have some hope. I do not believe that my efforts will of themselves carry me to Heaven, but Honey if we do that which is pleasing to Him, and believe that Christ can and will help those who so do; is that faith saving faith, if so, I hope a spark has been kindled in my soul. David wrote very feelingly upon the subject of his want of moral courage to be baptized.

. . . I am glad Jake has concluded to remain at home. The winter will be hard on our troops and he is not called upon to turn out. . . . Now my wife, the man has called for my letter and I must close. You will think that I make this an excuse lately, but I have to write on a few minutes notice, taking advantage of all chances. I am glad you continue in such good spirits lately, try to keep up so all the time and not let my little complainings worry you.

My love to all and a kiss for the boys. May the Father of us in Heaven watch over us.

Your devoted Husband

~❧~

Camp Fisher, Va., Nov. 3rd, 1861

My dear Wife

Yours of the 3rd came to hand tonight and was received with joy. It was the first for several days, for we have no opportunity to get our mail for four or five days. I am so happy to see you keep in such good spirits and health, and may you continue so.

We did expect an attack last week, almost hourly, but the anxiety has passed off. Our Generals fully expected a big fight, but things seem to have quieted down again, and we are where we were in every respect three weeks ago; but you need not be surprised to hear at any time of a big fight for it seems almost impossible to believe that after making such tremendous efforts and spending so much money, they will give up the idea of "on to Richmond."

I took my Regt. out Friday night on picket duty—at the battery 7 miles—and got back Saturday. It commenced to rain that night and rained incessantly 24 hours all of which we had to take as we had no tents. The men in addition had to wade two streams waist deep and you may be assured we were all pretty wet; and then had to sleep in wet blankets last night, but as yet I have not heard of any ill results. They took it very cheerfully and seemed to feel repaid by the look at the batteries and the firing at two small schooners that were passing.

As predicted, our chaplain, Mr. Mangum,[32] has resigned. I shall get an Episcopal minister if possible, and to further that end I think of writing to the Bishop for I know of none and none of my officers know any that would both suit and come. I got a Methodist to please some of the men. He has left and I shall try to please myself.

What you write about the boys interests me very much, and as you say, if we raise them properly they will be great comfort to us. I pray nightly that we may raise them as we should. Honey, do not fail to have Dorsey baptized as soon as possible, for if he should die suddenly I should never forgive myself. You

32. A. W. Mangum, D.D. After the war this Methodist Episcopal clergyman served as a professor at Chapel Hill for fifteen years.

say no one takes any notice of Dorsey, you know Turner is at that age that we all call interesting, so you must not feel hurt. I love Dorsey as well as I did Turner at his age, but you will be satisfied on Town Creek for I feel that he will be Mama's favorite. You must not let that feeling that he is neglected cause you to love Turner less. . . .

I am sorry to say that our court has been ordered to reassemble. It takes up all my time, or so much of it that I do not feel like doing anything after it is over. Besides this, sitting in judgement on men is not pleasant. I have [a] good many cases in my Regt. for sleeping on post and desertion. . . .

I am glad Jake has concluded to remain at home. I think someone ought for it would be awful upon Pamela and father to be alone [with] not one to wait upon them in the cold of winter. You will find it not so cold down my way, but if possible, more disagreeable. I am glad you have come to the conclusion that children can stand a little cold. Let Turner run, keeping his feet dry and his body warm, and he will be all right. Do not bare his legs according to the most approved style, but put something warm on them.

You have no idea how well and cheaply we live considering the high prices we pay for everything. Our mess expenses for two, including cook—$15, was only $44.50 for last month. Rather good housekeeping I think on my part, but still my money goes somehow. At the end of this month I shall have over one hundred dollars to send you. I want to earn money to pay up my debts. I never except to be rich, and I never think about it. I only want to pay what I owe, at least that is my feeling now.

We had a new arrival in camp today in the shape of a lady, the wife of one of the captains, married last May. Good many of the officers are meditating resigning this winter in which process they will find some difficulty if I remain in command of the Regt. for I do not think it right that officers who got their men to come, should go off and leave them.

I have finished Bishop Kipp's book and it has left me as good an Episcopalian as you could wish. I am now reading "Holy Living and Dying" by Jeremy Taylor. Honey, write me what week or Sunday, say next Sunday, it is, after Trinity Sunday. I have a book and cannot find the right place to commence regularly. I want a Prayer Book, and as I failed to get one from Richmond by Mr. Porter, I thought I would let you present me with it. You say right darling, I should not have been satisfied with any woman who was willing to give more to the world than to me. Her fascinations I should have wished reserved entirely to fascinate me and not lavished upon the world. One thing is certain, I am satisfied with my wife. Entirely and perfectly satisfied and could not wish her changed in any one respect.

Oh! my good Angel, you should be happy, for you have not lived for nothing, and my desire is to show in all my future life that I appreciate you. May God in his infinite mercy preserve us to each other, and give us Grace to please him as we do each other. Honey, if I do not have faith it is because I cannot. I try to and I do feel that my efforts have not been entirely without their reward. Honey, I feel as if my prayers and more particularly yours, have been heard. May I never be disappointed. You must not be disappointed when you do not hear from me, for our mail facilities are poor. My love to everybody in Tarboro and at home, and accept it all for yourself and the boys.

Your devoted Husband

෴

Camp Fisher, Va., Nov. 4th, 1861

My dear Wife

I wrote you last night which will probably reach you about the same time this will. I have but little to say that has not been said a hundred times, but if you are like me in this respect, and I know you are, it would be pleasant to hear it a thousand times. By the bye, we have one piece of news which if true is the most important event that has taken place for some time. That Gen. Scott, [Secretary of State] Seward, [Navy Secretary] Wells and [Postmaster General] Blair have resigned in consequence of the trouble growing out of Fremont's proclamation about the emancipation of slaves. If it be true, it is reasonable to expect some important results. . . . God grant they may have their hearts changed and offer peace. . . .

My dear wife, I never feel like writing to anyone but you, and if I were to follow my inclinations, I should do that at least once each twenty four hours. I also have written tonight to Bishop Atkinson asking him to recommend someone for Chaplain . . . I wrote the Bishop that the pay was poor, some hardships, and not much encouragement in the spiritual benefit to his charge manifested, but that it was a duty. . . .

I suppose father hates to give up Turner more than anyone else of my growing family. But Honey, Ham has got the inside track by naming his boy Augustine Henry.[33] Our boys must go on merit and not names, and surely with so much merit it cannot be hid or go unappreciated. I am very anxious to know how you will stand the exceeding quiet and dullness at Town Creek. I know I could not stand it and how you will I cannot imagine. They will ask you a thousand and one questions and then ask them over about as many times. You must not go amongst those Town Creek relations until they call upon you, for they have slighted our family since they became such strict Methodists—and I do not want my wife to let them feel that she desires their special notice.... This request is only to preserve proper self respect for your husband. Now my dear wife, I will close with a shorter letter than I have written in a long time. But I wrote you last night and have written two other letters tonight....

Your devoted Husband

∿✲∿

Camp Fisher, Va., Nov. 12th, 1861

My dear Wife

... We were again called out this evening, but got only about a hundred yards from camp where we remained about two hours and then returned to camp to prepare "two days rations and be in readiness to move, etc. as the enemy are in force on the other side of the Occoquan," that is about five or six miles off. We have been expecting them in that direction for some time. But I cannot think they will fight us near here, where the country is so much in our favor. Unless they are greatly superior numbers, we need not I think, fear the result of an attack.

I received yesterday your long and nice letter dated Nov. 6th. You will persist in thinking that I laugh at you for writing so much love, but you never were more mistaken in your life. Nothing could please me more than such evidences of your love and admiration. You know Honey, or at least I can tell you, that I am wanting in confidence. I have vanity enough, but singularly to say, not enough confidence, and your praise of me does me good. It makes me feel as if I could do....

Please send me a receipt for rice pudding. My own precious, I will try to write you a better letter in a day or so. But let me say that all you said in your letter is fully and completely recipro-

33. This child was named for Fanny's father, Augustine Henry Shepperd.

cated. I admire and love you as much as man can any woman. My love to all. May God in Heaven protect you and the boys. Kiss them for me. You say these cold nights that you do long to be in my arms. I seldom go to sleep without wishing that you were in my straw. I think to myself, altho I have nothing but blankets on straw, how happy Fanny would be to be with me on it. Good night.

Your devoted Husband

ঌ৵৵

Camp Fisher, Va., Nov. 18th, 1861

My dear Wife

I received two letters from you this evening. One dated the 12th and the other 14th, both of which afforded me great pleasure. I am glad to see you pleased thus far with Edgecombe and feeling as I do that they are pleased with you. As to Turner, I knew how Papa would do, as well as I know how he has done. It will be impossible to prevent him without making an enemy of him. Do not trouble yourself, Turner is too young to be spoiled for any length of time. You can soon get him out of it when you get away from the influence. Sister Patience will be of great assistance to you in taking care of the children, but do not leave them much when you are away. Keep them with you. I mean when you are in Tarboro have them there also.

As to giving music lessons, I leave it entirely to your own taste. I have no prejudice in the matter, but I do not want any of your relations to say that I brought you to [do] teaching. We can live without it as yet. Do just as you please in the matter. You will be doing Sarah and Anna[34] a great benefit to teach them, for they will learn more under you than they would under a regular teacher. Besides, it will be of service to you, and be returning some little the great many kindnesses brother Robert and his wife have done me. You have no idea how much he and David have done for me.

I shall be very glad to see David, and oh! how glad I should be to see my precious wife [if] it should be so she can come. Honey I have made up my mind to have you with me this winter if it be possible. If we go into winter quarters or move away from here, it would be imprudent and cruel to let you come as long as we are situated as we are in tents, and no place near to stay at. The

34. These were daughters of Robert Pender.

people in the neighborhood are such that you could not stay with them and you could not stay in a tent. We are rather expecting an attack upon this point, for the enemy declare they will take our batteries, and of course as long as there is a prospect of a fight here you could not come. The roads are so bad that when you may come it will be with the intention of staying some time. If nothing turns up in the meantime, I shall commence to build huts for the men the first of next week. Tell David to let me know beforehand when he expects to start, so I can then let you know what to do. Rest assured, if possible, you shall come, but you know not to what an out of the world sort of place this is, and how hard it is to get to. When I commence to build my hut it will be to hold you as well as myself. But Honey, try not to let the idea of coming get such a hold on you that a disappointment would be too great.

As to my religious improvement, it is I fear in the wrong direction. It is so hard to be a Christian. Today I got in a terrible passion and talked very improperly to a gentleman, but in half an hour I rode over a mile to apologize. It was all I could do and I did it. I was sorry for it, and felt ashamed of it. I shall try to do better in the future.

I am anxious to hear about Frank.

I got a message from Judge Ruffin, Jr. today saying that if I had any position I could give him he would be glad to take it under me. It is very flattering to have such men as he, think so well of me. Is it not? But do not fear I shall be spoiled, darling, for I know I have a poorer opinion of myself than many sensible people have of me. What they consider something extra I look upon as what any man with my experience and a desire to do right might do. If I could impress myself with the belief that I had any ability, I should be more aspiring. I do not claim any promotion, but think if I can get it and do as well as some who might get the position if I do not, I shall be doing nothing wrong. It is not because I feel so eminently fitted for it. I feel as I did about the Colonelcy. Doubts as to my capacity to do well.

I heard today through a young man just from Philadelphia by way of Washington, that there is great suffering in the latter place, caused by the blockade of the river. That they are unable to get sufficient supplies for the troops even. If we should maintain this position, and I do not fear but what we shall—what immense suffering it will cause them.

My dear child, why do you let the future trouble you so much. You say sometimes you feel that death would be a relief, but then the idea of my having a second wife comes up and you think you had rather not die. What useless trouble. No darling, let us live our alloted time and try to perfect ourselves for that terrible ordeal. Oh! I love life more than ever, for every day given me, I consider so much more time given me by our merciful Father to prepare for the future, and I do pray continually and endeavor to pray earnestly for Grace to prepare. Honey, do not say that Heaven would not be Heaven without me. We should love Christ more than husband or wife. We are so told and it is wrong to talk differently. I try first—I do not do it by any means—to do my duty to my Maker and then I know I shall do it to my wife. I am forced to say, if I say the truth, that my fear of death arises more from the disinclination to leave you, than the proper motive, fear of damnation.

Honey, you must not despond. Think how much better off we are than thousands of others. I am high in authority, comfort, and pay. You are comfortable, have friends and plenty, while so many have to suffer the hardships of privates, with suffering families crying to them for relief. My love to all at home. Tell Papa he must not spoil Turner. That he must not interfere when his Mama goes to whip him, but to think of his youngest son, see what a good boy he is, and think what he might have been if his Mama had not whipped him so much and kept him in such good trim. Tell sister Patience the boys take after their Mother, and of course could not be other than fine fellows, and tell Mama that she must not love Turner all and think nothing of poor little Dorse, because he is like me and bears my name. If I want anything from home I will let her know. I shall want some more sweet potatoes by the first chance. May God bless you all. Good night.

Your devoted Husband

∽❦∾

Camp Fisher, Va., Nov. 21st, 1861

My dear Wife

I hope your mail facilities are better than mine for I almost always have to write in a hurry, and leave something unsaid that I wanted much to say. I have not received any letter for several days now but hope to do so today. My camp was visited yesterday by Gen. Johnston. He came down the day before and went all around yesterday, and I am told that he was much pleased with our Brigade, and as I have the crack Regt. in drill, discipline, polish; I take something of the praise to myself. None of the Regts come up to mine in either of the three qualities above specified. They beat me in numbers and the enthusiasm of their men. My men are the sort who obey orders and make little fuss or pretensions.

We are beginning to give up the idea of a fight altho' the Yankee prisoners all say that it is to come. They [say] the batteries shall be theirs. I have given them this week and if they do not attack by the end, shall go to building huts Monday, if nothing else prevents.

Our numbers are being increased every day so we shall be strong in numbers as well as position. There were five Generals in a grand pow-wow night before last. Generals [J. E.] Johnston, [T. H.] Holmes, [W. H. C.] Whiting, [L. T.] Wigfall and [S. G.] French, but as to their determinations I know nothing. It was expected that the coming of Gen. Johnston would be attended with important results. But enough about Generals, that I know does not interest you.

I got a letter from brother Robert at Raleigh. Gov. Clark threw cold water upon my efforts saying—old Foggy—that I ought to be satisfied to have risen from Lieut. to Colonel. As if my being a Lieut. was anything less in the military than a private citizen. It does not trouble me at all. I shall try to let the thing pass from my mind. If any friends pursue it, all well. We lost another man yesterday morning, and our sick has taken another turn lower, but nothing serious, only jaundice and colds.

My precious wife I hope you are not very lonely in the back-woods of Town Creek. When Mary leaves you I know you will be. If you should want to go back home, do so for I know they have a better claim on you than they have in Edgecombe, but do not do so until I see whether you can come on here. I am very anxious that you should come with me this winter if possible, but it may be two or three weeks before I can tell. I do want to see you so much, and the children too. I think I should be able to be content on Town Creek even with you and the boys.

As to the music lessons, do as you please, but do you think it necessary. Can you not employ your time as well at something else while we are able to live without it. Read and improve your mind for the benefit of your children in their future education. It may be darling that we may have to educate our children ourselves. The man has called for the mail. My love to all. May God bless you all and give you the strength of body and spirit.

Your devoted Husband

~✿~

Camp Fisher, Va., Nov. 22nd, 1861

My dear Wife

I was beginning to get anxious to hear from you, as it had been several days since I had received a letter from you, but this morning your dear letter of the 19th came. It afforded me much pleasure to find that you are getting on so well. It was quicker getting to me than any I have yet received. I am so proud of you honey for more reasons than one. Least of all I see you are trying to adapt yourself to your surroundings and you will be repaid. I know how they at home will love you for it. You try to please and interest them and in so doing no doubt make your time pass more pleasantly than if you did not try to take any interest in what is around you. Turner must be getting on very fast in talking, the dear little fellow, I suppose he would call me Dorsey. I wish I could have been with you all last Sunday evening.

Oh! honey how anxious I feel that my parents should look to their future welfare. Particularly my father who I fear is not much better than an infidel for he has never taken any interest in those matters, never had any charity for God's ministers, and has lived a wicked life. Honey you must read to them. They have tender feelings and can be worked upon. Interest them by singing and then read portions from the Bible that will be likely to strike them forcibly. I believe some good may be done them and are we not bound to do that good if possible. This I feel, and moreover, I feel that it is my duty to try everywhere, but alas I do not which will surely be counted against me.

Fanny, I do thirst after righteousness but am too indolent and weak to gain. Of late I have almost despaired of ever becoming a Christian. I try but fail to arouse myself to that earnestness that one should have. I make good resolutions only to be broken. I think of God and His Glorious Son less than I did, but I think honey I have a better conception of some portions of His doctrine than I did. In reading Romans I am forced to see that by Faith and that only can we be saved. I had the thing changed about. I had some indefinite idea that if we did good because we were low-minded, etc. it would be well with us. But now I think I feel that to believe in Christ's ability and will to save us—not as [a] matter of reason—but to feel it and act it, is what we want. And here is where I trouble, I believe it as a matter of the mind, but do I feel it in my heart and act it in loving kindness to all. Alas no, but surely Christ who sees my feeble efforts will help, surely he who sees my ignorance of my wants, while in prayer—will ask those things that are necessary.

You speak as if David was coming on very soon. In one letter you speak as if you might come with him and in your next as if he might come right away. Please tell him to bring Harris[35] an overcoat. Sweet potatoes also. I shall show my appreciation of your promptness about the rice pudding by having one tomorrow. Harris is very anxious to learn and does so very rapidly.

I have about given out the idea that we will be attacked here, and shall commence to build as soon as I can get the tools, but it will be rather slow work. All my men have flues to their tents which makes them very comfortable barring a little smoke occasionally. I have just finished the life of Havelock and what a good and great man he was. A worthy pattern for any to follow. . . .

I wish I could hear you say "bless your old soul." . . . You, I hope, will have a chance of troubling yourself with me before the fire. How long do you propose staying upon Town Creek. I have about come to the end and said nothing. I knew you would not be frightened by my writing that we expected an attack or I should not have written. My own wife, if anything happens to me you shall hear it as soon as I can get the news to you. . . . May God bless and protect you and the children.

Your devoted Husband

Camp Fisher, Va., Nov. 24th, 1861

My dear Wife

Here we are at the beginning of another Sabbath which does not possess me with that dread of its loneliness as at one time. Honey I have received but one letter from you in the last week. Do you write as often as you did. At one time every mail was sure to bring me a letter, but now mail after mail comes in, and no letter. Then I felt certain but now I expect one only when I get it. And we are so much nearer too. Do not fear to trouble

35. Pender's manservant.

them to send your letters off.... Honey, I am not complaining, for I do not know what obstacles you may have to overcome, and always when I have complained I have been in the wrong.

I have no news of any kind and can only write the oft told tale of love and desire to see you and the children. If nothing happens I shall commence operations for the winter tomorrow. One of our Regts. has about finished, and some of the others have commenced. My great trouble is the want of tools to work with. You have no idea how scarce axes are getting in the Southern Confederacy. Scarcely to be had, but if we had a thousand they would soon all be lost or ruined. It worries me some times to see how negligent these men are. If they had been raised so, it would not be so bad, but most of them have been raised to make everything go as far as possible.

Gen. Johnston said to Gen. Whiting the other day while riding through my camp that it was the neatest in the Army of the Potomac. Gen. Whiting was very complimentary himself yesterday, saying he had chosen me for the position I occupy—left flank—and that I only had to prove myself as good a soldier in the field as in the camp and he should be satisfied. This is all gratifying but I hope it does not increase my vanity, for of a surety I feel that what I do is through God's mercy, having given me a desire to do my duty in all respects. Yesterday I experienced a palpable assistance from Christ, for evil thoughts were taking possession of me. I prayed to Him and the temptation left me at once. Should not such manifestations encourage me.

I am now reading "End of Controversy Controverted" and so far as crushing the Roman Church it is overwhelming, and as far as proving the number of priestly orders it is conclusive as to The Church. Is that enough to show that The Church is The Church. It is one of the finest written books I ever read....

I received a letter last night from a man in the 3rd which I will enclose.[36] I do not know when anything has so pleased or stirred me. The latter part of it was to me very touching. He was David's assistant while Quartermaster.

Honey, altho' I get up at reveille I have to hurry again to get this letter off. I am so much interrupted that it is very hard to do anything. I am going to try to get up every morning at reveille so

36. This letter from Charles D. Hill, dated November 14, 1861, stated: "I would like very to be transferred to your Regiment. Although I am socially very pleasantly situated, still your discipline and manner of doing things suits my views and habits much better than the way things are conducted here [at Camp Ruffin] now."

I can read without interruption. I shall write to your father the first spare time I get. Darling you must continue to be satisfied with your lot. Think how many are worse off than we are. O darling let us be thankful for what we have, for surely we are favored. Of all the trying times we have been through, no serious accident has ever befallen us. Instead of growing indifferent to each other, we grow in affection. Our children are healthy and good, and we have loving relatives. The Lord be praised. Honey I try to bring myself to rely upon him implicitly in all things, especially in what may befall me in this war. If I die I know He will take care of you. The leaving you is the only thing that troubles me when I contemplate such an end, but I pray that I may grow in grace until I feel that "to die will be gain." I do not write about death to trouble you, but to strengthen you, for in all cases we must submit to [His] will and if we can do it willingly how much better for us. I am in fine health and spirits. Things work well with me in every respect. My love to all. Kiss the children. I had a pudding yesterday after your receipt and it was fine. May our Heavenly Father watch over and protect us. I will write by every chance.

Your devoted Husband

◈

Camp Fisher, Va., Nov. 25th, 1861

My dear Wife

... Darling you must not be troubled at our separation. Try to bear it manfully. You may rest assured that if anything happens to me, you shall hear of it, for if I get too sick to write I shall most likely leave camp and send for you to nurse me, but I hope the same good health that I have had all summer may be continued to me. I certainly ought to be thankful that amidst sickness I have been spared. And you too my precious wife have been so well, better than when I am with you even. Do you know honey, it goes somewhat to reconcile me to our separation that you are always in better health when we are separated. ...

You will insist upon it that I make fun of you. You were never more mistaken than to suppose I make fun of you about the children, for I am as foolish about them as anyone could be. I cannot help talking and bragging about them. Darling, [give] up the notion that I am always making fun of you.

I got a short note from the Bishop today recommending Dr.

C. B. Calhoun provided he will acept. No, honey, I have not and hope not to regret being baptized, and I desire to be confirmed for then I shall not fail to do things which I feel that I hardly have a right to do now. I mean for the appearance of the thing. Not that I am ashamed, but not being yet a member of the Church it might cause remarks, etc.

. . . I shall be able to send home at least $150 the end of this month. My expenses this month . . . will not be over $65, and I started with $133 this month. Am I not improving. At that rate I shall soon be out of debt.

If David does not leave before you see him, tell him to get me two warm gloves and a winter cravat—and do not forget to send me some buttons—shirts. Tell Papa not to send any potatoes unless someone is coming on, for by express they cost too much and by freight they would be rotten before I got them.

I wrote your father Sunday but did not say anything about my desire for promotion, not that I would not ask him a favor, but I really feel a delicacy in asking anyone to recommend me for such a high position. I have not got the face to do it. You can better ask your father to do such a thing. A wife is excusable for saying her husband is capable of filling any position even if she should not think it. I have heard nothing or done nothing towards [the promotion] since I received brother Robert's letter. I feel almost indifferent about it. To tell you the truth, the knowledge that as General I stood more chance of having you with me, had I believe more to do with it in the beginning than anything else.

I know you, you go and say, well he is getting so he doesn't want me and has determined not to try any more. Not at all my dear wife, but I have done all I have the face to do. I wrote my brother to stir the matter and I do the best I can as Colonel so if merit has anything to do with it, it may recommend me. But I fear merit has nothing to do in the matter. . . .

We are apparently no nearer a fight than a week ago. My love to all. Day after tomorrow Turner is two years old and Dorsey six months. Good night my own dear wife.

Your devoted Husband

⚜

Camp Fisher, Va., Nov. 28th, 1861

My dear Wife

I received your long letter of Sunday this morning. I was happy to receive it, and was only sorry to think that you are so lonely, for I know you are and knew you would be, before you went there. You must go back to Tarboro [to stay with Robert] for it will be a little better there, and if [you] are still more discontented there than at home you had better go home for we have enough to trouble us without staying away from home when we can help it. Indeed my darling I want you to be as contented as possible and want you to go where you please. . . .

I am very much grieved to hear that Turner is still troubled with diarrhea. I had hoped the little fellow was over it. Honey I do not want you to wean Dorsey, but only suggested it because I thought it might be keeping you down in flesh and strength and that you would have motherly scruples about weaning him. As you say I sincerely hope we may not have any more children, at least for years. In the course of time I should like to have a sweet little flame haired Fanny, to make some man happy in the future, as you have done me. I fear Turner does not have good medical treatment. Please write me his symptoms and I will get Dr. Holt to give me a prescription for him. I have great confidence in our Dr. Holt. . . .

As to the Generalcy, I have given up all hope and scarcely ever think of it and then the thought passes away as soon as it sprang up unless someone is talking to me about it. But after your preaching to me about ambition, then get so yourself, Fanny, Fanny, that won't do.

If David comes on I shall send the mare Dr. Wharton gave me to Edgecombe. It will be too cold for her here without stabling. You must not go home until I can see about your coming to see me, which I hope will be soon. We have been deferring everything till after the big fight that was expected, but I am beginning to doubt of its coming off, but that [Major General George B.] McClellan will content himself with holding this Army here and carry on his operations south. If I should be promoted, I would like to be ordered in your direction some where.

It is rather strange they should not write you at home. Try them with the same trial . . . they give you and the chances are they will do better. I have written to Ham ten days ago, at least. I suppose Col. [J. M.] Leach caused the report to spread that [W. W.] Kirkland was the cause of so much sickness in his Regt. [Twenty-first North Carolina]. I have no doubt one cause of so much fatality can be attributed to the Governor for not appointing proper doctors, for one at least, of his, I have known was no account. I suppose some of these days I shall be blamed for the death in mine. If I am to blame it is due to ignorance and not to neglect. You will see when I come to run for Congress all these things will be brought against me.

Honey I fear if you were with me you would have more to prevent you from being a Christian woman than you have now. I fear I should fall so far short of what you would expect of one, that you would be discouraged. It is very hard, Honey, even to have the outward appearance of religion, let alone the all important the inner. I know I trust in God more implicitly than I did. I try to go to him for everything, but the sinner predominates so much in me that it is hard to do anything right. You have another task before you in Tarboro, it is time you should be attending to your choir.

I had got behind one day when I wrote you last, so it has been only two days. I try to write every other day, and when I think I may have no chance of sending it off, I write every day.

Tell Papa I am very much obliged for his offer to take care of my horse, and if I get a chance to send her, he will have to make good his promise.

My love to all at home and in Tarboro.... May God in Heaven bless you and the children and give you amongst other things good health.

Your devoted Husband

∾✤∾

Camp Fisher, Va., Dec. 4th, 1861

My dear Wife

... Things that used to worry me for days do so now only for a few moments, when I come to my senses and regret what was said or done and resolve not to be caught again, and I hope in some things I do do better. I try to make it a point to confess openly to the injured person when I find I am in the wrong. I do this to mortify myself.

Darling, I too enjoy Sunday more than I used to. It braces up my waning earnestness a little, and sometimes I really enjoy reading my Bible and other religious books. In fact, I have read nothing, nor have any desire to read anything else for some time— newspapers excepted. I do have such a longing to be a good Christian and to have some assurance of my acceptance. Sometimes I have a yearning for holiness and to see our Saviour, such as I feel to see you. I know of no other feeling to compare it to, but again I despair and read because I have set myself a task for each day. We are told that by constant prayer and humiliation we shall see the Kingdom of Heaven and in that promise I hope. God be merciful to us. I often think of the Publican who did not so much as dare lift his head to Heaven and pray to be as humble as he was.

I am glad you have gone back to Tarboro for I know you will be better satisfied there and I can hear from you and you from me more regularly. I know that what you say about their [Pender's parents] liking Mary [David Pender's wife] more than you, comes from your modesty. Old people like child-like frankness and that you possess to a greater degree than any grown and intelligent person I ever saw. But do not understand me as not wanting them to love Mary too.

I would not be surprised if we were ordered away from this immediate vicinity, but still I shall keep on building. My men still continue to die. One last night and one today. They are the most sickly men I ever saw. I have tried to do all in my power for them. We have [a] good deal of pneumonia, and I fear [a] good deal of it has been brought on by imprudence. One man died last night—was almost well of a bad case of fever and went out in the rain one night without his coat and shoes. . . .

Gen. Whiting gave my Regt. his Brigade flag to me today until further arrangements. He is rather partial to my Regt. for two reasons: 1st it is from North Carolina, 2nd it gives him less trouble than any of the others. They are remarkably orderly.

Mr. Frank [a sutler] has caused me some little trouble in one thing and unless he improves I shall be forced to get rid of him even if Ham is to retain a part of the proceeds, for I know Ham would not sanction his course. I told him he could not bring any liquor into camp. The other day in looking over his bills I found 1½ doz. [bottles] checked—when I reminded him of what I had told him, he assured me it was for his own use, but a few days afterwards he went to the General, and got him to say that he might sell it to the officers. The General was not thinking of what he was doing. All this after I had told him he could not and his saying it was for his own use, and besides being told before he went to the General that he had better not without speaking to me about it first. He went off leaving word with his clerk to sell to officers. When I found it out I ordered the clerk not to sell upon pain of being shut up and the store broken up. Since then I had some of it taken for the use of the sick for which I intend he shall only receive cost and transportation. I shall take it all if necessary and if he brings more—and I understand he said he was going to bring a large quantity—I shall take it without paying him a cent, and send him off. I will not have an authorized whisky shop in my camp. Some of the officers I understand have been talking about my not letting him sell to them. I am determined to break it up before it grows to such dimensions as to give me trouble. Do you believe Ham would be a party to such conduct? I know you do not, neither do I. Mr. Frank's whole existence seems to be bound up in money. Still he has some good qualities. He is very gentlemanly in deportment and very accomodating. I did not intend to tell you about it for I know it will trouble you, but I can not keep anything from you. You had rather be troubled had you not than for me to get into a habit of not telling you everything?

Honey, I have about finished. I would make some remarks about Turner's tricks but you would insist that I was making fun of you. But in good earnest, his window trick was precocious, little too much so, for his future prospects. If it shall be so you can come on, I do not want Turner left—he would not be much more trouble to you after you should get here, for I would take care of him, and he would be great amusement to me. I still hope I may get where it will be more convenient for you to come and stay than here.

... Honey, when one has persons applying to him for office it makes him feel as if he were somebody. I have had two this week and several since I have been here. One from Jerry Shallington a cousin of mine. ...

My love to all. Kiss the children and accept a thousand of the latter and inexpressible quantities of the former for yourself. May the Lord have mercy upon us helpless sinners. Honey, I knew when I wrote what I asked you to do for my parents was both a delicate and difficult task. Do you not think my Mother a good woman as far as she knows?

Your devoted Husband

❧

Camp Fisher, Va., Dec. 6, 1861

My dear Wife

Altho' I sent you a letter yesterday, still as I do not know when I may get another chance, I will write as much as I have time. But what shall I write about. Winter quarters and the prospect of a fight and difficulty of transportation have all been completely lifted.

I am well, etc. etc. Was delighted last night to learn that we had been largely reenforced. Nearly as many more Regts. than we have had here were sent down to help us. We are now strong, ready and willing for the long talked of fight. It is talked about a little that after the fight, provided all goes well, that we may move from here to some point near the [Orange and Alexandria] Railroad. It now takes 4 days to make a trip of 20 miles there and back with half loads of provisions.

The bearer of this is waiting so I must close. My love to all. I will write you again not counting this as [a] letter. Write me Turner's symptoms so I can ask Dr. Holt about him. God bless you all.

Your devoted Husband

Camp Fisher, Va., Dec. 7th, 1861

My precious Wife

As I have an opportunity of sending a letter tomorrow I will anticipate one day. I am now looking anxiously for the mail, hoping to hear from you. I was a little unwell yesterday for the first time this campaign, but thank the Lord I am now well again. I was fearful that I should have dysentery but [by] dieting slightly it has passed off. I was not abed at all but about as usual. Have I not a great deal to be thankful for—good prospects in a worldly view, good health and my family well.

Some others are coming to the same conclusion that I did several days since. That is that McClellan does not intend to attack us here, but wishes us to think so while he carries on his operations south. Here we have our largest and best army, and as long as he can keep it in check it will be better than to risk a defeat. He can gain no additional rank but might lose a great deal of power. We have been led to think for the last four weeks that each week we would certainly be attacked, and now I do not see how they could move a large army against us with artillery and provisions. It looks to me next thing to impossible.

We shall get into our tents next week if we have such another as we have had this, and nothing prevents our working. I have mine all planned and shall commence in it Monday. Two good size rooms. Won't we be comfortable and happy. If you come you must bring something to housekeep with such as sheets and pillow cases, knives, forks, spoons, salt cellars, half dozen plates and two or three cups and saucers. You would have to get in Richmond a mattress, one pillow, two or three camp stools and some few spices, etc. for cooking. We would do with but little. I have blankets, one pillow, three stools, buckets, basin, mess chest, cooking utensils and some crockery candlesticks and that is about all. But we could not have much here. You see I am getting in earnest provided nothing turns up to mar my plans and provided you will leave the comforts of home, for the hardships of camp and log huts. Gen. Whiting has or will apply to get his Brigade south, but to apply is one thing and to get another.

Capt. [E. D.] Scales, Dr. [A. C.] Avery [and] possibly some other of my officers are expecting to have their wives come on. We shall have quite a little town. About one hundred houses, seven or eight hundred men, ladies, children, horses, cows, dogs, etc. And if the Yankees will let us alone we shall be so happy.

I am anxious to hear how you are getting on since you got back to town. Honey, have you not found out by this time that I cannot write tonight. I have and will stop until I get in the mood.

I have just finished a letter to David in which I wrote a little on the subject of religion. Do not think darling that I am getting to be a babbler on that topic, but I know David is a good man, but wants moral courage to avow religion. If he does not like for me to write him about it, please let me know and I will do so no more, for I know we often do harm by writing people about it. I feel a deep interest in the future of my family, and when I can do anything it is my duty, not that I have not more than I can attend to keep myself from sin, and if God is not merciful to me I shall certainly rise to the resurrection of damnation. I try but oh with what small success. If possible I get more cross and ill tempered every day. I cannot help from brooding over and talking of my little crosses and I cannot take that interest in religious subjects that I desire.

I fear your letter is not coming tonight and I shall have to go to sleep without reading one of your sweet letters.

Honey I have undertaken, I fear, a difficult task, that is to Christianize my boy Joe.[37] He seems to be a good boy and desirous of doing right and says he likes for me to read and talk to him, but he is rather unlearned as a darky would say. If I could bring him to a true Christian condition I should feel that I had

37. Pender's Negro servant boy.

done some good in this world. I read and try to explain to him as well as I can. He seems very sorry when I tell him he has done wrong, which however is but seldom. Last night I laid down and told Harris I was not well, but to wake me when the Doctor should come, but when he attempted to waken me I was in one of my old sleepy moods and he could not do it, the Doctor came to his rescue, and told me [he] never saw such a miserable negro in his life. He was frightened nearly to death. I try to be kind to them and they seem to be attached and are as faithful as they could be. I could not have better servants. I trust Harris entirely with my money in mess business.

Now honey let me talk a little about you and not so much about myself. How are you getting on in Tarboro with the children, with your music and the girls' lessons. Where are you staying, etc. . . . You must not think of coming here without a grown nurse. Get David to try to get you one. Joe says he has four sisters. Nice girls and you might get one. They never nursed any but you could soon teach her and it would be cheaper than getting a slave. How would you like a raw girl from the piney woods. Speak to David about [it] and if you like the idea get him to see about it. The family has a good reputation and Joe is certainly a good willing boy and has learned fast. I would not have a better boy. He did not know how to black boots, never had curried a horse or anything pertaining to waiting on a gentleman, but now he is quite a reputable valet. The idea is worth some consideration. It will not do to come here without a grown woman.

Now darling I must close. Rest assured I am perfectly well, or I should not have told you of my slight indisposition. I did not even take my medicine. Kiss the boys. Give my love to all. I send to David $100 for you to draw upon, so do not hesitate to ask him for money. God bless you and the little ones.

Your devoted Husband

~✻~

Camp Fisher, Va., Dec. 9th, 1861

My dear Wife

The mail came that I wrote you I was hoping for so anxiously, but no letter from you. I look for another mail tomorrow and live in hope of one then. I am still in the same predicament as to anything to write you, except what is purely personal, that I was in the last letter. The weather being a fruitful topic and one I seldom draw upon, I will state that we are having the finest I ever saw on the Atlantic slope, for the month, particularly for daubing log huts. You see my mind seems upon huts and nothing but huts. I commenced since today. Two rooms 13 ft by 14 ft. Will have a floor, one window and door to each room and a door between. None of your pine logs either, but as a gentleman facetiously remarked, today, *a popular house.* Next after a double house will be a double bed and next after that I hope will be two of us doubling in it, and possibly three as you have taught Dorse (prince) the very bad habit of sleeping with grown up people.

Gen. Whiting is still of the opinion that we are to have a fight and that soon. He has information to the effect that they have recently crossed over with what they had before from Washington, between 75,000 and 100,000 men, ammunition, and wagons, provisions and transportation therefore, with various other warlike demonstrations.

Speaking of battles, have you read Lincoln's message. A poorer thing I never saw. One would suppose it was written as a burlesque. He commences by informing them that the North had enjoyed good health and a splendid harvest. I have just this minute heard that his Congress had adjourned for seventeen days in consequence of a peace party in their body, hoping by the end of that time to have broken it up. A victory is the only thing, but if they should be defeated what may we not hope. Fernando Wood, the peace candidate in New York, was only beaten by a few hundred. These things look ominous for Lincoln and Crew. Oh what a blessing peace would be to our country, and how ardently I hope for it.

Honey I have written tonight for two copies of the Southern Churchman, one for you and one for myself. In it the other day I was sorry to see that Bishop Atkinson voted in Convention to change the name of our Church to "Reformed Catholic." Some of the members wished to call it American Catholic. I must say that in this case there is [a] great deal in a name. If we believe that the doctrines and disciplines of our Church is that of antiquity as well as the only proper system, of course we wish to see her supporters increase, but as surely as they call it Catholic with whatever prefix they choose, her members will be decreased and [a] great many who may come within her protection would not. Our people will not go the word Catholic any further than used in the creed. The motion was lost. Three Bishops voted for it, seven against it. What is your view upon the subject. Had you rather not remain a member of the "Protestant Episcopal" rather than the "Reformed Catholic" even if their principles are the same.

Honey, I feel in the mood for writing and I think I am doing pretty well. Darling, I have had such pleasant but quiet feelings this evening. I have really felt as if I may call myself a Christian. I never felt more happy, quite calm happiness. O God, thy service surely is the only life that brings any comfort, and may we continually worship Thee day and night. . . .

∽✻∾

Camp Fisher, Va., Dec. 11th, 1861

My dear Wife
. . . We are still in a perfect state of quiescence, waiting for something to turn up. I cannot feel as if we were to be allowed to enjoy our labors of the axe. My house progresses slowly but surely as Mr. A. Hart would say. It is the remark of all what a pretty house you have.

I received two letters from you last night and one long one from your father. His was rather rare in some portions. He said that Turner is certainly a remarkable child, but that Dorsey was a quiet dignified fellow, sometimes astonished at Turner's rather lively tricks. That he had remonstrated with you for endangering your health, but you would do that or anything else that you thought would give you a stronger hold on me. That if any woman could possess too great admiration and love for her husband, that you did. Oh honey how I did love to hear such from others. That my wife's love and respect for me is so great as to be thought, if possible, too great. If he knew more of me he might think my love had me almost as far as yours. That I consulted your opinion and wishes more than was manly. Darling, what is it you are going to ask. Do not keep me in suspense. It has struck me that it is to name our youngest William Dorsey—if so and you desire it, it shall be so. Why should my whim deprive you of a lively pleasure. I say if that is it, for you may not care enough about that to take the trouble to write about it. But what is the favor. Honey you may send me some shirts if you have them ready, by David, some of those I have are pretty well worn out.

. . . If Turner shall ever get over his puny look as his father has and learns to try as hard to do his duty as I have, he will not give us a great deal of trouble, for I have tried always to do my duty in whatever position I have found myself. My success will have to be determined by someone else.

I am afraid, Honey, Christmas will find you in Tarboro, for it seems that we are not going to be allowed even to imagine ourselves in a state of prospective quiet. After the 1st of January the chances are that it will be impossible for armies to move however anxious their Generals may be to have people killed. You speak of your fears for my safety. I thought you had gotten to be more of a philosopher than to have more than a personal feeling of disquiet on my account. You must not let it trouble you, for all these things take place, however individuals may feel on the subject. I had to take a big dose of blue moss last night for my old bilious trouble. It has served me pretty badly today but now I feel as if I should be all right for another few months. Notwithstanding the medicine I worked hard all the morning cutting and sawing. . . .

Do not let David forget my gloves. If none can be bought, someone must knit me some for I cannot do without them; however, he will have no difficulty in getting them in Richmond, I suppose. . . .

Honey, I must close as I have nothing to say that is worth saying. My love to all. May God protect you all. Kiss the children.

Your devoted Husband

Ask David if he is able and will accept the Quartermaster position in my Regt. Capt. [E. D.] Scales in a pique has tendered his [resignation], which I quickly approved. If he will, let let him telegraph me to Dumfries.

෴

Brook Station, Va., Dec. 24th, 1861

My dear Wife

I wrote you last night not to come on yet, thinking we were to change from our present position, but I learned this morning that we will not. So if you can, come at once. I telegraphed you last Wednesday night, wrote you last Thursday and yesterday about coming. I came down here day before yesterday expecting to meet you but have to go back this morning. If you should not have left, come by Bristol Station, telegraphing me from Richmond as soon as you get there, to Camp Fisher where we have an office. Buy all the things I wrote you and do not forget the shirts. I was very much in hopes to have you with me Christmas and made preparations, but our plans are not always carried out. I am very well. I have not written you lately as I have been expecting you every day since Saturday. My house is all ready. Mrs. Scales and Mrs. Avery are in Camp. Please come as soon as possible.

Your devoted Husband

∝❧∾

Fanny, Turner, and young Dorsey did come and spent a prolonged visit with Pender at Camp Fisher. In February, Pender obtained a leave during which he accompanied his family to Richmond where Fanny and the boys entrained for Tarboro to visit Pender's folks. Upon returning to camp, Pender described the wrench of parting.

∝❧∾

Camp Fisher, Va., Feb. 21st, 1862

My dear Wife
    I reached home last evening, and I can assure you it was anything but a pleasure. I do not recollect when I disliked so much to return to a place. If I could have found a good excuse to have stayed out my leave I should have done so. It was dreary and solitary enough last night, here all alone. I almost wished you had never come, for then I should not have felt so keenly my loneliness. But I must get used to it. I am glad to say that I found the basket and bag here, but no spoon in the basket. I will send the carpet bag by express. You will find the key tied to the handle and put inside.
    My dear wife I hope you got home without much inconvenience and not only in good health but at least tolerable spirits. You have one advantage; that of having the dear boys with you. Poor little fellows, I wonder if either of them will know me when they see me again. I hope so. I stayed with Custis Lee after you left. His sister Mary expressed great regret that she had not known that you were in town. There were various rumors in Richmond after you left, all of which you will have seen in the papers. We have been stirred up here this morning with a report to the effect that the enemy are landing above us and have driven in Col. [Wade] Hampton's pickets and we are accordingly called

upon to be in readiness. Col Lightfoot had an attack of apoplexy in my absence and came near dying. With that exception everything has been as when we left.

I found Dorsey's cradle in my room and I think I shall let it stay. It will only remind me still more forcibly of what happiness I did enjoy and how cheerless I am. I wish I had but one room. Oh! darling, did we not spend seven happy weeks together. They were as so many days, but I shall not forget them soon. Honey, I felt while in Richmond that you might think because I said so little to you about your entire movements for some time to come you might think I took no interest in it, but I disliked to remind you of our separation any more than was necessary, for I saw that it troubled you. My dear wife I believe I never missed you as I do now. May God protect us from all danger and allow us to meet again and not soon to be separated. I bought "Sacred Biography" by Hunter. It contains the lives of several of the Old Testament fathers commencing with Adam and winds up with that of our Saviour.

Judging from Mrs. Scales' appearance this morning she will not have to wait long to be confined in camp. She looks very large. At least seven months gone.

It was rumored in Richmond the night before I left that Gen. Johnston's Army was to fall back to Gordonsville; how true the report was I of course cannot tell. I suppose it got abroad simply because the General was in town at the time. You need not, however, be surprised to hear of our falling back at least to the Rappahannock. It was also reported in Richmond—and upon better grounds I suppose—that the enemy were trying and about to get in the rear of Gen. [T. J. "Stonewall"] Jackson at Winchester.

However much darling I miss you—and I can assure you it is more than you will believe—I do not regret taking you away from here. I am more convinced than ever that it is no place for ladies. I am perfectly astonished at Capt. Scales allowing his wife to remain here particularly in her condition. Please let me know of your hopes, as to your condition on the day you left Richmond turned out to be as you thought, or if it was a false alarm. I sincerely hope it was bona fide, for we all have enough to contend with in these times even when we are free from continuous nausea and have to look forward to nine months of pain and general ill feeling....

My dear wife, write me often, and keep me advised of your movements and plans. I will not let an opportunity pass to send you a letter. Kiss the dear boys and do not let Turner forget me. My love to all at home and in Tarboro. And accept a thousand kisses and bushels of love for yourself. May God bless you.

Your devoted Husband

ન⁂

Camp Fisher, Va., Feb. 26, 1862

My precious Wife

I am anxiously looking for a letter from you today. I am anxious to learn how you got along after I left you. Better I hope, than I started out at Bristoe, but I am thankful that everything except the spoon has turned up. I have at least one piece of news that will give you a malicious pleasure. All the ladies have left but Mrs. Scales, and even she is going as soon as the ambulance returns. I shall send my trunk either to cousin Robert to keep or forward to you.

We are upon the brink of something, the men hope an advance but which I doubt. At least I do not wish to lose my trunk unnecessarily. I have not ceased to congratulate myself upon having taken you away just when I did, notwithstanding my loneliness, which does not diminish as time glides on. I never had such difficulty to pass time and I am always glad when bed time comes. If I had something active to do it would be much less irksome.

We look to Weldon [N.C.] for the most important news that we can hear now. I see by the Northern papers Gen. [A. E.] Burnside has been largely reinforced.[38] What the results can be no one can tell. I do not fear any invasion so far inland as Tarboro, but it is possible if not probable that they might cut off communications between this and the south and I will now give you a piece of advice for all future. Never remain if you can help it where their armies have control. I do not write you this because I fear where you are, but you know I am a prudent man and always like to look out for contingencies as much as in man lies. Their policy has changed of late and the only thing we have to fear when they get a footing is their kindness, and not as of old their cruelty. They are trying to wean our people from the cause by their kindness.

38. Early in 1862 Brigadier General Ambrose E. Burnside transported 12,000 soldiers by boat to the North Carolina coast where he launched a successful expedition to wrest control of the coastal waterway network.

...It is no fear of anything of that sort that makes me desire to keep you out of their reach, but to have you where I can hear from you, and my antipathy to having my wife near them. Our people are much more frightened than they would be if the enemy were nearer. Danger always looks more dangerous in the imagination than in reality. I suppose the Virginians looked upon their approach with as much fear and trembling as the people at home, but they seem to have become used to it and think nothing of having their pickets around. Our people would be frightened to death.... Let me know when you expect to go upon Town Creek for I will prepay my letters to save you any trouble. According to present arrangement I can write you three times a week. Mailed at Bristoe Wednesdays, Fridays and Sundays or Mondays.

My dear I believe I have about expended myself upon my long dissertation upon the Yankees and their peaceful policy. I have but little more to say than assure you for the thousandth time—which I know from experience is sweeter the oftener repeated—of my devotion and love to the best wife in the world. Darling, we have lived together with as little to trouble the smoothness of our intercourse as but few have been blessed with. And most of the credit can undoubtedly be ascribed to you. May God protect and cause our future to be as happy as the past. May we increase in grace so that our lives toward God be as uncorruptible[?] as it has been towards each other. If we ever attain to such excellence in Christianity as our happy union would indicate that we had in domesticity—we might hope for a future more blessed than any existence could be in this life of probation. We can hope for nothing better in this world than a happy married existence and to see our boys—only two—grow up in wisdom and virtue. The ills of this life are too great for anyone to wish to entail it upon many of his own seed. Two are as many as I want....

Camp Fisher, Va., March 4th, 1862

My dear Wife

I really know not how to commence my letter only by lamenting my ill fortune in not getting anything from you. I felt certain yesterday that today I should hear from you, but again I am mistaken. Darling, I am not complaining of you for I cannot help from thinking that my dear wife is too sick to write. I have never

Samuel Turner Pender, the General's eldest son
Courtesy of William C. Pender

William Dorsey Pender II, affectionately known as "Dorse"
Courtesy of William C. Pender

felt so restless and uneasy when away from you. The idea haunts me day and night and I fancy all sorts of trouble to me through you. I cannot read, sit still, or do anything else for any length of time. I have put off my "muster rolls" in part because I [cannot] bring my attention to anything. I hope I shall not have to remain in this state long. I shall make another effort tomorrow to get a letter by sending a man specially for that purpose. I pray God all my fears are groundless. Surely if anything is the matter with you, some one would write me. I have been to headquarters every day except Sunday and today, for the last twelve days, simply because I cannot stay at home. Maj. [R. F.] Webb will be here tomorrow and I expect and hope he will have some marvelous stories to entertain me with.

Honey, after we move I shall try, if it is possible, to go to Richmond to be confirmed. In reading today I came across something that was better and more conclusive to my mind than anything Bishop Kipp said in his book, as to the Episcopal Church being The church. It was the part of the pilgrimage of Israel and the comments thereupon—where some of the Jews accused Moses of assuming too much to himself in claiming to administer in the Tabernacle and claiming the right, and the punishment for their attempting to do so. It showed that some particular persons should be properly set apart for that task, and we have no other than that left us by the Apostles and the race they give us. Honey, I think the VIII chapter Romans 28 verse and IV 2 Corinthians 14 verse may be read with consolation by those situated as we are.

I think I can say candidly that all things have been for the best in my case, so far as time has allowed me to judge; not in worldly only, but in spiritual matters. It is certainly a matter of consolation to know that our crosses and sorrows in this world, provided they are properly borne, will more surely enlist the sympathy of the Saviour than continued prosperity and a smooth current, for he was a Man of sorrows and knows how to feel for others in like positions.

Tell brother Robert please not to neglect to get me a cheaper boy than Joe unless his father will consent to let him stay for less. He is very anxious to remain but in these times when servants are so low I cannot begin to pay $15 per month for what Joe does. I shall also try to do a little better than give Harris $15. No one in the Regt. gives so much. I will probably write again tomorrow night.

Kiss the boys. Love to all; and may our merciful Father watch over and protect my little family from sorrows and troubles and bring us to a good old age together and then to die in the Lord.

Your devoted Husband

∾✿∾

Camp Fisher, Va., March 6, 1862

My dear Wife

I was rendered very happy yesterday by the reception of your letters of the 25th and 28th ultimo. My mind was very much relieved to hear that you were not as I had imagined, very ill. A miscarriage—surely if you do not want children you will have to remain away from me, and hereafter when you come to me I shall know that you want another baby. If it is not sinful—and I cannot see why it should be as it has been brought about in a way beyond human control—I must say I am heartily glad you had a miscarriage. If you should have gone on with it for some months you would have been sick and felt little like being troubled by outside affairs, as we all must expect to be, and for I do not know how many months your nervous condition would have been all out of order. The best thing that could have happened except not to have gotten in that condition, as after all you did the next best thing *you* could.

You can go to the commencement and all that sort of thing. I hope you did not get up too soon and injure yourself. Ham wrote you the letter received yesterday—that he was going to send Mary to N.C. and wanted to know when you expected to go and if . . . she might go with you. I was very much amused at him; he said he should send Mary off on account of certain expected events to come off, and intimated that I did not and could not possibly know anything about affairs up that way.

Maj. Webb returned last night. He says he was asked ten thousand questions about me as to my looks, color of hair, etc. and that some of them rather gave me fits. He says Judge Ruffin, Jr. is trying to get up a Brigade and that I am to be the Commander. I put no faith in the report at all. I have given up all idea of promotion since I was in Richmond—not my dear that I tried to get any influence while there as you once or twice accused me. I shall rest perfectly satisfied with what I have. If it were possible I feel sometimes as if I should like to get rid of everything like military. I feel confident that my recruiting officers will get enough men to fill up the Regt. sufficiently for all practicable purposes.

My Darling I am about through. I commenced this to let you know that I had heard from you. May our merciful God protect and watch over us all and continue us in good health. We have been expecting to move every day for awhile. Do not forget to tell brother Robert about the servants. Write me as often as you have the chance. I hope we will leave here soon. I am tired of it. My love to the old folks and sister Patience. . . .

Your devoted Husband

ᘏᵂᴥᶅ

Camp Fisher, Va., March 7th, 1862

My dear Wife

My dear wife my last [letter] I sent to Joyner's [Depot][39] supposing that by the time it got to N.C. you would have stayed from Turner as long as you could, and would consequently be in Town Creek. He was in bad hands on Town Creek without you. . . . It is not much pleasure to furnish them [Pender's parents] the pleasure that having him with them affords, for they abuse the trust so in the kindness of their hearts. . . .

What you write about Col. Lightfoot I feel to be true, at least so far as his being a bitter enemy of mine, and I do not see why he should not respect me. I feel that I have respect of most of those with whom I am thrown in contact. It seems that he is about to lose one of his strong supporters in the Regt.—Lt. Evans Turner. As his friends around Hillsboro are trying to raise a Company of which they propose to make him Captain, I am sure I have no objection of his leaving the Regt., and all his admirers may do the same so far as I am concerned.

Maj. Webb says that the Colonel [Lightfoot] is completely dead around Hillsboro where he used to have a great [many] friends and admirers. . . .

Would you believe that homesickness could make such hypocrites and fools as it does. Hundreds of our men have nothing in the world the matter with them but a crazy desire, as I told them the other day, to get home. I told them that no other man of this Regt. so long as I should command can expect me to

39. Joyner's Depot was the post office near Pender's parental home at Town Creek.

approve of his going home so long as he was on the sick report. It seemed to please those who have been doing their duty very much. I let about forty loose the other day and told them to get to Fredericksburg as soon as possible, and although some of them pretended they could not carry their guns, they, I think, all reached there in about two days with gun and knapsack. I am beginning to believe that there is nothing the matter with about half of them and most of the others injure themselves by imprudence and neglect.

One piece of news. Dr. C—— is supposed to be on his way back with a wife. If he got her they had to run away. Honey, what a sad thing that a lady should run away against the wishes of her parents to marry a man they cannot like. Runaway matches are, I believe, generally unfortunate in the end and I do not see why this shall be an exception to the rule. Dr. C—— is coarse and rude in manners, rather uncleanly and lazy in habits, deficient I think to some extent in the milk of human kindness, conceived out of wedlock and has risen I fear as high professionally as he ever will. Now from the picture above drawn—which was either gotten from other parties or corroborated by them—how could a beautiful, intelligent, refined and well turned woman be expected to [be] bettered in the end.

Well honey our long looked for orders to move are out. My surmises as to the point were correct. Our wagons go in a few hours. We shall not leave tonight. I cannot help but think it will be better for us in the end as we shall gain time enough to get our Regts. filled up. I shall try to get to Richmond as soon after we settle down as possible. I shall not be able to write you again before Monday night, 10th. I hope to have a letter waiting for me. As I have filled my sheet and have to attend to getting ready, I must close. May our wise and good Father have mercy upon us and bring us to a state of Grace. Pray darling that I may not take the step [confirmation] I hope soon to take unwittingly. My love to all . . . and kiss the children.

Your devoted Husband

ন্ধ্রুঃ

On March 8, Pender's Sixth North Carolina, in accordance with orders, burned the regiment's winter quarters together with considerable baggage and supplies and joined the rest of General Johnston's army in a general withdrawal to the south bank of the

Rappahannock River. Here the Sixth established quarters at Camp Barton near Fredericksburg.[40]

ຕະນ

Camp Barton, Va., March 11th, 1862

My dear Wife

I had the extreme pleasure of receiving two letters today from you, and a very unexpected pleasure at that. This will be handed you by Harris who goes home for the benefit of his health. I notified him today that I could only give him $12 after this month. He says he will come back. You ask him if he is going to return and if not ask brother [Robert] or David to send me a cook.

Honey, if Jake comes on soon I can get the position of clerk in Maj. [J. F.] Hill's office. If he would like it he can then learn more about office matters but less about drill. It would be better for some reasons than being in the Company. His associates would be better, for the clerks are very nice gentlemen.

I knew Turner would be spoiled at home and the less he is there the better your future ease. I am delighted to hear that your health is so good and to have you write in such good spirits. Honey, you need not have apologized so much for that letter for I knew you were sick and unhappy generally and only wrote you as I did to have the effect it did of making you bear up better.

We are delightfully situated here, about the right distance from Town, nice camp, lots of troops, etc. The only drawback is the 11th Miss. Regt. is too near me for quiet. We fell back to this position for what special and pressing reason I know not. Gen. Whiting has three Brigades consisting of twelve Regts. and Hampton's Legion. Gen. French's Brigade is also near us and four Light Batteries.

My dear wife, I am very glad you went to call on so many of the ladies, for if you had not, they would have been miffed. Did I tell you that when all of my recruits get here, we should have over a thousand men besides officers, and when we get them around and set up, won't I be proud of my Regt. I should be tempted to do as Col. [J. J.] Pettigrew, refuse promotion. The more we hear of the Virginia's exploits, the more brilliant it gets.[41] What a glorious affair it was. It beats anything in history. Col. Lightfoot

40. *N.C. Regts.*, I, 300.
41. On March 8, 1861, the Confederate ironclad *Virginia* sank two wooden Union men-of-war in Hampton Roads.

and myself have been as jovial as you please since we left the other camp. I do not know what to make of it. He works and volunteers to do on all occasions. I hope he has determined to do better.

Honey, go home as soon as you please for I know you must want to see them, and they you. You have done more than I could have expected of you and I know none of my family can complain of you for not going to see them. Honey, I have about got to the end of my letter. I can write you often. You must notify me when to address you at Salem. Tell papa to send me a box of sweet potatoes by Harris. My love to them all. Kiss the boys and do not let them forget me. May the Lord bless you all and preserve us for each other to a good old age.

Your devoted Husband

ᘇᘺᕽ

Camp Barton, Va., March 13th, 1862

My dear Wife

Your dear letter of the 10th was received today, and very much to my surprise you were still in Tarboro. I have been directing my letters to Joyner's [Depot] for more than a week under the supposition that you were on Town Creek, and had begun to think of sending them to Salem. Honey, your letter made me feel badly to have you praise me so for what's never deserved since I feel deeply my sinfulness and my inability to be as I wish and ought to be. I have not had that love for Christ in me that I ought to. I know I am grateful for all the mercies He has shown us, I love his name, but it has not a part of my existence like my love for you. My feeling for my Savior partakes more of that arising from a sense of duty, but for you it exist[s] and how it commenced and upon what principle high up I hardly know or think about. I know you are my wife, that I love you and am anxious about you and desirous of pleasing you because I love you. Oh Darling, I so desire to be a Christian, but I know and feel that I am far from being one. Here lately I have, in scrutinizing my own conduct, come to the conclusion that my efforts have been almost worse than useless, but when I remember the promises made us, I can but hope that however sinful we are, He can and will save those who believe on Him.

By accident I happened to be in town Wednesday just as the service commenced and went and enjoyed most of it, but the pleasure was considerably marred by some soldiers who were drunk and disturbing people. . . .

The enemy are now in the country that we occupied a week ago. They hardly let our places get cold before they were there. The Valley of Virginia is all in their possession, Centreville, etc., etc. Let them give us one fourth the time we give them and we can give them a warmer reception than we could now.

. . . You do not tell me anything about Dorsey. You could never get it out of your head that I did not care anything for him, in which you are very much mistaken. I am not only proud of his looks, but love the child as much as any father. It is true I took more notice of Turner because he was at a more interesting age. Wait till Wm. Dorsey get to be "over two years old" and see what a pet I will make of him.

. . . God be with us and keep us in health of souls and bodies.

Your devoted Husband

ᐯᴥᐯ

Camp Barton, Va., March 15th, 1862

My dear Wife

I received a nice long letter from you informing me that you were still in town, and here I have been sending letters to Town Creek more than a week. I was so glad to find you so well contented. The Yankees are this side of where you were a month ago, but I did not leave my houses very comfortable. The roofs, doors, floors, etc. were burned. The logs would not burn. . . .

I brought off your two chairs and my stove and consequently I am very comfortable. The Doctor brought two hospital mattresses and as we have no sick in [the] hospital, I have one of them. The Regt. has never been in anything like as good health since I have been with it, as now. I have changed my tactics. I tell them we have but two places to shelter men, the company tents or guard-house, and as I have a good driver over the inmates of the latter, the sick list has considerably decreased.

I have been exceedingly hoarse and attended with my sore throat—for three days, produced by drilling and cold, but today the soreness has improved very much. I have not attempted to drill but once, and that soon after I got hoarse. I did not write you that I took a big dose of oil after you left. It was an awful dose at that.

The arrangements for an escort will do. When I wrote, I thought you were suffering with one of your nervous attacks, and I could not bear the idea of having you travel while under such mental depression without a proper escort.

What a lucky thing it seems to me that you had that mishap. It would have worried me very much if you had gone on to maturity in that condition, for I should have known that you were very unhappy. Honey, get brother Robert to go as far as Goldsboro if Jake is to meet you there. There are so many soldiers there and at High Point—I have a horror of drunken soldiers, particularly when ladies are about, for it would appear that men do not act so badly until they get to be soldiers. What is Jake going to do?

I shall try to go to Church tomorrow if it does not rain all day as it has today. I have seldom seen so much rain in one day.

I have not answered Jake's letter asking for advice. I hope you wrote to him after getting my letter. I have not written because I did not like to advise him. I should hate to have him join my Regt. and then by any chance I should be removed from it. Do you know that it surprised me very much when you wrote that you were going to write him to enlist under me. If he should come on I will keep him with me until the spring opens. I have owed your brother a letter a long while and I must try to answer it tonight. I will try to write you again tomorrow night. Good night and may God bless you all.

Your devoted Husband

Camp Barton, Va., March 18, 1862

My dear Wife

I will commence by saying that I am in a precious humor. I got back at 11 A.M. and have done nothing but pitch into everybody and everything that has come near up to this time, 3 P.M. I can assign no reason, but my own dear wife shall get none of it. I was sorry, Honey, to have to write such a hurried letter last evening. I wanted to see Mr. John Norfleet to take $75 home for me. I have had no dinner—and had to see the Sec. of War and ordnance officer. I went after muskets, accoutrements, but only succeeded in getting the promise of half I wanted.

My letter cost 80 cents. They had no writing material at the hotel so I had to buy one package [of] envelopes [for] 50 cents.

Ten sheets of this paper 25 cents, postage 5 cents. You see it was a very heavy outlay.

Col. Lightfoot has been assigned to duty outside of the Regt. and I hope he will stay altho we have gotten along very well lately. Gen. [Robert] Ransom asked me to whom he might write at Salem about quarters for his family and I told him I know none better than Jake, and he said he should write him. Mrs. Col. Chilton may possibly go up there also. I held out the advantages of Salem in the strongest light. I know you would enjoy the society of older army ladies so much. Mrs. Ransom has the reputation of being a very nice person....

Oh, Honey, I hope my Regt. will do well when we may get into a fight. N.C. troops stand so low in that way, but I believe it is because they have been so badly handled. I can manage my men in camp, on the march, and at drill, but it remains to be seen how I can manage them on the field. They all seem to have the utmost confidence in me and I hope I shall not disappoint them. If I live twelve months I feel that I am bound to be promoted. I believe I could get it now if I would get political influence.

The enemy seem to be making preparations to come this way. The big men in these parts think this is the point. These war times you must be prepared for anything. When one goes to war he must expect to stand his chance of being numbered in the list of casualties. Honey, never let us forget one thing, education is far more precious and highly appreciated even in these days of money loving, than money. I want to educate my children if nothing else. Either of us is capable of carrying them pretty well along in the English branches, so if necessary we could educate them on small means. And above all I want to see them fully imbued with reverence for things Holy. I had rather see them Christians than princes.

I have never suffered more from cold than for the last few days. I cannot drill at all. My throat has been very sore, cough, etc., but it is getting better slowly and in time...I hope to be well. Do you know honey I have not heard from you since your letter of the 10th, but I do not blame you. I always find that you do your part. Honey, I hope this will find you all ready to start home. My next will be directed to Salem. I wrote your father a few days ago, but it was a short and poor note. I hope you will find Mary all comfortably domiciled at Good Spring. You would do a good business to open a house of retreat for refugees. The Yankees will never get up your way.

We have it reported here that they have unaccountably recrossed the river. The papers of today state that it is rumored that the people of Md. have risen up in their rear. As to their recrossing, Col. Hampton told me and he keeps well posted with their moves. We are certainly in a blue way, but I never have any apprehensions as to the result. If we can hold them in check one month more, we will be all right. And if they have retreated to the other side it would look as if something was going wrong with them.

Honey, how are you and the children? Well I hope.

I saw John Pegram last night at Richmond.

God bless you all.

Your devoted Husband

~☙~

Camp Barton, Va., March 21st, 1862

My precious Wife

I hope this will find you once more at home and feeling better than when I last heard from you. I have entirely recovered from my sore throat and hoarseness, but still have some cough. I have nothing in the world new to tell you honey, but can say as I have said a thousand times how dear my wife is to me.

I know you would be glad to see Harris and for that reason I made him go by Town Creek. I am getting anxious to have him back. I do not like the present arrangement. I invited Maj. Webb to eat with us when he first came back as I had sent off his mess—but he seems to think it permanent. When Harris returns I shall draw out and leave him and the Doctor as I prefer to be alone. I like the Doctor less every day, as I see his character develop. He tried to put on some airs the other day in consequence of the position he thinks he occupies above, but I told him plainly if he had any such views to carry out that I wanted him to resign and make way for someone else. Capt. Lea told me this evening that he treated his wife most shamefully and I should say beastly. I do not like to keep company with such a person. . . .

Honey, I do not know when I shall ever get a chance to be confirmed, for things look cloudy for me to leave home in, and I should hate very much to leave the Regt. in the hands of Maj. Webb.

I am glad you have gotten away from Edgecombe for I knew you wanted to—for I should—and know you can do something for

Turner, and you will be farther from all the excitement. As to being able to come to see me ... you may have a chance next winter. I find [a] great many Colonels got leaves this winter, so the first good opening, I shall apply, not however, I think before next winter if the Lord permits us to live. Tell Pamela I shall certainly write her soon. As to Jake, he can clerk either with or without enlisting if he come on at once, but if he stays away long he may lose it. As long as the Headquarters is near me he can stay with me provided he does not enlist, and if he does enlist and I should be promoted I would take him as volunteer aid. I do not advise him to enlist, mind you. I will write again in a day or so. God bless you all.

By the bye we hear that McClellan has been removed as commander-in-chief and assigned to the command of the Army at Fairfax—that Lincoln has taken the field and that Richmond is to be taken at once. Their troops have all left the river and they have but few troops in all of which is good if true. Fremont has been given the command of Western Virginia, etc. etc. My love to all. . . .

Your devoted Husband

ঞ৸৳ঌ

Camp Barton, Va., March 23rd, 1862

My dear Wife
You will allow me to commence my letter by stating that I have not heard from you since your letter dated 16th. I try not to allow myself to get uneasy but I cannot but help fearing that your cold has caused you more trouble than a headache. It is true the mails are exceedingly irregular.

Gen. Holmes left here today for N.C. with five splendid Regts. and another Brigade goes from Gen. Johnston's command besides what they already have and are getting from other places. Gen. Robert Lee commands in the state. You may look out for stirring times in N.C. I do not believe they will march to Goldsboro, but tackle Wilmington. I should have liked very much if my Regt. could have been one of the five.

I went to church today and heard a most excellent sermon from 9 chap. Deuteronomy. The church was crowded with officers and soldiers and it was preached at them entirely. I should have gone tonight but that I was absent most all day and the road is so muddy that I hated to ride in the night. Then it would not have been very prudent with the cough I have.

I hope sincerely darling that you are safely at home and enjoying as much health and contentment as you did for a few days in Tarboro. If I only knew that you were at home I should rest much easier.

... I would have sent you a few pounds of coffee if I had thought of it in time for I suppose you are getting none of the articles these days in the back woods. I feel that I could do it as we are allowed to any rations for our family. I took a family dinner in town today. Two gentlemen, one married lady middle aged and one old maid so you need not be jealous. It was the first hospitality offered or received by or from anyone in this vicinity. I would not do much violence to the truth if I should say after being here that the people are not hospitable to strangers. . . .

Honey, tell me about things in Edgecombe, what they talk of doing if the Yankees get near, etc. I think our prospects altho' bad enough, look a little better for recruits are joining all parts of the army. Just now we are stronger up this way than anywhere else, comparatively speaking.

How are the dear boys. Have Dorsey christened Wm. Dorsey as soon as you have a chance. I should like to pay you all a flying visit. Give my love to all. May the Father of all mercies protect us for Christ's sake.

Your devoted Husband

ন্য়েঃ

Camp Barton, Va., March 25th, 1862

My dear Wife

I was rejoiced today to receive two letters from you dated 19 and 21st, the first for eight days, I last night wrote to you enclosing it to David and asking that he forward it to you at once. I could not but fear that you were sick in Edgecombe. In the box, honey, that I sent you, I sent all your letters to me, every one of which you sent such love for me. You must not destroy one for I sent them to you for safekeeping. In one of your letters today I found a little piece of reed—about as long as the envelope. What was it for? I shall keep it until I know for what it was intended.

Gen. Whiting had out eight Regts. today in review, and mine was the largest of them all, 500 men. . . . All said I had the best Regt. I felt very proud of it. About 100 of them were recruits at that.

. . . I would have a Brigade of N.C. troops if I were promoted and could be allowed. I feel a desire to try them anyhow. We have heard here today through a . . . refugee that Washington has been burned by the Marylanders, but I do not believe it. . . .

Tell Pamela I shall make it all right on Stephen's [S. D. Lee's] part if I can manage to get her mind prepared for waiting and their being there together. . . . My love to all.

Your devoted Husband

໖໖

Camp Barton, Va., March 30th, 1862

My dear Wife

I am glad I have more time to write than you did when you wrote the last that I received. We have been expecting to move for several days and have had our provisions cooked for two days. We may be called out any moment but where to is to me a profound mystery. We are ready and feel that we shall be a match for them. Darling I hope I shall soon have the pleasure of getting a letter from you written at Salem.

I went to town to go to church today, but as there was no service at the Episcopal Church, I called on Mr. Randolph, the minister and sat with him awhile. He told me they would have communion in two weeks. I hope I may be able to partake of it. I feel very anxious about it and really feel as if I might dare to do so with some benefit. You may think that I do not get confirmed because I do not desire it, but really I am very anxious to do so. My desire is to do everything that may gain favor with Christ and insure my salvation. I feel sadly the want of true religion in my soul. That little and perverse member, the tongue, has not by any means been conquered, neither has my angry passion. I feel more and more every day the total inability to do good by one's own efforts.

Honey, you are to be envied by most people in our country. You have a home to retire to out of the reach of the enemy, plenty to live on, a husband whose position affords him all the benefits that one can have as a soldier, friends and relations willing and able to help you. When I look over my past life I feel that I have achieved nothing but favors.

A poor woman came on here from Alamance County to see her husband who she supposed was in [the] hospital, but poor creature, she came to find that he had been buried four or five days. She spent her last cent to get here. She walked out here from town—two miles—through the rain and mud to see his Captain. I sent her back in the ambulance and gave her $5—I knew I should spend it better that way than any other. She had only a female friend to come on with her, but I am a poor comforter. Wasn't her case a hard one. Many is the poor heart that will be broken by this war. May God spare yours is my daily prayer.

Please write me at once whether Jake is coming so I may let Maj. Hill know. Mind you I do not advise it. I see some strong resolutions passed at Edgecombe about burning cotton and destroying whiskey and remaining at home in case of invasion. They all sound all right. Bigger talk in the paper than at home I imagine. How are the Union people up your way? Any danger to a secesh wife?

Honey if you can buy me a couple of silk undershirts reasonably, please do so. I do not want them now, but they are handy to have on hand.... Write me how everything is going on at Good Spring. I hope you have given Turner a good settling and that he is now fine in every respect, and Dorsey how does the big boy flourish. Do not forget the William for I shall want someone to hand down the name. I will write whenever circumstances permit, but if you do not get a letter don't be uneasy....

Kiss the children and Pamela and tell her I am bringing Maj. [S. D.] Lee on ... and that she must wait and give me a chance to show her and him to each other. I gave him a look at her picture the other day with the assurance that it is nothing to the original. God bless you my darling.

Your devoted Husband

✧

Camp Barton, Va., April 3rd, 1862

My precious Wife

I received your sweet letter dated the 30th today, and it made me feel bad to think that my last was doomed to make you unhappy. Darling, look over it and forgive the hardness of it. I love you dearly and I am surprised that I should ever allow my bad disposition to so far overcome me as to allow myself to hurt your feelings. Darling, forgive me this time and write me that you have done so.

As to naming Dorsey, I really have no objection in the world to his having a double name, and to do anything to please you even against my prejudices . . . let me ask you to name him Wm. Dorsey.

. . . We had a grand turnout today of 12 Regts. and 3 Batteries for Gen. [J. E.] Johnston. Gen. [G. W.] Smith rode my horse. . . . We had a rainy review and my Regt. was the [most] observed of all the Regts. One of General Johnston's staff said he had heard it complimented [a] great deal during the day. It has the reputation of being about the best in the service.[42] Now if we can only maintain our reputation in battle. I sometimes feel quite anxious when I think of how we should behave on that occasion.

. . . I cannot imagine what they propose doing here, but cannot help think they are fooling with us to give their army a chance at Gen. Magruder at Yorktown. Frank ought not to resign for he is not the only unused officer who has nothing to do. He had better get on some General's staff than resign. Good many of them hold such positions. Gen. Whiting has two. It will do to talk of serving as private, but he would be sick of the trial.

I pray this may find you better than when you wrote. Honey had you not better wean Dorsey. . . . He is old enough and nursing him will wear you down more than the birth of two. . . .

My dear wife forgive me for writing as I did, and let me know that you have. I met the wife of the minister the other day. She is a sweet little blonde and asked me very particularly to call to see them. I have been to call on him twice. He is a very nice man and very able too. . . .

I pray that we may be spared a good long life to make each other happy and be a material help to each other spiritually. I too long to have you to read to me. I have read my lessons aloud since we left. It seems more like when you were here.

Your devoted Husband

Camp Barton, Va., April 5th, 1862

My dear Wife
. . . I have not been without my little Regimental troubles, but strange to say I have not allowed them to annoy me as usual. I have learned, that altho' Col. Lightfoot is so smooth to me, he has not ceased his plottings against me, which proves your judgement

42. Major A. C. Avery reported in his sketch of the Sixth North Carolina that "when on review at Fredericksburg General Johnston declared it [Sixth North Carolina] superior in drill and discipline to any other regiment in the Army of Northern Virginia." *N.C. Regts.*, I, 349.

to be, as always, right. He will not make much of it, I *think*. Happily, he is still absent.

Tell that dearest little sister that I love her more dearly than ever, and that if she wants to take a husband of my choosing she shall have a man to be proud of. One far superior to the stale and rough husband of her sister. You say my earnestness amuses you. I am not as Mrs. Ely would say, terribly in earnest. I know now so well that I am convinced that few of them are worthy of any sweet, innocent and Christian girl. You know darling how unworthy I am and was of you. I know I have improved some but still for an innocent girl to be contaminated by the intimate association with young men generally is distressing to think of. Take my word for it, young women such as you were and Pamela is should not be thrown away upon any sort of a fellow. Now [Stephen D.] Lee is the pink of honor, in morals above the ordinary standard at least, in sobriety unquestionable, and in goodness of heart unequaled. His whole life would be one continual effort to render any good woman happy. When I mention his name I do not mean to be understood to be pressing his claims, for I have not the remotest idea that they will ever see each other, but to give you my idea of the sort of man that is worth having. I see [a] great deal of him these days.

You say you fear you will have to wean Dorsey, that is just what I want to see you do, so you will have a chance to get strong and well once more. He is old enough to drink for himself. I shall be happy to hear that you had been guilty of such an act. And do not fail to prefix the Wm. Honey, have him baptized the very first chance. By all means go to the Convention if nothing turns up to prevent. I will finish in the morning. God bless you all and give you refreshing sleep and renewed strength in body and soul. Tell Turner that he is papa's good and dear boy, indeed. Bless the dear children. Good night.

April 6th

My dear I have nothing to add to what I wrote last night. I will try to write again tonight. I am getting ready to go to church, which it is to be hoped will be of benefit to me. I wish we could go together. To think we have never been able to go together since I have begun to take some interest in the matter.... God bless you. Good bye.

Your devoted Husband

The Shepperd family homestead at Good Spring, North Carolina
Courtesy of William C. Pender

*W. D. Pender (left) and unidentified comrade during the early
days of the war*

Courtesy of William C. Pender

Camp Barton, Va., April 7th, 1862

My dear Wife

We have just heard of the glorious victory in Tennessee,[43] saddened however by the fall of Gen. A. S. Johnston. Ten hours fighting, we taking 6000 prisoners and 100 guns—artillery—and of course [a] great many small arms. Now if we whip them at Yorktown where we are bound to have a fight if it has not already commenced, they will have their plans considerably disarranged again. Gen. McClellan is there with nearly all of his army. We have an insignificant part to play here for we have scarcely no one in our front. They will make a desperate effort on "on to Richmond" at Yorktown, in which I believe they will be foiled again. I hope father will be a little cheered up if it is as we have heard. Our news came from Gen. [P. T.] Beauregard through the President to Gen. Smith.

I did not write last night, Darling, as it was late before I got back from church. I heard two sermons yesterday. I have but little to write about this time having given you all my views of the war in my last, as well as having expatiated quite extensively on another prolific subject of mine: Pamela's matrimonial prospects. I am looking anxiously for Jake every day. If I find he needs a horse I will send home for Fan for him. I hope, Honey, you will find the medicine beneficial, and soon get strong again. . . .

I find that my clothes are getting so seedy that I will soon have to buy me a suit, but I tell you it goes against the grain. It will cost about $100. I [never] contemplated the purchase of anything with so little pleasure in my life, and if I were not ashamed to go so shabby, I would not do it. I am getting to be quite a miser these days. The mail has not yet come, which deprives me of my expected letter. It was due here six hours ago.

April 8th

A few minutes after writing the above Jake came in very much to my surprise, bringing me in addition to the general gossip about you all, a will. . . . You shall have the money as soon as I can make the arrangements to send it.

We are up, 3 A.M. getting ready for the march, but where to is the question, but I suppose in the direction the Yankees are so desirous of going, Richmond. I will write you on the march if possible but in the meantime do not be uneasy about me. You might write to Henry's care in Richmond. Tell Pamela I will

43. Pender's reference is to the first day's reports of the battle of Shiloh.

take care of Jake as well as I can. Kiss the boys, and may God bless you all and protect us from harm. Love to all.

Your devoted Husband.

∽✤∾

To meet McClellan's advance up the Virginia Peninsula aimed at taking Richmond, Johnston puts his troops in motion toward Yorktown. En route Pender wrote a brief note in a scrawling handwriting that betrayed his excitement.

∽✤∾

Ashland, April 14th, 1862

My dear Wife

We are all packed for the march towards Yorktown. I can merely say I am well and in fine spirits. Jake is well and shall be taken care of. We all go and expect work soon. Do not believe any rumors you may hear, or feel uneasy if we should have a fight and do not hear from me. We have no regular mails even from here. You shall hear as often as possible. I think we can give them a pretty lively time as we have three armies concentrated. We are all right as to numbers and Generals—Johnston, Smith, Longstreet, Magruder, Whiting, etc., etc. With the help of God we shall save the country for they are making their grand move in our front. My love to all. God bless you and the children and let them know that their father has tried to do his duty both to God and his country, and may he shield us from harm.

Your devoted Husband

∽✤∾

Camp near Yorktown, Va., April 19, 1862

My precious Wife

We have at last arrived at our destination for the present. We are encamped about a mile from Yorktown. We are to be the reserve of the army—the troops from Fredericksburg. We have a magnificent army here; the largest and finest we have ever had at [one] place. We have our best Generals also. We all believe and hope we shall whip them. In all the skirmishes that have taken place—and they occur nightly and daily—we have had the best of it. We hear firing in the distance all the time, but not near enough to do us any damage. We have [a] great many N.C. troops here. Those Regts. from near Smithfield have come over. Col. [R. M.] McKinney of the 15th N.C. volunteers was killed the other day in a skirmish. He was surprised.

. . . We had hard but pleasant marches to get to this place. Our men and officers thought it very hard that they should have to march 75 miles instead of coming on the Rail Road. I think it was probably right for they have as much as they can do with their limited rail and water transportation.

I do not know whether I can get this off or not and shall not write much until I find out. At Ashland I had my pistol stolen out of my tent.

Honey, I try to prepare myself for the worst, but I am a great sinner and can only trust in the great mercy of God and the atoning power of the Blessed Saviour. I fear I do not improve any. I do not know of any glaring sins that I am guilty of, but you know how far one can fall short of being a Christian, even when he appears to those of this world to be good. The Lord be merciful to us. Jake is well. My love to all. I write again tomorrow if I can get this off.

Your devoted Husband

Camp near Yorktown, Va., April 25th, 1862

My dear Wife

I have but [a] few minutes to write. We are well and doing finely. No fight nor more chance of one than the day we reached here one month ago. It is said I believe by many that McClellan is moving his forces back toward Fredericksburg, but in that he will be foiled as our President is taking steps to meet him there. My only wonder now is where we get so many soldiers.

I have a chaplain at last. The Rev. Mr. Stuart who was dragged out of his pulpit last year in Alexandria. He seems to be eccentric but I have no doubt is an able man. About 50 years old. Please let me know when you get the box of clothes I sent you. I have not ceased to condemn myself since I sent it off, for I fear I shall be out before I get them again.

Your letters of the 11th, 14th, 16th and 19th were all received as also your father's to Jake. I have advised Jake to wait a few days to see how my old Regt. will organize. If Capt. Ruffin should be a captain and they get a good Colonel, I shall advise him to enlist there. I hate to leave him in the ranks in my Regt. I will look out for him to the best of my ability.

The accounts I receive about Dorsey delight; as to Turner's ability I send no confirmation. I know he is all a fond father could wish. I hope you will go to the [Episcopal] Convention, for I know you will enjoy it. You must take Pamela with you. But what gentleman or lady will go with you. Have you weaned Dorsey yet—if not had you better not? He is getting old enough to get along by himself now. You must not fail to let me know when you want money and do not suppose you are drawing on brother Robert, for I send him all I save. He is my banker.

I worry Jake nearly to death by telling him he asks too many questions. He has got so that he will ask and then take it back. He is the most open and candid boy I ever saw, but gets along with everyone remarkably. You never need be troubled about him.

I suppose Frank is delighted now he has fighting about the lower Miss. He stands more chance of a fight there than anywhere just now. Do you not see that I was right about Goldsboro being in danger. They are not going so far from water.

Now my dear I must close as the carrier is about ready and I have to go to drill. May God in Heaven bless you all. My love to all at Cold Spring. Write me regularly.

Your devoted Husband

~❧~

Camp near Yorktown, Va., April 26th, 1862

My dear Wife

Your letters of the 7th and 8th were received yesterday. The one of the 7th I can say I had rather not have received, for before I did not know how much I had injured you and also how much you were hurt by it. The letter was unjustifiable and deserved the strongest condemnation, and I have heartily repented of ever having written it. I can only hope the feeling and indignation it must have produced have as entirely passed away as the feeling that caused it to be written. I have felt very badly about it since yesterday. I will only say in David's defence that however unjustifiable in writing what he did, I cannot think he wished to produce trouble between us. I was as much to blame for causing it as he was in writing me.

Harris returned yesterday bringing my shirts. You will not believe me when I say that they are just the thing in every point: color, material, and fit. You could not have hit it better. I am perfectly delighted with them. I think of sending Harris to Ashland Monday after the balance of my things. . . .

Our troops are suffering [a] great many hardships here. We are very comfortable compared to most of them. We have no picket or trench duty. Nothing but to rest and enjoy ourselves preparatory to finishing the fight when the others have been in it some time. The reserve have to give the final decisive blow.

Honey, I really did not mean anything when I wrote that I thought Jake had been very undecided. Maj. Hill [was] so anxious for him to come on. Gen. Whiting I think stood in his way, saying he would not allow it; for what reason I know not unless it was because they had a man who had been doing the duty for nearly a year, who he might have thought ought to have it.

I am getting very anxious to see you my dear wife, more so than I have for a long, long while. I do not know why just now, but I long very much to see you, probably because I want to see for myself that you have not lost your love and good opinion of me and that my unjust and foolish letter is not to be the cause of any future disturbances or disagreement between us on any point. We are about as near cut off from all communication with the world as we could well be. Our mail all seems to come by chance and I have not yet been able to find out from what post office it came. Jake wants Pamela to account for her silence towards him as she has not written to him yet. He send his love to all.

We are in considerable uncertainty as to the safety of New Orleans. Will not the danger it seems to be in probably hurry up Helen's movements northward. I am glad you are getting so much stronger. Now do not stop taking the iron as soon as you get a little better, but continue until you get very strong, sufficiently so to walk miles. You need not trouble yourself about the shirts, for when these I have wear out, you can make me some of flannel which will be just as good. What are you going to do about your machine. I think you had as well keep it, for there is no certainty of getting another as cheap when you want it. I did not suppose my indebtedness to D. Pender & Co. so great myself, but I had no idea of what it was. I will write again tomorrow night if I send Harris off. My dear wife, good night and pleasant dreams to you. God bless you all. Our love to all.

Your devoted Husband

~❧~

Camp near Yorktown, Va., April 27th, 1862

My dear Wife

According to promise I write you again tonight altho' I have but little to write about. Today was passed about like all Sabbaths do in camp. I should be very glad to be able to go to church but that is not allowed us. I hope we shall have service Tuesday by Mr. Stuart. I hope he will administer the sacrament for upon the eve of what we suppose is to be a great and bloody battle. I should like once more to partake of that means of grace, altho' I feel totally unworthy. I could only trust in my sincere desire to accept it worthily.

We have very cheering rumors from Richmond today. If only half of them are true. One that Jackson has whipped [N. P.] Banks in the Valley, one that Beauregard has whipped [D. C.] Buell, another that our gunboat Louisiana has destroyed the two Federal boats reported to have passed the Forts, and the fourth which is said to be from the President that the Steamer Nashville had gotten into Wilmington with 7000 rifles. Pretty good for one day, is it not?

Captain Ruffin has been reelected Captain of his old Company and Dr. [D. A.] Montgomery 1st Lieut. The men of the Company are superior to most any I know from N.C. and I think I shall advise Jake to join it. I know he would be taken good care of there.

Do you know Honey I feel very solemn tonight, possibly more so on account of some singing which is going on near. Oh! Darling I do so long to be a Christian and I do find it so hard even to have the outward semblance of such. It is impossible for me, I suppose I trust too little to Christ and expect to do too much myself.

Have you seen any account of the dream a soldier had at Pensacola. We were to have a big and severe fight the last week in April, in the first week of May peace was to ensue, and that the day after his dream at a certain hour he was to die. The latter part of his dream was fulfilled and I cannot help from being superstitious enough to think a part at least of the remainder is to come true. May the Lord, if it be his good pleasure, protect me from harm. I cannot contemplate leaving you with any degree of composure. My dear, excuse this laborious strain I am in tonight and set it down as worth nothing, but you know how impossible it is to prevent ourselves sometimes from indulging ourselves far enough to communicate our feelings to others. To none would it give so much pain but at the same time none can sympathize so fully with me as you will. God bless you my more than guardian Angel.

I sometimes treat you badly and am cross to you, but I love you none the less. Fanny, it seems to me that I can want no other blessing conferred upon me in this world than to be allowed to live quietly with you and the children. I may appear to be restless, etc. when you are with me, but it does not arise from not being satisfied. You always say I do not talk to you. I talk but little to anyone, but it always seems when with you that I am content to sit down and enjoy my happiness in quiet. Live on my dear wife in consciousness that you have been a true wife a good wife and a devoted one. That you have inspired in me the desire at least to be better than I was when you married me.

Matters militaire stand about the same with the exception of a little activity on the part of the enemy in throwing up some dirt last night, [a] good deal nearer our works.

Honey, won't you write me that I am the same to you that I was before I wrote that unfortunate letter. I feel guilty and therefore uneasy. I am scared at the calmness with which you wrote that reply. Darling, I cannot bear to lower myself in your estimation. Kiss the children. May the Lord have mercy upon us miserable sinners.

Your devoted Husband

ᔋᔍ

Just as McClellan was poised to batter the 56,000 graycoats ensconced around Yorktown, Johnston evacuated his lines and fell back toward Richmond. After four days of trudging through Virginia mud Pender found time to write Fanny.

ᔋᔍ

Camp near New Kent C.H., Va., May 8th, 1862

My dear Wife

I know you have been in great trouble about me, but I had no possible means of sending off a letter. I had one written last

Saturday but had to tear it up not having any conveyance and not wishing to run the risk of having my letters read by any Yankee. Honey you will have to be satisfied with a short letter, for I have seldom been much more sleepy, hungry, or tired than I am just now. Up nearly all of two nights and in the saddle for two days, few hours will cover the sleep I have had in forty-eight. We were in a pretty tight place last night [but] are all right now.

We are out of the Peninsula which was a perfect trap for us. We had some hard marching . . . and two skirmishes and one battle. We with inferior numbers beating them badly. The battle lasted about all day commencing with two Brigades on our side and winding up with ten [or 25,000]. We beat them badly again. Our loss was over 1,000 killed and wounded, theirs much heavier besides some hundreds of prisoners. These two were at Williamsburg. Skirmish was near West Point. The two former I was not near, the latter I was near but not engaged. I was seeking one all day but failed. Three or four Regts. each engaged. We whipped them badly again, 65 prisoners taken by us [and] 30 or 40 killed. We lost 25 killed and some wounded. I did not have a chance to test my courage. I saw enough to satisfy me of my men's pluck.

The big battle will come off yet. They are following us up slowly and more so since we whipped them at Williamsburg. McClellan was [in command] there. Longstreet commanded on our side. . . . Jake is well and was skirmishing some yesterday during our little affair, trying to get a chance. He is all right and as good a young man as I ever saw. My love to all. Kiss the children. May God bless us all.

Your devoted Husband

⚜

May 9th, 1862

My dear Wife

I wrote you last night but for fear it may not reach you I will write again . . . to let you know that I am still in the land of the living. We are about done falling back, I suppose. Tomorrow or next day will place us where we will make a stand for Richmond. No one amongst us fears the result . . . our men have shown superior fighting qualities. Of 44 prisoners I saw today only four were Yankees, the rest foreigners. . . . We are only about 22 miles from Richmond but march very slowly, only about 4 miles today.

Honey, I will write again as soon as I can send off the letter, but we have no facilities for writing as we scarcely ever have our wagons. May our merciful father protect us. My love to all and take my whole heart to yourself.

Your devoted Husband

 ∿❧∾

May 11, 1862

My dear Wife

You may imagine what a monotonous time we are having only marching 1½ miles yesterday and 4 the day before. I wish we were at our journey's end where we could have what few comforts we can have along. I can have neither change of clothes or writing material. Jake is all right.

My dear wife, notwithstanding the grand operations going on here I have nothing to write about. I hope you will receive my letters written a few days before in due time, but when you do not hear from me do not feel uneasy for it is difficult to write for many reasons. And do not believe the reports you see in the papers about battles, for three-fourths of what was in the Richmond paper the other day was every word false. We had but one General wounded and only two Colonels killed. The heaviness of our loss was caused by the bad behavior of the 23rd N.C. and 38th Va. in common with the rashness of the others.

Honey, I long to see you. Now nearly one year ago we were under the shade tree [at Good Spring] sitting on the grass, the happiest hours of my life. I shall never forget it and I do not wish to. It was complete earthly happiness.

How are the dear boys getting on. Honey do you not feel very different from [what] you did last year this time, but about the same [as] you may [feel] the next year this time.

I have not heard from you for nearly two weeks, over, counting from the date of your letter. How do you pass your time, now [that] you have your summer outfit made. I hope you will go to the Convention if you think you would enjoy it.

Honey, I have to write always so hurriedly that it is but little satisfaction to me, and I fear less [to] you, but it cannot be helped.

It is distressing to pass through this country. Nearly every farm is deserted and what our soldiers do not destroy they will.... My love to all the folks at Good Spring. I must now

close. May our merciful father have mercy upon you all. Accept
my undying devotion.

Your Husband

~✤~

Camp near Baltimore Store, Va., May 14th, 1862

My dear Wife

I have no ink or pen so you must excuse pencil. We are still
waiting for the coming of the Yankees, but strange to say I
believe we do not even know where their main force is. Stuart is
looking after them but is not doing himself much credit as he
does not find out anything. Gregg is Captain of the 6th Regt. of
Cavalry and Cal of the 8th Penn Volunteer Cavalry. Stuart's
father-in-law is General of the cavalry on their side and Stuart on
this. Stuart says he wants to catch him and that he expects to do
so.

The Merrimac you no doubt know has been blown up. Does
it not seem a pity that she had to be lost, but I suppose it could
not be helped. The people of Richmond are frightened to death
and believe that the Yankees will have possession in three days,
but I apprehend it will at least take them longer than that. If they
come this way they will be much longer.

How is it that Frank gets as much salary now as I do? What
new position has he? I should like to see him pass this way for
I suppose his occupation is now gone near New Orleans.

I shall try to send some money home today. Those merchants
up your way who have refused to take Confederate notes should
be made an example of at once. Hanging would not be too good
for them. I suppose you all will have a jolly time at Good Spring.
Now at least a noisy one. What you write me about the children
is very gratifying, but I should much prefer to know of their
perfections from personal observation. I suppose you have strawberries now while we are barely subsisting upon meat and bread.
Our men have to go upon short rations nearly every day and the
officers are not much better off. I have managed to keep a little
coffee and tea yet.

Jake is now a soldier and seems to get along very well. He is
with Sgt. [C. M.] Mebum and Rev. Holt, two very nice and intelligent young men. You may rest assured that I will take as good
care of him as I can. He endeared himself very much to the
officers with whom he has been associated. He is a very superior

young man and if I ever have an opportunity shall not fail to advance him, but I have about as much as I can do to hold my own.

I am fearful that Gen. Whiting is doing something that will cause me to take some step that may appear rash. He has been ordered to place some one in the command of the Brigade, and if he places any Colonel over me— for I am by right entitled to it unless they put a General in his place, or if they promote anyone connected with us now—I shall deem it due my self respect to resign and look out for some other position. He has not asked me in a maner to heighten my opinion of him. I am entitled to the Brigade, and if he would give it to me it is a step towards promotion.

You could direct my letters to no better place at present than Richmond, for we do have occasional communication with that place. I must now close, my dear wife, but will write again soon. My love to all. May God bless you. Do not fail to send the likeness on when you have the chance.

Your devoted Husband

Who are the merchants that refuse Confederate notes?

∽❧∾

Camp 5 miles from Richmond, May 17th, 1862

My dear Wife

You see the enemy is on to Richmond with us, but do not think we have been running all the time from McClellan, for it is not so. Our Generals have been very anxious for him to attack us. . . .

We hear it from the best authority that the Monitor was so crippled in her engagement with our battery in the obstruction [at Drewry's Bluff] that she could not make the tower, in which her guns are placed, revolve. . . .

Lee [Major Stephen D.] is considered the best artillerist in this Army. We make short but very hard marches, not averaging a mile an hour, and it generally rains when we have to march. I felt as tired and badly yesterday as I ever did from a march. It is a tremendous job to move a large army composed as ours is. The whole country ahead on either side and rear is literally filled with stragglers. The only consolation is they will nearly all fight. . . .

I was glad to hear yesterday that Col. Lightfoot would certainly be reelected in the 22nd N.C. His previous election was only for the unexpired term. I never want to have him back here. I think Capt. [I. E.] Avery will get his place here. I shall recommend him and so will Gen. Whiting.

Honey, I hope you will excuse the poor and short letters I write you, for it is impossible to write a decent letter the way we are living. I try to make up by the number. My love to all. God bless and protect you. Tell Turner papa says he must be a pretty boy.

Your devoted Husband

∼❧∼

Camp near Richmond, Va., May 21st, 1862

My dear Wife

I know you have thought fifty times, why cannot I go to see him, he is at Richmond, and my dear such thoughts have crossed my brain, but had to be given up in their infancy, for it would be imprudent for a lady—especially with children—to come on here now. Every nook and corner is filled with soldiers dirty, etc. etc, and then again there is not telling when the city may have to suffer what New Orleans was only threatened.

By the way, have you seen Gen. [B. F.] Butler's order or proclamation in which he says if another lady dares treat a Yankee officer discourteously they shall be treated as women of the town— that is, women of bad repute. Did you ever hear of such brutality, trying to frighten our poor women into showing respect to his miserable drunken rabble. Can such people succeed. I pray not. May the Lord have mercy upon us and make our hearts brave and theirs more cowardly than they are. What can we expect when their chief officers—and one who pretended to be favorable to the south before the war broke out, act as Butler proposes if we should be subjugated.

McClellan is making his way slowly towards us but unless he travels faster than he usually does, it will be some days yet before he gets here. He was 12 miles off yesterday, with a little stream between him and us. He will make every effort in his power to beat us, but he will have a hard time of it.

I received a very desponding letter from David two days ago. Each individual seems to think that when their little village is within reach of the enemy that the country is gone. I rather gave him a piece of my mind yesterday. I do not think one should allow anyone to know if he thinks so that he fears for the ultimate result. Everyone weakens the cause who allows himself to doubt of our success.

...Mr. Stuart went into the Convention yesterday with the intention of having the Bishop come to camp and preach for us today. I hope he will come. We have the most beautiful place around my tent I ever saw, for him. I have my tent in a beautiful little nook of the hills. Beech and honeysuckles all over and around a nice little stream we have dammed up to make us a bathing place.... It is perfectly charming I just wish you could see it. Mr. Stuart is a regular trump. I like him so much. He seems to be a most excellent Christian and an agreeable and industrious companion. He makes himself very useful instead of troublesome as I feared. I feel that association with him will be of great benefit to me.

As drill is about to come off I must close but will write again tomorrow or next day. My love to all. God bless you and the children.

Your devoted Husband

෴

Camp near Richmond, Va., May 22nd, 1862

My dear Wife

You may know that I feel anything but easy in mind when I tell you I have received no letter from you of later date than the 8th. I do not for a moment suppose that you have failed to write, but attribute it all to the mail. Write me as soon as you get this and put down the Regt. as well as Whiting's Brigade. All mail to officers or soldiers are now arranged according to Regts. I asked at the office the other day five times, hoping by getting them to look often they might light upon one.

I was in town again today hoping to get something. I called to see Custis Lee and was sorry to find him quite sick and in a fair way of getting worse.

My dear child when I sit down to write I find so little to write about that I feel you will see the effort I make to interest you and that it may have the contrary effect. I could write always of my love and desire to see you, but when I get on that tack you always pretend, at least, not to believe me. There is nothing in this world I so much desire as to be able to live quietly and constantly with you and this you know from past experience....

I am now getting old enough for I really feel as if I were

getting along in years. I am told so often that I look thirty-five. I pass with those who do not know for anywhere between thirty-five and forty. You must not feel worried at the idea that I am getting too old for you. I wish to get old faster than you at least some years to come. It looks better. I am quite bald also, but I hope all these signs of old age will not give you any trouble or make you love me less. I cannot help it and my heart is as fresh and tender for you as if I looked only twenty. If I get much less good looking and you continue so young and fascinating—remember the young preacher. I shall get to be a jealous old husband.

Honey I hope you have gone to the Convention for I know you will enjoy it. Gen. Whiting is to have a $1000 horse presented him this evening by the 4th Ala. Regt., and the 11th Miss. have $1200 to buy him one and I believe the 2nd Miss. are going to do likewise. High appreciation of our superiors is all very well, but such toadyism as has been shown in this matter, except by the 11th, is rather too much of a good thing. . . .

My love [to] all. Tell Pamela I am waiting quite impatiently for that letter she promised. Honey please try to get a letter to me, for you must know how anxious I must be to hear from you. I pray our Father in Heaven to protect us and grant us strength to bear all troubles with which we may be afflicted. Kiss the dear boys.

Your devoted Husband

∾✿∾

Camp near Richmond, Va., May 25th, 1862

My dear Wife

I this evening took the finishing step towards making myself a member of Christ's Church in this world, and may I prove myself worthy of the privilege. I was confirmed this evening at the Monumental Church by Bishop [John] Johns. I know you will be pleased to hear of this pledge of my earnestness in trying to be a Christian steward, tho' darling that it is much easier to conform to the outward forms than the inward, and all important, man, but by God's help I pray I may come in the future to everlasting salvation. I find that the company of Mr. Stuart is of great benefit to me. He is a good man with good men.

Darling do you not pity me. I have not heard a word from you since the 8th. I am so anxious to hear but I will not allow myself to think there is anything wrong except in the mails.

Our affairs have about come to a crisis. The bubble must burst in comparatively a few hours. We all look for the all important battle to-morrow, as our troops are only a mile or so apart and there has been great activity in movement of troops on both sides today. I write to you fully because I know you are a woman of too much good sense to wish [otherwise] or for it to be prudent to retain from you anything. I know you are brave enough to look the thing squarely in the face. Let us hope for the best. All our people feel very confident, but a great many, of course, will bite the dust before the battle shall be ended. They have [a] great many more men than we, but at Williamsburg they had more than twice our number and were fresher than our troops and still they were badly whipped. They admit a loss of over four thousand while we did not lose two thousand. If you hear of fighting and should not hear from me, do not feel uneasy for it will be impossible for me to communicate until things shall quiet down a little. Be of good cheer and rest assured that He who knows of the falling of a sparrow will direct all things for the best, however hard they may be to bear. I can truly say, that in my life I can see wherein He has directed it has been for my good. When it has been to the contrary it has been the result of letting the evil one get dominion over me.

My dear wife I should so like to see you, if for only one moment to give you a good embrace and to assure you of my undying love and admiration for you. Kiss the dear little boys and tell them of their father and how he intends to raise them to be good men. My love to all the family. Jake is getting on famously, much better he says than he expected. His mess has a negro to cook for them. Write me often and do not forget to address to the Regt. and Brigade. May the Lord have mercy upon us.

Your devoted Husband

❦

Camp near Richmond, Va., May 27th, 1862

My precious Wife,

We are still going on in the usual way; two large armies lying within three miles of each other, apparently on good terms for we scarcely ever hear a gun for the last three days, but the real opening will be the more earnest. If we are victorious here it will bring some months of quiet around Richmond at least, for if we are successful it will be such a bad whipping for them that it will take some time for them to recover. And we contemplate nothing but a defeat for them. How can people who threaten to treat ladies as harlots because they will not bow and smile upon their low rascals, succeed? There is [a] great deal of real piety in our army and a much more Christian spirit than formerly. We do not depend so much upon our own superiority as upon the help of God. Every man who has any manhood should and does feel the absolute necessity of fighting to the death.

You need not be surprised to find some of these days, our Chaplain Rev. Stuart drive up to your door. I told him yesterday how I should like for him to go and take and bring me some letters and that I would promise him he should enjoy his visit and he jumped at [it] and says if nothing prevents he shall start next Monday. I know you would be delighted to see him, particularly as he would be from me. He is a most capital fellow. He got his commission yesterday to date from the 1st.

Do you want the prescription for Turner, for fear you do I will send it in my next, the Doctor not being here just now. As the bearer is waiting I must close. No letter from you yet. My love to everybody. I am getting on finely. May our Heavenly Father protect us.

Your devoted Husband

❧

5 miles from Richmond, Va., May 29th, 1862

My dear Wife

I yesterday received two letters from you, one of April 30th and the other May 20th, and honey I must say the last left me more sad than I have been for many a day. It was very evident that you had been very sick and would not only let me know nothing of it at the time, but would not have the confidence in me to write me when you could about it. You ask me to write or let you know if I should get sick or wounded. Why do you not set me the example. Darling here I was making myself believe that my dear wife was well and that it was only the mail, when probably she was dangerously ill. Darling do you never forgive or retract? Do you really intend to carry out what you said last summer and not let me know when you get sick. Honey be more confiding next time under similar circumstances.

My dear how can you have any respect for a man who acts and talks as Joe Williams? Would you like for me to do as he does.

Refuse to fight but want to make money by the worst calling but one—negro trading—making that curse of man more than curse of a wife, whisky. Fanny, write me no more about such a miserable degraded creature. Let his name never be mentioned by us to each other only to condemn. I am sorry that his family pretentions so blind you as to allow you to respect such a man. I do not write how I like the idea of his being Pamela's husband. That is her business, but Pamela will have to come down very much from my opinion of her before she gets low enough to marry such a creature....

We came out last night fully expecting to move on and attack the enemy this morning, but something prevented. I hope the attack will not be delayed many more hours. We can whip them without their artillery, but with them the things become more difficult. My dear, never allow yourself to doubt our ultimate success. We can never be conquered unless the Laslens [?] and Williamses do it. The Yankees cannot. I slept not a wink last night and but very little for the previous 48 hours. I have felt anything but bright today. We occasionally have pretty rough times, but generally it is not bad. We lived very well at Richmond. I got a bin of nice sweet potatoes from home two days ago. We are here with only what we brought on our horses and boys.

Your description [of] the progress of the children is very gratifying. I am very sorry I did not get your letter asking for powders for Turner until a few minutes before we left yesterday, but I will send them as soon as possible....

... Do not let your father make you despond. My dear wife one more word about Unionists. You love me and think I act from a sincere conviction of the justice of my cause and you did approve it. Here I am not only risking my life in battle but by any of the various camp diseases in a cause which really primarily affects me but little, while they [the Unionists in North Carolina] are giving aid and comfort to the enemy by creating trouble at home, etc. etc. etc. Now my dear how can you not only treat these people with anything but frigid politeness, but appear to consider a lingering liking for you as desirable. Erase the apparent harshness of my letter, but I say no more than I am justified in.

May our Father have mercy upon us. Write me often. Love to all.

Your devoted Husband

∾❀∾

When McClellan's blue-coated legions had leisurely advanced to within ten miles of Richmond, Johnston seized the opportunity to pounce on the divided Federal Army as it straddled the swollen Chickahominy River. In the ensuing fierce but inconclusive battle of Seven Pines Colonel Pender distinguished himself by cooly and skillfully extricating his regiment from a precarious predicament.

Ordered to lead the advance on the Confederate left, Pender pressed ahead through dense woods with the assurance that his regiment would be supported. After crossing a road Pender espied three Federal flags to his left and rear. The enemy troops in the area were "so posted that they could in five minutes have moved rapidly down the road which the Sixth had crossed and cut it off from retreat or support."[44]

With quick presence of mind Pender in "the ringing voice which would always be heard and was always heeded," shouted the command, "By the left flank, file left, double quick!" This directive, according to a lieutenant at his side, "was the only possible combination of commands that could have saved us from capture, and they were molded into a single order without hesitating for an instant."[45]

On reaching the road Pender charged the Union regiments on his flank, throwing them into confusion long enough to allow the Sixth to fall back a short distance and form on the right of some Mississippi regiments which Pender had summoned upon first realizing his plight.

President Davis witnessed the execution of this bold maneuver, and riding up to the Colonel of the Sixth North Carolina said: "General Pender, I salute you." Gratified by this reward for his conduct in his initial engagement, Pender confided to Stephen Lee: "I could have coveted no greater honor than to be promoted by the President on the field of battle."[46]

Two days after the struggle at Seven Pines, Jefferson Davis' battlefield promotion of Pender was formalized in General Orders No. 71 which stated that "Brigadier General Pender is assigned to the command of General Pettigrew's brigade [Pettigrew was captured at Seven Pines], and will at once enter upon his duties." Pender's brigade, which became part of A. P. Hill's newly organized Light Division, comprised the Thirteenth, Sixteenth,

44. *N.C. Regts.*, I, 351.
45. *Ibid.*
46. *N.C. Regts.*, I, 352; Montgomery, "Life and Character of Major-General W. D. Pender," p. 12.

Twenty-second, Thirty-fourth, and Thirty-eighth North Carolina regiments plus the Second Arkansas Regiment and the Twenty-second Virginia Battalion.[47] *In his first letter, dated June 6, to Fanny following his promotion, Pender inexplicably fails to mention his new status save in a fleeting oblique reference.*

∾❦∾

4 miles from Richmond, Va., June 6th, 1862

My dear Wife

The Rev. Mr. Stuart left me this morning to take Jake at least a part of the way home. I tried to persuade him to go on and think he will. I wish him to see you, and then you can find out a great many little points that I never think to write. He will appear a little eccentric but when you know him you will like him. He has rendered Jake invaluable services. They heard at home that I was killed and David put off immediately, reaching here last night, but instead of finding me a cold corpse he found me standing in all the dignity of a Brigadier. David looks very badly and is suffering very much with a cough. He will leave this evening. I sent Harris off last night for my mare.

Honey, I promised you a description of the fight, but I have had to talk and write so much about it that I will have Mr. Stuart and Jake to give you a description of the whole thing. Mr. Stuart not only will give you what took place, but ought to have taken place. He is a great warrior in theory.

Honey, I wish I could see you and the children very much, but I am still of the opinion that my leave will not take effect until the winter. Darling, you ask my opinion of our prospects. They are in some adversity now, but I do not and cannot believe they can ever conquer us. Let them take Richmond, what then; we can still fight and will fight. Let them take every large town and still we are not conquered. Did not the English have all the towns in the Revolution, and did [not] our fathers fight on until the end was gained? We have fewer tories in our midst than they had and more facilities for conducting a war, and I do not believe that our people are one whit less patriotic now than then. No, my dear wife, never despair; we men will never give up as long as we have the brave and angelic women of the South to cheer us and depend upon us for protection.

47. *O.R.* 11, pt. 3, 569 and *O.R.* 11, pt. 2, 487.

But to go back, Richmond has not been taken yet and before it is they will have to fight many a battle and desperate ones too. We have nearly as many troops around Richmond as they and I know they are as brave and determined. They fight, it is true, but in the most cowardly manner, behind earth works. Our men and officers showed the most wonderful bravery and determination the other day. Darling, keep up your spirits. Cheer the men portion of the population. The ladies of the South have, morally speaking, done much more in this war than the men, but for them many a faint hearted soldier would long ago have given up, but so long as we have such wives, mothers, and sisters to fight for so long will this struggle continue until finally our freedom will be acknowledged. Do you supose we are going to submit to see our wives etc. insulted for all future by brutes they would send amongst us? No! No! Take a few examples and see how hard and almost impossible it is to subdue a people determined to be free. The Netherlands when Phillip tried to crush. Spain against Napoleon. This country in '76. . . . Most of us may bite the dust but our children with the help of God will be free. I am not so brave or fearless, I wish this war could end without another shot being fired, but I will continue as long as it or I last.

Listen to Mr. Stuart, he will cheer you. Doctor up Jake and send him back. I shall try to get him as my clerk where he will be with me, mess etc. I wish very much that Frank would come with me. Great many of our naval officers have been acting as staff during this war. He might be able to look around and see something better if he wished. I shall hold a position open for him awhile as you write that he expects to be thrown out of command. What has become of Ham? I suppose he is in Jackson's glorious campaign [in the Shenandoah Valley].

We are now resting for what may come at any moment. I must now close as I have some business to attend to. My love to all. Write me as often as you can. God bless you all.

Your devoted Husband

Tell Jake when he returns I want him to bring me a pr. of waterproof boots with long legs, size no. 6. . . . I want a nice pr. of riding boots, serviceable at the same time. . . .

∼✺∽

Camp 5 miles of Richmond, Va., June, 8th 1862

My dear Wife

I hope by this you have had the pleasure of seeing Jake all fresh from the battle. I can write but little as my mind is pretty well taken up with pickets, abatis, roads, rations, and such small sanitary details. My Brigade is on advance duty and I consequently have but little time to think of outside matters, but always time to think of, if not to write to, you. The enemy kicked up some shims this morning as if they wished to make an attack upon our front, but Col. [S. D.] Lee with some of his shell soon put them to flight, but with what loss we cannot tell. Our people found on the ground after they had left, 10 or 12 dead and one wounded.

I hope to get off this duty tomorrow when I shall have time to rest and write and fix up generally. Here I sleep with boots and all on. I did not tell you that I was indebted I believe to Gen. Whiting for my promotion. He took advantage of the first opportunity to press my promotion upon the President. He is going to try to have Stephen Lee made Brigadier. So I fear Mrs. Lee, née Sheppard, will be as big a lady as your ladyship. I hope you have not put on the airs you threaten me with. And honey, what about the velvet cloak, can you not wait awhile longer? Money is very scarce and debts are heavy. Please let me off with such an expensive one.

We have heard by Flag of Truce that Gen. Pettigrew is not dead. He is said to be severely wounded but out of danger. Cols. Lightfoot and [J. O.] Long both of the 22nd N.C. of this Brigade are reported as prisoners and well.

Mrs. [Rose] Greenough [Greenhow]—the celebrated [Southern agent]—came to City Point below Richmond by flag of truce on Sunday, May 1st [Pender obviously meant June 1] and she states that the loss of the enemy Saturday was very heavy and that they lost two Generals of Division killed. You will hear that our Army lost 10,000 and all that sort of thing, do not believe a word of it. We did not have 1000 killed in the whole affair. 5000 will more than cover the loss—as officially reported, but a great [number] were put down as missing, who had run back to Richmond, and it was remarkable that the wounds were very slight. Mostly in the limbs and but few, very few, of those had to be amputated. Gen. Whiting told me that from what had been heard, the enemy lost two or three to our one. I give you the above to show what exaggerated reports get out.

I am very sorry Darling that things should have turned out so you cannot feel towards David as you did. I know he was not actuated by any mean or ungentlemanly motives and he is to me a devoted and kind brother. I know him to be a high minded, generous man. He said when here the other day that they never heard from you except through me, meaning I suppose rarely heard. He said it in a sad way. The whole thing seems to have been unfortunate. It has caused me many unhappy moments to think that my wife, the dearest object on earth, and my most beloved relative are never to get on well together, for entertaining the opinion of him that you do, the less you have to do with each other the better. But I will drop this unpleasant subject. I do not desire to draw you out upon it.

I hope you like Mr. Stuart, and have had your likeness taken so as to send it to me. Today is Sunday and how I wish this horrible war was over so we could be about this hour returning from some village church with our boys in the door waiting to welcome us. May God grant us yet such earthly happiness and in the world to come life everlasting. Give my love to all and to the young lads a kiss apiece.

Your devoted Husband

June 13th, 1862

My dear Wife

I have been so very busy the last few days that I could not write. I am now enjoying quite an easy time considering what we have been doing. Our men were completely broken down. Our position is very pleasant and not much annoyed by the enemy. I begin to think there will [not] be any more fighting for some time unless we again make the attack, which we ought to do. Jackson is and will continue to walk into them. Gens. Whiting and [J. B.] Hood of Whiting's Division went to him two days since taking two of the finest Brigades in the service with them. It left me in command of the Division, but being satisfied just at present with five Regts. I made arrangements by which Gen. [A. P.] Hill, to whom I had to report when getting here, relieved [me] of all but my own Brigade which consists of over 5000 present and absent.

My dear I am so mixed in my mind that I cannot write. I am well, in good spirits and still in love with the finest woman in the world. I was delighted by your account of Turner's health but sorry to hear that your son [Dorsey] was falling off. My dear I hope you continue well and hope Helen will be able to enjoy this fair weather. I am still anxious to have Frank, he is just the fellow for the position, the ornamental and agreeable part of my life.

I will write again tomorrow and more in full. You would be proud to see me with my new coat, plain but becoming. Let me know how Jake is getting [along], and tell him not to forget my boots. Write often. God bless you all.

Your devoted Husband

~~~~~

In Camp 5 miles of Richmond, Va., June 14th, 1862

My dear Wife

Your long and agreeable letter was received yesterday in which you complain that I did not let you know of my promotion. My darling I certainly intended to tell you in my first letter after it took place if I did not, for I always like to write everything that I think will give you pleasure, and I was sure that would. It was not intentional, and you must not think hard of it.

I hope Mr. Stuart stayed long enough with you all for you to overcome the first bad impression he usually makes. He is very amusing, as well as instructive. It was very kind in him to take Jake home. Jake I hope is improving and will soon rejoin the service. You all must not keep him after he is able to [come] back.

I am having quite an easy time compared to what it was a few days ago, but how long it will remain so is the question. The Yankees seem to all outward appearances as far from attacking us as ten days ago. We are making some preparations for them. They admit in the [New York] Herald a loss in the recent fight of 7,000 thus showing contrary to my expectations a larger loss than we sustained. They had all the advantage of position, preparations and artillery.

May has passed and they have not taken Richmond yet. In some of the letters taken on the field they were quite facetious about marchnig to Richmond. Some said they had not time to write more as they were in a hurry towards the city. Others said their next would be dated in Richmond, etc.

I received a letter yesterday from Col. [A. M.] Scales[48] asking

48. Alfred M. Scales of Rockingham had succeeded Pender as colonel of the Third North Carolina Volunteers [subsequently the Thirteenth North Carolina] when Pender became colonel of the Sixth North Carolina. *N.C. Regts.*, I, 654.

me to try to get his Regt. in my Brigade and congratulating me upon my promotion.

I went to see Almond Heart today and found the poor fellow in a bad plight. Altho' looking fat he said he was completely broken down and that the Doctor had promised to send him to hospital tomorrow. He said he had not a clean white shirt or drawers to his name, having lost a few days ago, for the second time everything he had. You will excuse me for offering him one of the shirts you made me. He said he would accept it and a pr. of drawers and seemed very grateful. I then ventured to ask him about his finances upon which he said he had not a cent for three weeks and I pressed him to take $15. He said he was so tired of salt meal and bread. He has [had] diarrhea since leaving York-town. We talked about when I was married and he said he was sorry when the affair was over as he was enjoying himself very much and that he often thought of Miss Mary Lilly. It felt like old times for Almond was always a great favorite of mine.

... Honey I must close sooner than I anticipated, having some pressing business on hand. May God in Heaven bless you all. I have just gotten through part of my business, I will now give you a few more words to show you that even the duties of a general do not make me forget my wife. Good night.

Your devoted Husband

In Camp near Richmand, Va., June 22nd, 1862

My dear Wife

I received two letters from you today dated the 10th and the other the 4th inst. I was much pleased to find you [in] so much better spirits as to our prospects, and particularly to hear that you are in such good health. I suppose Dorsey must be *cutting teeth*. I was sorry to hear that Helen is so unwell. May I ask if she is in an interesting situation. Honey as I was all wrong in my explanation to myself as to why you did not write, please tell me the reason. You wrote that you had not written for some time but had been very anxious to do so. My dear I can take a joke altho' you think I cannot, but those Williams' are my abomination, they are traitors and ought to be treated as such. You will recollect that Joe has the reputation of being vindictive and you know he bears us no good will. He has said we should rue the day we married. Keep him at a distance.

You will see by the paper of this morning that Jackson has been gaining more victories. He and Gen. [R. S.] Ewell together have completely routed [Major General John C.] Fremont and [Major General James] Shields. If we could get these people away from their breastworks we could make as short work of them as Jackson has those in the [Shenandoah] Valley. It seems that Norfolk and Portsmouth have both been evacuated by the Yankees, thus showing that they feel their weakness here. McClellan has been calling lustily for re-enforcements since the battle, we hear. Their list of killed and wounded in the recent fight show a big list of high officers. They admit 800 killed and 300 wounded. I saw the Herald of the 5th. The Herald claims a grand victory but the [New York] Tribune calls it a reverse and wants to see the thing explained.

I am very anxious to have Frank join me but from what you write I fear there is no chance. I do not know who to get on my staff. I want about two in addition to those now with me as they will leave whenever Gen. [J. J.] Pettigrew may be exchanged. I hear that Dick Dodge is a prisoner in Salisbury. A gentleman told someone in the 6th that he saw him. I hope it is so. We captured men who said they belonged to Col. Dodge's Regt. and we also got his camp.

I now have five Regts., and a Battalion, in all present about 2400, but the Regts. are bad off for field officers in consequence of casualties in the battle and sickness.

I must close darling. I hope Jake is improving as fast as [we] were led to hope he would.

I have no fault to find for the last week or two about getting no letters. My love to everybody. Tell Turner his papa hopes to come home to see him some of these days and in the meantime he must be a good boy.

I must not fail to tell you what a sumptuous dinner we had today. Mutton, garden peas, asparagus, rice, etc. We have been living on ham and bread since the battle. Mutton 50 cts. per lb. I will write as often as possible. May God bless you all and protect you in all your afflictions. You must not worry about me too much. I can now communicate with you better than before as I have several mounted men entirely at my control so I can at any time send to Richmond. Good bye.

Your devoted Husband

Camp near Richmond, Va., June 25th, 1862

My dear Wife

I commenced this with the intention to write you [a] long and egotistical letter. The same day I received your letter saying that Sarah had gone home, I received one from David giving me the intelligence . . . that Sister James[49] could remain in this world but a few hours. She had six doctors all of whom had given her up. What a terrible blow it will be to brother Robert, for she has been to him a noble wife and to her children an irreparable mother. She has certainly done in a worldly point of view at least her duty as a wife and mother. . . . What in the world will brother Robert do with all his little children? Charles and Georgia had just gotten out of danger and Bob was still very sick. I wish you were there—not with the children—to help him, but it is too late now. Sister Patience I know has done all any woman could do. David wrote that he had suffered very much with a cough since I had seen [him]. Do you know honey that I am fully impressed with the belief that he cannot live long and then there will be poor Mary, with her cross old Aunt and worse brother. I shudder when I think of the consequences to her.

I am getting on finely. My Brigade has improved very much. I shall be able to take in the fight about 2700, and as we are preparing for marching orders which we expected tonight, it may not be long before we have to try it. It seems to me that we can with the favor of God expect a most decided victory. We will probably join Jackson who is now supposed to be near Richmond ready to fall on McClellan's rear. Jackson is undoubtedly near but no one knows where he is or when he came. It has been done in the most miraculous and secret manner. Our Major Generals know nothing of his whereabouts, only we all feel convinced that he will be about when the battle comes off which must be in a very few days.

Our Generals who have access to General Lee are beginning to gain a great deal of confidence in him. Everything, darling, around Richmond looks bright. McClellan has undoubtedly lost a great many men since he left Yorktown, and he is crying very lustily for more. We are getting reinforcements from all directions . . . intent upon making this one battle decisive. We have, I am convinced, more men to bring into the fight tomorrow than he has and when that is the case—unless a miracle should be performed in his favor—what must the result be but victory. May

49. Emeralda James Pender, Robert's wife, died of scarlet fever on June 20, 1862.

God give it to us, is my nightly prayer. I want one grand battle and have the thing settled. Some of the Northern papers begin to talk as if they thought a defeat to their arms here would not only be disastrous but decisive of the contest. They begin to fear for McClellan instead [of] exulting over our fall and are crying that if he should be allowed to be defeated here that [Secretary of War E. M.] Stanton and his crew should be made to suffer for it. I have written for Sam Ashe to ask him to take the Adjutant Generalcy in this Brigade, but have not heard from him.

You wish to know all about me these days. It can be said in a few words. I am about as when you used to know only I am less dignified, and more lazy as I do not get [up] before 7 A.M. I have really but little to do myself, having so many others to do for me. The only fear is I shall become more helpless and too grand in my notions to retire to a small farm after the war. The scheme I have not yet given up, and unless they bribe me by giving at least a Colonelcy in the Regular Army there is some danger of their losing me. I am sick of soldiering and especially the fighting part, particularly as I have no desire to be killed. My uniform is very unassuming, so much so that I always have to tell the pickets that I am a General before they will let me pass. The next coat, however, shall be more stylish. I was glad to get any when I got this.

If Frank should by any means get away from his present position I shall always have a place for him. My staff as yet being very moderate, only one volunteer aide, and he likely to leave at any moment. Do you know any real clever fellow who is desirous of serving his country at his own expense?

Would you believe it, we pay 50 cts. per lb. for all the mutton we get and 50 cts. per quart for milk. We concluded as soon as we found out what we had to pay for the latter that we would not encourage any such rascality altho' a Mrs. *Christian* did practice it. Now really I have told you about all I know of myself unless it is, Honey, that I know I am falling off in order to be a Christian.

As I now have to attend to some business I must close. You must not feel uneasy if you do not hear from [me] for several days as it will be impossible for me to write.

My love to all. May God bless and protect us.

Your devoted Husband

∼❊∽

The next day General Lee launched a massive week-long offensive which swept McClellan's Army of the Potomac from the outskirts of Richmond to a tenuous refuge at Harrison's Landing on the James River. In the Seven Days' Battles as these engagements were known, Pender's brigade played a prominent role. At Mechanicsville Pender led his troops in line of battle through the village in the face of heavy Federal fire to assault Porter's heavily fortified left at Beaver Dam. The next day his brigade pursued Porter's V Corps and engaged the enemy in a fierce struggle along Boatswain's Swamp near Gaines' Mill. Then as McClellan withdrew his entire army toward the James, Pender joined in the attack on the retreating column at Frayser's Farm in Glendale.

The day after the battle of Gaines' Mill, in which Pender proudly claimed his men "fought nobly and maintained their ground with great stubborness,"[50] the aggressive young brigadier hurriedly penned the following note to Fanny.

June 29, 1862

My dear Wife

I can merely say that I was not engaged yesterday. Some of our troops were and the Yankees have retreated it is supposed towards James River.... The troops we fought here were all the Regulars they had.

I did not tell you yesterday that I was slightly wounded in the right arm. Merely a flesh wound which has not caused me to leave the field. One of my aides was killed the other just wrecked. We took two Brig. Generals lots of Colonels and Majors, in all about 4000 prisoners and any quantity of small arms and between 12 and 20 cannon. I saw Ham yesterday. Willie was left near.

We will try to see each other if God should spare my life through this, for if I do not go to see you, possibly you may come on to see me if you can leave the children. We may follow them [the Yankees] so far from Richmond that I cannot get there, in that case it would be useless for me to come on. I will let you know.

May God bless and protect us.

Your devoted Husband

50. *N.C. Regts.*, II, 568.

July 1st, 1862

My dear Wife
God has spared me through another day's fight. We drove them again from their position [at Frayser's Farm], taking one General, McCall, and two batteries of fine rifled guns. My Brigade took one of them and drove the enemy until after dark, holding the field until 3 A.M. this morning when we were relieved. We have marched from the flank and are after them on their flank as they retreat. They have destroyed immense stores. There rout has therefore been complete. We have had four big fights with them in none of which my Brigade has taken part. We are still after them, Magruder is in our front and Jackson is coming up. I must close. My arm is much better.
My love to you all. May God protect us.

Your devoted Husband

~⚜~

With Richmond secure, Pender turned his attention to rebuilding his brigade which had lost approximately one-third of its original 2,400 effectives.[51] During this period he enjoyed a reunion with Fanny. After her departure he wrote the following letter.

~⚜~

Richmond, July 29th, '62

My dear Wife
I got here today about 11 o'clock. I wished very much yesterday I had waited with you until the evening train, but the President of the Road and Conductor both said they would make connection at Raleigh. I am just in time here, for my Brigade left last night to join Jackson. I shall go with Gen. [A. P.] Hill tomorrow night. I know you will hate to hear this. . . .
David writes that brother Robert had been dangerously ill, but was up about at present. He has moved with the children to papa's and is going traveling west with Anna[52] as soon as he gets able. I feel much better than I did when I left you. I really feel about well and have no doubt getting up where the water is good will cure me, especially as I shall have two or three days to

51. *O.R.* 23, pt. 2, 899.
52. Anna Pender was the fourth child of Emeralda and Robert Pender.

loaf. . . . I had a very pleasant crowd coming on and all seemed to see how kind they could be to me. There is no news here at all. It is not believed at Headquarters that McClellan is moving his forces away as you will see stated in the papers.

You will see that Beaut Stuart has been promoted to Maj. General. With the single drawback of getting where our hearing from each other often will be interfered with, I like the change. I dislike very much sitting down before a place so long as we have been before Richmond. Gen. Hill has been released from arrest.[53] I failed to get the appt. for Jake but shall try [to] have him transferred to my Brigade. I have just written begging brother Robert to let you have Anna and told him you would write him about it. . . . Honey, I must close as it is late. I will write you from Gordonsville. Direct [letters] to the care of Maj. Gen. A. P. Hill, Jackson's Army. My love to Helen and regards to the Doctor's family. May God protect us.

Your devoted Husband

I am making application to have Jake ordered to duty with me upon the plea that he will not be fit for duty on foot. Tell him not to leave home until he hears from me. If I succeed I shall make him my volunteer and which will give him a Government horse to ride. His board should be nothing so his expenses would be comparatively nothing. . . .

Maj. E. A. Palfrey wants to get board in Hillsborough for his wife, three children and servant, in [a] private house. I offered your services to look out for him and write to him. He wants to know the terms, what sort of place, name and in fact all about it. I told him you would write him as it would be so long before he could hear through me. He is a very nice man and no doubt his wife is a nice lady. Palfrey was at West Point with me. Write to him at once, Maj. E. A. Palfrey, Adjutant General's Dept, Richmond.

∿❧∿

Shortly after Lee relieved Richmond from McClellan's threat, a new Union offensive developed to the north. The middle of July a Federal army 47,000 strong under pompous General John Pope marched toward the vital Virginia Central Railroad, the

53. A. P. Hill was placed under arrest as a result of a quarrel with General James Longstreet over the division of credit for the feats of their divisions during the Seven Days' Battles.

only line which linked Richmond with the ripening crops in the fertile Shenandoah Valley. To counter this threat, Lee dispatched A. P. Hill's Light Division, which included Pender's brigade, to reinforce Jackson at Gordonsville. In his next letter Pender described his new situation.

ન⚜ૐ

Camp near Gordonsville, July 31st, 1862

My dear Wife

We left Richmond last night and reached Gordonsville about 10 this morning, being 10 hours coming 77 miles, Ham was one of the first I met at Gordonsville. He asked [a] great many questions about Mary and the baby and pretended to be surprised when I differed in thinking her better looking than your precious self. At present there seems to be no prospect of a fight. We have quite a force here and unless Pope should be or has been reinforced we will probably be too much for him.

I find Capt. Sam Ashe[54] a very nice modest young man. I like him very much. Mr. Young will be up tomorrow. Capt. [S. S.] Kirkland is 1st Lt. of ordnance on my staff. Willie[55] is well and very anxious to be transferred to the Cavalry and seems to think that I can have it done. Gen. Hill has been released from arrest. But what will interest you more, I am well and exceedingly comfortable, having a nice room and a seat at a very nice table. Mrs. Walker came up last night. She stopped about 16 miles from here. The Colonel is with us. Mrs. Hill also came up. You will have to excuse a short letter for I slept none last night. I sent you $100 by Mr. Thomas Webb. I had the money and did not know when I should have another chance to send any. I will write you often enough to make up for the shortness of them. Tell Pamela her letter came to hand and yours my dear, in which you make me out such a hero, was received yesterday.

Ham wanted to know how you managed to get me home. Honey, I must close with the earnest prayer that God in his infinite mercy will preserve us to each other to a good old age.

Your devoted Husband

ન⚜ૐ

54. Pender's Assistant Adjutant General.
55. William H. Shepperd, Fanny's thirty-two year-old brother.

Camp near Gordonsville, August 4th, 1862

My dear Wife

Yours of the 31st ultimo was received yesterday. I was very glad to hear from you, but I do not think I needed to have taken so much trouble to apologize so much about my short letters. You call me [an] obstinate man for not waiting Monday morning. The President of the road and the conductor both assured me that we should make connection. It was well I was in a hurry to get back for my men were dissatisfied and deserting. The Regts. were without officers, etc. etc. I have filled them up by promotions, appointments, and elections. I took it in my own hands to make appts.

About the horse, darling, I am bound to have a horse for I am now riding a Quartermaster horse. You saw what sort of thing Chaffin asked three hundred for, here $300 won't buy any sort of horse. I wish you would ask Capt. Kirkland to try him and if he thinks he will begin to do for $300 take him, telling them they may have to wait a month for their money. If Capt. Kirkland is not in town ask the Doctor to decide for me. I do not expect to get a tip top horse for that money these days. I will send Harris for him as soon as I hear he has been bought.

We had orders at 2 A.M. to cook rations for one day and are now waiting orders to move, but do [not] know if they will come or where they will take us. None of Jackson's old officers ever try to divine his movements, and some of the old Army like him. It is rumored that we are to have more reinforcements. I have but little doubt but that this is the commencement of a move into Md. or Penna. If we should ever get there what nice things I will buy you and cram Confederate money down their throats for them. You shall have the cloak, corsets, shoes, baby shoes, etc. so send me your no. [number].

Honey you seemed to be out of humour with me, or sick, or something. You know what I mean, there was something wanting.

I went to church yesterday and who should show himself in the pulpit but Mr. Stuart, very much to my surprise, for I saw him in Richmond a few days ago.... He says he thinks the 6th will be sent to me, the matter being before Gen. Lee upon a unanimous application of the officers to leave Gen. Whiting. I am glad Turner is behaving himself so well for your trouble on that score will be somewhat relieved. I must now close. May God protect us and save us to each other. My love to Helen. You will not believe me when I tell you how anxious I was to remain in Hillsboro. Regards to the Doctor's family.

Your devoted Husband

∾❦∾

August 6th, 1862

My dear Wife
We are now ready loaded up to move, but where to is not for those of my low rank to know. . . . I do not anticipate anything in the way of fighting just yet. I was much disappointed yesterday at not finding a letter, but that I lay to the change of the Postal arrangements, the mail failing. My dear wife I am, if possible, more anxious than ever to hear from you often.

Honey, give as much as you can afford to charitable purposes. I am beginning to feel that I have been sadly deficient in that respect, for once I gave cheerfully, but now I allow myself to believe that I ought to give. Oh how I do wish I could be a Christian. I feel now how far I am from what I would believe myself and what we should be, particularly one who has taken such solemn vows as I have. Oh, that I could be filled with the living Faith necessary to salvation. We are taught that the prayers of the just avail much—honey, pray for me continually for my conversion and that I may not go astray. The life I had is becoming more and more irksome to me, for the less chance I see of getting away from the army the less hope I have of that quiet and happiness on earth and that security . . . that I so much long for. God have mercy upon me, for I feel that I am not only a sinner but a perjured one. I made vows that I have in no way kept—only in a careless way of hoping to keep . . . this time. I have been very loose lately—not so much externally as spiritually.

We heard various rumors yesterday which if true may help to end this war. I pray sincerely as I can—night and morning—for a speedy close to this war. I am tired of glory and all its shadows for it has no substance. We work, struggle, make enemies, climb up in rank and what is the result—nothing. It is very much like gambling, money is won but soon spent and nothing left behind. I have not the slightest idea what we are to do, but cannot but believe that this army is the nucleus of any invading one. The quickness of Jackson—so contrary to his previous course—makes me think that it is so. The enemy seem to think so too.

I hope, Honey, that little indisposition on your part that we both looked forward to, has overtaken you, but if not bear up bravely in the consciousness that all things are directed from above and for our good. I can sincerely say that I believe such to be the case, and recur to things that I thought grievous and hard to bear at the time, that now I see were the very best that could have taken place. This is a part of my creed that I believe in fully. You may say I have none of the suffering, but I have for I know that I love you well enough to be troubled at anything that causes you suffering or unhappiness. Honey, I know I appreciate you very highly and love you dearly, but I sometimes feel that my cold and unfeeling nature prevents me from feeling as much of it as I ought, or even showing you what I have. May Heaven bless you for you are indeed dearer to me than anything on earth—now, ever was, and I hope ever may be. You will not allow yourself to have full and undoubting faith in what I now tell you because I do not do what you wish sometimes and what I ought to do oftener, but it is true if I know myself—as I live and hope for your whole heart. You will be astonished at this outpouring of senti-ment. I am not always devoid of it when I fail to express it.

...You ought to make yourself easy at the Doctor's for would you not feel hurt if any of your relatives were at your house and were making themselves uneasy and trying to go to Salem to board especially as they did not expect to remain more than a few weeks. Do unto others as you would be done by. You are too afraid of feeling under obligations. None of us can be entirely independent.

I have not seen Ham or Willie for several days as they went off Friday [with] their command. I am still of the opinion that I can not do better than buy the gray horse unless he is unsound and I am obliged to have a horse. I am now riding a quarter-master horse, Fan's back being sore and Jim's foot not being well.... I feel as strong as ever....

Sam Ashe wishes to be remembered to Helen and yourself. He thinks very highly of her. I think he will make me a fine officer. Give my kindest regards to all the Doctor's people. Write me often and tell me all about yourself and the children. My love to Helen. God bless you my good wife.

Your devoted Husband

August 14th, 1862

My dear Wife

Your letter of the 6th was received yesterday, and I was sorry to see you were so unhappy. You would have done better to have stayed at the Doctor's. About me, you must be more content for it is only one day further off and as for the danger here, it is no greater than anywhere else. The specimen of fighting shown us the other day by the Yankees does not compare to that of the rascals around Richmond. In fact, Pope's men did not fight at all.[56]

I wrote to Capt. Kirkland to bring me a horse he wrote to Maj. Scales about, instead of getting the one owned by Maj. Huske. Tell the Capt. if he can possibly find a good cook to bring him on at any price for we cannot get on without one. Mr. Young is going to leave me as soon as Gen. Pettigrew returns to duty which will not be long hence. I shall write at once asking that Jake be made my aide. If the cloth will make as nice a coat as the one I have, buy me enough to make me a coat and enough to make a sack for Mr. Young. The cloth my coat was made of sells for about $15 per yd, and so if you think that you spoke of is cheap buy it anyhow and send by Jake. Do not fear you will not please me for it will. I must soon have another coat and cannot afford to pay $100. Tell Capt. Kirkland to call at the Clothing Department in Raleigh when he comes on, and get my coat they were unable to make for me, paying the bill if he pleases and if he should be bringing me any boxes to call on Tom Webb of Hillsboro for some whisky he promised to send me. I hope Frank has reached you, but had he better not let Helen stay where she is for she will not get well if he continues to carry her around the country.

Pope seems to be satisfied for the present with having caused Jackson to fall back, but let him wait a little while. Longstreet with his Division is up and others on the way. He [General Pope] will take to thinking about lines of retreat yet if he does not mind. Our people got [a] good many spoils. I ride a Yankee horse, Harris [has] a Yankee saddle and bridle, Gen. Hill a fine horse and equipment, Col. Fray of my Brigade ditto, a Lt. of Archer's Brigade ditto, etc. We got about 100 firearms, wagons, etc.

Tho' I have not heard so, I expect Gen. Lee will take com-

56. On August 9, 1862, Jackson met and defeated Pope's advance guard under General N. P. Banks at Cedar Mountain near Culpeper, Virginia.

mand up here, for it does not look reasonable that they would take the command from Jackson to give it to Longstreet who has been sent and who ranks him.

. . . Gen. Jackson has ordered that military duties he suspended today and divine service held to render thanks for our recent success and to ask for a continue.

I received a letter yesterday from Mr. Porter who baptized me saying that through the request of friends he had prepared a tract and was publishing it based upon that incident. If I had known it in time I should have objected, for I do not sincerely consider myself a fit subject for any such publication. I know I am a great sinner and not worthy to be held up to others as a light, or one to be followed. I know I am desirous of doing good and am sorry when I do not, but I can only try to repent. Oh! that little member the tongue, it will carry me to perdition I fear.

We have a busy camp and are living well. Col. [R. H.] Brewer, an old friend who was Lt. in the 1st Dragoons, is now on my staff temporarily. He is a very nice fellow and a great acquisition. His only objection, he swears so much but is trying to stop it. I think if he stays with us he will break himself for he is really anxious. I could not help remonstrating with him about it when he came. You see I am getting as many around me as Whiting had.

Now I must close. You did not hear from me as soon as you should, but I could not get the letters off. I wrote one dispatch and several letters but none went as soon as I expected. God bless you and the little ones. How is Turner getting on. You say nothing about him in your last two letters.

Your loving Husband

ঝ

The next day General Lee arrived at Gordonsville to take command of his reunited Army of Northern Virginia. After assessing the situation, Lee decided to crush Pope before string Federal reinforcements arrived. To accomplish this objective Lee undertook a bold offensive whereby Longstreet pinned down Pope on the Rappahannock while Jackson swept wide around Pope's right flank and struck his base of supplies and rail line far in the Union rear. This eminently successful maneuver forced Pope to retire to Manassas where the furious Second Battle of Manassas was fought at the end of August. During this whirlwind campaign Pender had scant opportunity to correspond with Fanny. As Jackson's flank movement got underway Pender managed to send the following brief note.

Jeffersonville, Va., August 24th, 1862

My dear Wife
   I wrote you this morning but for fear it will not reach you I will merely tell you that I am safe and well thus far. Yesterday I was at Warrenton Springs but tonight our Division fell back to this place 2 miles east. We are not yet across the Rappahannock River. We had today the most terrible artillery duel, but we did not have fifteen casualties. It lasted from 11 A.M. till night with slight intermissions. I can form no idea of what we are to do but suppose to advance. Pope has been running from us but seems determined to make a stand behind this river. I saw Ham this morning. He and Willie are well. My love to all. May God in Heaven bless us and protect. I would write more but it is late and I have not slept but little for the last 48 hours. Good bye.

Your devoted Husband

August 31st, 1862

My dear Wife
   We have been fighting for several days. I am safe and sound with the exception of a small cut by shell on the top of the head.[57] It will be well in a few days. Willie was shot near the knee and above—only a flesh wound. Ham had been placed at a comfortable private house. You need not be uneasy about him. I saw Ham a few moments ago. He is well. Our first skirmish was at Manassas day before yesterday. Jackson's Army had quite a fight maintaining our position. Yesterday we had a general action and whipped them badly making almost another Bull Run affair. They had about ninety thousand, we had not that number in action. Their loss was tremendous and ours very heavy. We are now pressing them and our Division will move soon. My loss

57. Pender considerately refrained from alarming Fanny with the additional information that a wool hat he wore prevented the ball from inflicting a serious if not fatal wound. S. T. Pender's account.

has not been very heavy. I have not time to write but little. May God have mercy upon me and protect me as he has thus far and may he keep you in health and spirits. I am very anxious to hear how Dorsey is. Please write to my home and tell them that I am well. My love to all.

Your devoted Husband

ᘒᴥᴥ

Near Fairfax C.H., Sept. 2nd, 1862

My dear Wife

We had another fight yesterday in the midst of the most pelting rain I was ever in.[58] The Yankees had rather the best of it as they maintained their ground and accomplished the object that was to cover their retreat. Two Regts. of my Brigade were entirely used up by straggling from the field. . . . I am sick and tired of hearing of guns and hope I may never see one after this war is over.

Our fight on Saturday was I suppose the largest ever fought on this continent. The Federals were supposed to have about all McClellan's and Pope's forces commanded by [Major General H. W.] Halleck. They had nearly 3 to our 1 and were badly whipped. Every man except stragglers leaving the field and crossing the run. I flatter myself that I had more to do with the success of the day than my rank would indicate, for I saw their position and sent [word] to Gen. Hill [that] if he would order his Division to attack the thing would be up with them. He did so and they fled precipitately. By our move their right flank was turned.

During the fight I commanded three Brigades and parts of two others. I presumed to direct and the officers seemed very willing to have someone who would take the responsibility. My command took several pieces of Art[illery], my Brigade taking two. I flatter myself I did good service. The day before, Jackson's Corps alone was engaged, principally Hill's Division, and for service in that fight I was complimented by Gen. Hill for the manner in which my Brigade behaved, and everyone in the Division speaks of the handsome manner in which they went in.

As for yesterday, I have but little to say, but that none of us seemed anxious for the fight or did ourselves much credit. I have

58. Pender refers here to the engagement at Chantilly or Ox Hill on September 1, 1862, where Jackson overtook Pope's rear guard fleeing to Washington.

written so much about myself because I suppose you had rather hear of that part of the fight where I was than any other. Longstreet's Corps and Anderson's Division were also in the big fight. I rode out in the edge of the field the enemy were formed in and never saw such a magnificent sight in my life. As far almost as the eye could reach they had one continuous line of troops, with artillery it seemed to me for every fifty yards. It looked fine but was not Generalship for their line was nearly perpendicular to our left and as soon as attacked were turned.

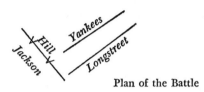

Plan of the Battle

My head is well but [a] little more bald than of yore, a small quantity having been shaved off [by a Union bullet]. I have certainly been most fortunate thus far. I have not heard from Willie lately. Gen [Philip] Kearny was killed yesterday. He was one of their brave Maj. Generals. We marched 42 miles in two days getting entirely in Pope's rear, taking his trains, and burning their Depot at Manassas containing an immense amount of Quartermaster and commissary stores. Marched [to] Centreville and . . . crossed back to the other side of the run, fought, bled, etc, and in fact performed the most brilliant and daring feats of Generalship and soldiership ever performed. The boldness of the plan and the quickness and completeness of execution was never beaten. Lee has immortalized himself and Jackson added new laurels to his brow—not that I like to be under Jackson, for he forgets that one ever gets tired, hungry, or sleepy.

We are resting today but move again tomorrow morning. We [are] only seven miles from Fairfax C.H. I have no idea when they will make another stand. My love to all. May God protect us all and may we show our gratitude by obeying his laws.

Your devoted Husband

❧

As Pope's routed divisions scurried back to Washington, Lincoln, in desperation, summoned McClellan to rally the troops and gird the capital's defenses. Realizing the exorbitant cost which would be incurred by a direct assault on Washington, Lee craftily marched his army to Leesburg where he crossed the Potomac and marched through Maryland toward Pennsylvania. Lee's strategy was to lure McClellan away from the capital in order to overwhelm him in the field. On September 7, Pender wrote Fanny from the army's bivouac near Frederick, Maryland.

∼⋆∽

Near Frederick City, Md., Sept. 7th, 1862

My dear Wife

Are you not surprised to find us in Md. We crossed day before yesterday and now have possession of this part of the State. Our Cavalry are hovering around Washington and it is said they have gone into Penn. Gen. Lee is in good earnest and the Yankees are terribly frightened. May the Lord have mercy upon us and give us success, not for glory or conquest, but as the only way to peace.

The people here are about equally divided in sentiment, which is more favorable than we expected. It was rumored yesterday that the citizens and soldiers of Baltimore were fighting. I hope not as I think it would be very foolish in the people to commence any such thing, but bide their time and come to us quietly. Honey, the only thing I could find yesterday to buy you was a pr. of shoes and also a pr. for Turner which I fear will be too large, but 4 were the smallest they had. The first chance I get I shall buy you some nice things and take the chances of sending them.

We had a small fight Monday in which of course it was my luck to take a hand and lost heavily. Col. [R. H.] Riddick [Thirty-fourth N.C.] was wounded in two places. Gen. Kearny, one of their best Generals, was killed. Their army had been totally demoralized by the recent whippings we gave them and are now in and around Washington behind their fortifications.

It was rumored here before we came that four of the six members of the Cabinet were against McClellan's being again placed in command of the army, but that the soldiers refused to fight unless he was, and there is some truth in it. We killed in the fights around Manassas eight Generals besides wounding several. We had paroled 7000 prisoners up to Tuesday. Their total loss could not have been less than 30,000. I saw their whole army at one view Saturday, drawn up in battle array to meet our attack, we having driven back theirs.

I see Ham nearly every day. Willie is getting on finely. My head is well, but I am minus the hair, it having been shaved off. Tell Helen I gave her letter to her sister to Gen. Jackson, who said he would try to get it off for me. It was the best I could do. I want you to write to brother Robert to pay Dr. Strudwick for the horse. It is impossible to get money to him now, and it is so hard to get a letter off—every one being laden down who starts for home—that I have to get you to write to him for me. Tell them all how I am and my dear if you do not hear from me do not be uneasy for it is next to impossible to get anything to the post office.

I got your letter of the 17th August two days ago and was grieved to learn that Dorsey was still so low. Poor little fellow, I hope before this he has recovered. Say to Helen that she need not be surprised to hear of our being in Philadelphia in less than ten days. Md. is rising, we have a victorious army, and no troops in our front. Gen. Lee has shown great Generalship and the greatest boldness. There never was such a campaign, not even by Napoleon. Our men march and fight without provisions, living on green corn when nothing better can be had. But all this kills up our men. Jackson would kill up any army the way he marches and the bad management in the subsistence Dept.—Gen. Lee is my man.

I captured the most beautiful horse at Manassas, and Harris was riding him the other night & got captured horse and all. Sam Ashe was captured at the same time and is now in the old Capital at Washington. I shall try to get his exchange. Where is Jake? If he has not left, let him write to Col. Custis Lee in Richmond and tell him when he will be on and if he can bring my horse. He can get to us only by having a horse. Tell him to hurry on [and] never mind the appointment. He might call on the Sec. of War and ask for it. Now my dear I must close. May God bless you all and bring us together soon. We must soon have peace or it will be an indefinite time before one more big fight must settle the thing one way or the other. My love to all.

Your loving Husband

Frederick, Md., Sept. 8th, 1862

My dear Wife

I went into town today and bought some little articles for you and the children, but it has been so long since I shopped that I fear the whole thing will prove a failure except the handkerchiefs. I recollected the last time I saw you, you had very coarse ones, so I bought you the best I could find. Let me know honey what you want and if we should remain in Md. or go further I can send them. To show you what things bring, the handkerchiefs were $2.00 apiece and the shoes $2.00 for yours and 75 cts. for the others. I thought and thought what I could buy that would not make much bulk and could only think of what I send.

Dr. [W. A.] Holt [Brigade Surgeon] has been ordered on duty with me. The 6th distinguished itself the other day.... We do not know when we shall move but it cannot be longer than day after tomorrow. Our army is improving very rapidly and are in fine spirits and feel confident of success. We ought to succeed and I think will. May God grant we may, in bringing them to stop this war by recognizing us. Their delay in advancing upon us shows how totally disorganized their army must have been. Did I tell you we killed in the recent battle eight of their Generals besides several wounded, and have you heard of Kirby Smith's victory in Kentucky the same day we fought the big battle at Bull Run?

Sam Ashe is in Washington. I see Ham nearly every day. We have nothing new to write. I am in great distress as my trunk has been taken off and will not come to me for some time and I am without clothing. I cannot hear from you but do not complain as I know it is the fault of the position we occupy. I partook of the Holy Communion yesterday in company with about fifteen others. I pray I did so in the right spirit. Oh! how I did wish for you. Shall we never be able to join each other in that blessed sacrament. God bless you and the boys and may you all be spared so we can meet again in this world. My love to all. Ask father what he thinks now of our chances.

Your devoted Husband

※

On September 10, the army broke camp and resumed its march. Lee accompanied Longstreet's troops as they headed west through South Mountain toward Hagerstown, while Jackson led

*his "foot cavalry" by a circuitous route to capture the Federal
garrison at Harper's Ferry. In the meantime, McClellan, who
cautiously left the capital and circumspectly followed Lee, fortuitously came into possession of a copy of Lee's orders wrapped
around three cigars left on the campground at Frederick.*

*With Lee's plans in his tent, McClellan issued orders designed
to overtake and destroy Lee's divided army a half at a time. However, Lee managed to reunite the bulk of his divisions before the
"bloodiest battle of the Civil War" on September 17 along Antietam Creek at Sharpsburg, Maryland. Here McClellan's daylong
attack was on the verge of breaking Lee's attenuated line when
A. P. Hill's division, including Pender's brigade, arrived late in
the afternoon after a forced march from Harper's Ferry and
staved off defeat.*

*Pender participated in the engagements at Harper's Ferry and
Sharpsburg, but the fragment of his letter written just after the
Army of Northern Virginia recrossed the Potomac provides only
scant information on the campaign.*

༺❀༻

[Fragment of letter apparently
written September 19, 1862.]

... I envy you all the fruit you have. I cannot get what I
ought for fear of starting the men. They will clean out a big
orchard in half an hour. ... My dear such a filthy unprincipled
set of villains I have never seen. They have lost all honor or
decency, all sense of right or respect for property. I have had to
strike many a one with my sabre. The officers are nearly as bad
as the men. In one of my Regts. the other day when they thought
they were going to get into a fight, six out [of] ten officers skulked
out and did not come up until they thought all danger over.
More than half my Brigade went off the same day. Oh dear, oh
dear, our army is coming to a pretty pass. The only thing is if the
enemy does not run before the fight, they do when the fight commences. Gen. Hill gave me command of half his division when
we attacked Harper's Ferry and two [Brigades] this morning on
the retreat. We are off tomorrow at 5 A.M.

I will now close. My dear the prayers of the righteous availeth
much, pray for my deliverance from the enemies balls, but darling
if my fate should be that of too many, you must rest in the hope
of our meeting in a better world. I try to do my duty to God and

my Government and am desirous of harming or injuring no man. May our Father have mercy upon us. My love to all.

Your devoted Husband

෴

Near Martinsburg, Va., Sept. 22nd, 1862

My dear Wife

I write but never have the satisfaction of knowing that you receive my letters. I have [heard] from you since August 13th but once and that through Mr. Stafford. Ham came by this morning on his way to Winchester to return tomorrow. Our Division had a hard fight day before yesterday. Some of our miserable people allowed the Yankees to cross the Potomac [near Shepherdstown, Virginia] before they ought and ours ran away making it necessary for us to go and drive them back. We did it under the most terrible artillery fire I ever saw troops exposed to. They continued to shell us all day. It was as hot a place as I wish to get in. It is considered even by Jackson as the most brilliant thing of the war. The fact is, Hill's Division stands first in point of efficiency of any Division of this whole Army.

We have so little of change or variety that it is difficult to write even so far between as I do. The whole of our time is taken up by two things, marching and fighting. Some of the Army have a fight nearly every day, and the more we fight the less we like it.

I wish Jake was here as I am about to be left alone. Col. [R. H.] Brewer I had much rather was gone for he has become so dissatisfied and talks so much about wanting to go to Richmond that it is disagreeable to have him around. Capt. [S. S.] Kirkland ought also to be along.

I gave you my views on the Md. question in letter Mr. Stafford has for you and will not repeat only to say that I have heard but one feeling expressed about it and that is a regret at our having gone there. Our Army has shown itself incapable of invasion and we had better stick to the defensive. I think if it were hinted around in Yankee land that we would be satisfied with the Potomac as the line, that the people would soon bring the Government to it. Some of our officers have been asked by them if we would consent to such an arrangement, showing at least that it has been talked of in that country.

My dear wife, I should like to know what you are all up to, how you are getting on, etc. Mr. Stuart heard in Md. that the

Yankees had five Generals killed and wounded in the recent big fight. Three of them Division commanders that I know of.

I wish you to see Mr. Stafford or send him word for me that I wish him to let you have enough calf skin to make me a pair of boots and you have them made in War Towne or some where else. My love to all and may God have mercy upon us all.

Your devoted Husband

⁓✻⁓

Camp Branch near Martinsburg, Sept. 25th, 1862

My dear Wife

You will probably be surprised to receive two letters from the same place, and in fact we have been surprised at remaining here so long, but our Generals seem to have realized at last "that tired nature needs repose, etc." We may be here several days yet, as the last report I have heard places McClellan still on the opposite side at Sharpsburg. They admit a loss of 13 Generals and 30,000 men killed and wounded.

Ham has just left me after a long harangue on politics and war. Ham is always ready to argue about the merits of Jackson and the election of Vance [as Governor of North Carolina]. He had received your father's letter of the 7th in which not one word was said about you or the children. I am getting very anxious to see a letter from you once more. I sent off a courier three days ago, with orders to go until he got me some letters. Do you know, Honey, I am afraid ambitious notions are getting into my head and that I am aspiring to another step. And between us I do not see that it is so preposterous for me to look forward to promotion. I think my chances pretty fair if many more should be made. But really and truly if the Lord will be pleased to bring me through this war safely, I will be satisfied to end up as a Brig. General.

You have no idea how anxious I am to see Jake for really I am without any assistance. Brewer is here but seems so much dissatisfied at having to remain in this part of the Army that I have ceased to ask him to do anything. I need assistance very much. Capt. Kirkland has not yet joined.

I am reading Uncle Tom's Cabin and really you have no idea how nearly we [i.e., Stowe and Pender] agree on the subject of slavery. I tried to whip Joe the other day but could go only three stripes. He is thus far a very smart boy and much improved. You would be amused at some of his trades. The rascal seems to have plenty of money, but I have ordered him to allow me to be his treasurer. He has managed to dress himself in a nice gray uniform, french bosom linen shirt—for which he paid $4—has two pairs new shoes, etc., etc. If he continues as he has commenced his clothing will never cost me anything.

The same old song in your father's letter. "Pamela and Jake are expected from Mrs. Williams." Do they go as often or is it the same old go that I heard of soon after I left you. But no better business could be found for them, while one part of the family is being shot at and cuffed about on the head and knees, the other to keep up the good feeling with the sympathizers of the cuffers. Isn't it a pity we don't need but one magistrate in the same muster district or that some of our Post offices have been broken up.

I am sorry to see the conscript law so ineffectual in its results. Of all the Regts. here from N.C. only a few have as yet received any conscripts, and I hear that in some sections the men swear they will not come out. I need them badly for I have in my Brigade only about 850 all told present. I have been in several fights with not more than 300 men. One consolation, the Yankee Regts. are no better off than ours, except the new levies of which they have many. The Yankees admit that they were whipped on their left—that is where Hill's Light Division fought [at Sharpsburg]. You have no idea what a reputation our Division has. It surpasses Jackson's old Division both for fighting and discipline. Hill told me that I had the best discipline of any Brigade he had. But when I tell you that this Division has lost 9000 killed and wounded since we commenced the Richmond fight at Mechanicsville, you can see what our reputation has cost us. We started in that fight with 15,000, now we have 6,000, 9,000 disabled. My Brigade has lost between 12- and 1500. One would hardly believe it that the percentage of the killed in the list of casualties is only about two per cent. For instance, in the Friday's and Saturday's fight at Manassas I had 165 wounded and only 12 killed. Several of the former have since died however. Let me cease to write about war and killing.

I am really anxious to hear of your having received the dry goods, and that they are such as you need. I felt very proud of them and if they only suit I shall be very happy. I was sorry I could find nothing to send Pamela, but she must take the will for the deed.

Please do not fail to get the sheep skin from Mr. Stafford and have me a pair of boots made. Long legs and not to come above the knees. I want a good stout waterproof boot. If you can get them, hold on till you get a safe chance to send them. My horse is still in Richmond so far as I know, but hope to get him soon as I send Maj. [N. E.] Scales [Brigade Quarter Master] to Richmond tomorrow. Would it not be nice if I could get ordered south with my Brigade this winter and be in Charleston or Savannah. Gen. Hill says he intends to ask that his Division be sent south as soon as the campaign is over here and he stands high in the regards of Gen. Lee. The campaign in this section cannot, it would seem, last more than a month.

Now my dear, I must close by asking God's blessing upon you all. You know my dear that every time I go in my trunk it makes me sad, for nothing so forceably reminds me of you. My love to you all. God bless you.

Your devoted Husband

♦

Bunker Hill, Va., Sept. 28th, 1862

My dear Wife

As I have another opportunity, I will write a few lines. We moved to this place yesterday and are now only ten miles from Winchester. The enemy are said to be crossing at Harpers Ferry. It will take them several days to cross and march to us if they are inclined to do so. If they do not come soon we will in all probability fall back nearer Staunton, for I do not see how we can supply our Army [here] so far from railroad. . . .

Our ranks are being filled by the returning of men from hospital and those who have either broken down or wilfully straggled. This straggling is becoming to be the curse of the Army and unless Congress pass some law to stop it there is no telling where it will end. Men find it safer to get behind [the] lines than to fight. We will have to shoot them before it stops.

Jake's appointment came this morning and I shall not send it for fear it might get lost. I send the form of oath for him to have filled up and submitted. He is required to notify the Adjt. Gen. of his acceptance. Reporting when he sends the oath back, his age, residence, when appointed and the State in which he was born.

My dear, just imagine my pleasure at having to stop above to read the first letter I have had from you for a month. Not one letter between one dated August 13th and Sept. 16th. You say not one word about Dorsey, but I will take it for granted that he is well. Your last told me of his almost hopeless condition. I shall not send the oath as Jake would miss it. I am glad Frank has at last [come] home and wish he could come up this far and see us. I shall look up Ham today and give him the news.

Honey you must not be so low spirited. . . . I am in the keeping of God at all times and in all places. As to battles, I cannot know, we shall have many more but most of the fall in my opinion will be taken up maneuvering. If we live I shall try to see you some way this winter and early in the winter too. We are not the only ones who have to be separated but that is poor consolation, I know.

Capt. Kirkland came on two days ago much to my gratification, and the appearance of Jake will be hailed with pleasure. I am sorry, Honey, I could not get more things for you. I could have bought some calico and coarser articles, but sending them back was the trouble. I will try to manage to pick up something else for you. You will see what a hard time I have to get any when I tell you that I have not been able to get a hat, pair of boots and but one undershirt in all my travels. I have made arrangements by which I shall get on very well with undershirts.

. . . I am glad Gov. Vance has taken such a strong war stand. You all may be proud of him if he continues as he has started. Honey, you must not believe much you see in papers on either side. H. B. Davidson—old friend of San Francisco—sends from Staunton a dispatch [that] 10,000 Yankees crossed at Shepherdstown, Jackson's Corps contesting, etc. . . .

. . . My only regret [about the Maryland campaign] is that we ever crossed it [Potomac] in the first place. They cannot drive us from any position we choose to take, but by reinforcements they may cause us to draw off after the battle. You must not be gloomy if you hear of our leaving this part of the state, for [if] it is impossible for our Army to remain still here we must either advance or fall back which we propose to take our time in doing.

I must now close. God bless you my dear wife and bring us together again. I should like to write how much I love you and think of you and admire and worship, etc. . . . My love to all.

Your devoted Husband

My dear Wife

As Maj. Scales will leave tomorrow or next day for N.C. I will commence with the intention of writing you a long and affectionate letter, feeling some assurance that you will get it. I envy the Major very much, but if we cannot enjoy a pleasure ourselves the next best thing is to have our friends do so. He goes after clothing, etc. for my Brigade. I send by him six pairs shoes, none of which I fear will do, two pounds of tea, three pairs drawers and three shirts. The drawers I send Ham and the shirts to father. One pair of the shoes I thought might do for Pamela. I sent Jake off 18 miles hoping to get [a] good many things, but the shoes and tea were all he could get. I will get the Major to try in Richmond for the linen and corsets.

We are getting on very nicely but no orders for a move yet. I should like to be a little nearer the post office if we can serve the country as well. I cannot but allow my desire to have you this winter make me feel as if I should like to winter nearer Richmond.

Tell Mary that I fear that I am to some extent responsible for some very unwarrantable indulgences. He [Ham] was over to see us this evening and took his drink of apple and honey with the rest of us. The other evening I went to see him and he was out with the band making music for the ladies, one of whom I was sorry to hear had fallen in love with him, being under the impression that he was single. I do not know how she is, but my wife would hold me responsible for such weakness on the part of any lady. The fact is, my wife is so particular that I hardly dare go where young ladies congregate.

I was very much gratified today to find in conversation with my very esteemed friend Tom Ruffin that he is about to give himself to our church. He used to rather sneer at our church but now he has become interested in such things he turns to it with great interest. He will make a most enthusiastic member of the church if his life—which I pray God may grant—is spared. I know no one that I have a higher opinion of than him and feel that I have the regards and good opinion of such a man as he is. Oh! my dear wife, if I could live a Christian life. I try but it is so hard that I almost despair. I want charity and humility above all things. It is hard, almost imposible, to love our neighbor as ourselves and to forgive and look kindly upon the weaknesses of others. "If thou shalt say thou fool thou shalt be in danger of hell fire"—what a terrible thing and I say it of some every day, nay almost every hour and feel the next moment that I have violated the order of our blessed Father. Honey, do you know that I sometimes believe fully that my life has been spared thus far to reward the prayers of a Christian wife. I cannot realize how I could otherwise have escaped than by the kindest interposition of God, and I cannot see why he should take me under his especial charge but to reward your prayers. If I could be what I believe you to be I think I could look forward to the prospects of death without fear—almost with pleasure. May he hear you so far as to save my immortal life. Honey, my nightly prayer is that we may be spared to a good old age and live to His Glory.

We are getting on very pleasantly and I am getting very worthless. I have lost all energy. We were strung up so long that any little quiet completely lets us down. I was getting very feeble under the continued hardship and excitement, and had fallen off [a] good deal, but this rest has improved me very much and I am fattening every day. I was upon the point of giving out several times but by taking to brandy kept up. I think the hard work is over, but if it should commence again I am strong enough to stand it. I do not believe I have thanked you for the nice shirts —if not you have received in my heart often enough. Darling I fear I should not be able to get you either the woolen or silk dress except in Richmond where they would cost a fabulous price, but if you absolutely need them you shall have them let them cost what they may. The articles I sent you which cost about $35 or $45 would have cost at least $200 in Richmond. By the way Honey, you must send me word what distribution you and Mary made as Ham and myself cannot settle until we hear from you and Mary on the subject. As my paper is about filled I will close for the night. Pleasant dreams to you, my own dear wife.

Oct. 12
Sunday has passed and I feel that I have passed it very unprofitably for I have not even read the service as I usually do on this day. I commenced but was interfered with. I shall do so before I go to sleep. I always miss you so much on such occasions. Tell father he will be indebted to Mary for the drawers and shirts as she wrote Ham to buy them for him. My love to all. God bless you and the boys.

Your devoted Husband

Oct. 21st, 1862

My dear Wife

We have at last moved for a change but not in the direction I had expected for we are nearer Shepherdstown—only six miles—but we only came down to tear up the [Baltimore & Ohio] railroad and not to fight. They have very few troops on this side the river and those at Harpers Ferry. My dear, is it not precious news from Kentucky.[59] Everything looks bright for us. The Democrats of the North are helping us by their speeches, etc. I cannot but have some hope of peace this winter. It would of all things be more to my taste than anything else.

Honey, I fully appreciate your feelings about housekeeping and am perfectly willing, but I shall be rather particular about the locality, and really I cannot see how you could get a house for all the desirable places in the middle and Western part of the state are filled and in the Eastern it would be unpleasant, owing to the proximity of the enemy. But look around and find some place and let me know. Col. Ruffin wants you to and housekeep with his wife. What do you say to that? I hope, Honey, that the most of the winter at least we shall be able to be near each other, and if peace is made by spring we can then be together, and when I say if peace, etc., I only say what is fully believed will come about by great many.

Your last letter makes me rather uneasy about your *unaccountable* growth. I hope it will not turn out to be anything wrong, but [by] the time this reaches you, you will be able I suppose to tell what is the matter. Are you entirely well of the trouble you wrote for a prescription for? You spoke about Jake's likeness, did you discover that he had his moustache dyed. He would not own for some time that they were, but when the dye wore off he had to admit it.

I am sorry Turner gives you so much trouble, but you tell him that when he gets under his respected papa he may look out for he will catch it. Your father will not deter me from whipping him and that soundly. As to the boots, Darling, I sent to Richmond and by Maj. Scales hoping to get a pair from one or the other. I shall soon know if I fail, then you can try Forsythe. Honey I wish I could get all the things you want but it is impossible.

What do you all think of Stuart's last raid [around McClel-

59. This news concerned General Braxton Bragg's abortive success against General Buell at Perryville.

183

lan's army]? It was nip and tuck with him. They [the Federals] knew before he crossed the river that he was going and had plenty of time to make all their arrangements to get him as he returned [but] he was too quick and sharp for them. Capt., now Gen. [Alfred] Pleasanton was after him but he [Stuart] just hours ahead of him so the Yankee papers state. They express great mortification at it. Beaut [Stuart] is after a Lieut. Generalcy. I did not write you that Gen. Hill proposed the other day to write and recommend my promotion and told me to use all my political influence. He said he should write anyhow. Col. Scales Regt.—old 3rd—is now in my Brigade making me five Regts. I am going to try to get the 6th before I am done.

You were grieved at our hard living [but] for the past month we have lived splendidly.... Now my dear wife, I will close, not because I wish to do so, but for want of time. Recollect when I do not write love it is not because I do not feel it for you know as well as I do that I love you as much as any husband ever did his wife. My love to all. Tell Mary I saw Ham a few days since and he was well. God bless you and the boys.

Your devoted Husband

You need not feel uneasy for we are ordered not to make a fight here but fall back if they attack us.

☙❧

Camp near Bunkerville, Va., Oct. 24th, 1862

My dear Wife

Your letter of the 15th inst. came last night much to my gratification. I am delighted that you keep in such excellent health. My dear wife, I will do anything in my power to render you happy and contented and if I can find by inquiry where an eligible house can be rented I will rent it. But my dear the children are too young to receive much damage by the interference of others with your discipline, and to rent a house and furnish it now, would take a great deal of money. Can you not think of some place where you would be willing to board, you may come to any safe part of Va. which will furnish you with an excuse to get away from your father without hurting his feelings, and then you would not be any expense to him. Let me know when you wish to go. I have made inquiry of all my friends and some of them can tell me of any chance for getting a house. You shall do as you wish and I will be satisfied, for you have enough to worry you without my interfering in that matter. I fully agree with you that it would be well not to live on your father and am desirous of bearing the burden of your support. Rest assured that I do not think it a mere whim on your part.

Ham came over to take dinner with us today. He had received Mary's and father's letters of the 14th.

We returned to this camp yesterday after tearing up over 20 miles of the Baltimore and Ohio R.R. Our troops worked to within 4½ miles of Harpers Ferry and were not disturbed. I had supposed we would have left here before this, but strategy or Gen. Lee's great dislike to give up Md. prolongs our stay beyond what looks to us inferiors as useless. We have not only eaten up all of last year's crop that remained over, but have about used all the corn of this year's growth. We have various rumors as to the future but know nothing in reality. If the keeping of our own counsel goes to constitute a General, Lee possesses that to perfection.

It would appear that our people have gotten to be as bad as the Yankees, for after all the big reports from Ky. are sifted down we took no prisoners and but few pieces of Art[illery] and had to fall back. Bragg it seems did no doubt whip Buell, but the latter was so heavily re-enforced that he had to fall back to form a junction with Kirby Smith. I fear my darling that your ambitious designs for me are destined to be destroyed. My name has been mentioned in army circles and it has been several times reported that I had been promoted, but I am too young and have no one in Richmond to push my claims.

Honey, I have been giving you credit for writing oftener than you do. The fact that my letters sometimes miscarry makes me write oftener so you may hear as often as possible. Darling, how about that "unaccountable fattening" up of yours. You caused me some uneasiness.

My dear wife I am so proud to know that your love instead of abating continues to increase. I know I ought to be more affectionate in my letters, but you need not fear that I do not feel, for indeed the longer I know you the more excellence I see in you and the better I love you. Honey, whenever I try to reflect upon the future and to resolve to do better, I think of you first and your image rises up and intrudes in upon my thoughts of Christ and the future so that I have almost come to feel that you are a part of my religion. Whenever I find my mind wandering upon bad and sinful thoughts I try to think of my good and pure wife and they leave me at once. My dear wife you have no idea of the excellent opinion I have of your goodness and sweetness. You are truly my good Angel. May God bless you for the good you have done in thus far bringing back one sinful erring creature to at least a sense of his sin. I am now reading Zenaida and although a poor book with lots of nonsense, she is an angel and all the time I am likening her to you.

I am glad to hear you say what you did about [Stephen D.] Lee and only pray that it may in the all wise Providence of God turn out that he may be our brother. No nobler man lives than he. I am going to see him tomorrow to get him to come dine with me Sunday. You have no idea of our luxurious living. We even have a milk cow and what my dear wife has not, coffee and sugar. You will be surprised to hear that I gave Joe a tremendous whipping last night. I had been promising him some time and finally he got it. He is a good and smart boy but like most young negroes needs correction badly.

You seem to think that I would be glad to hear that Joe Williams was to be married. Indeed it was a matter that I cared not a thing about. I do not like the family but his marrying or not did not disturb me, as I was not jealous of him. I feel myself to be more worthy of you than I think he is and moreover I think you are a woman of enough good sense to see it. I did feel some fear that Pamela might be trapped into an alliance with either Nick or Col. Conally, but I do not now.

Honey, I hope Mary was not deprived of a dress if she needed it, and at the same time I am glad Pamela got something out of the bundle for I have been reproaching myself ever since we left Md. that I did not get something for her.

Darling, what is the state of your finances. Do you need more money. I heard today from David. He was better. Sam Ashe has tendered his resignation and really I do not know who to get in his place. I fear I have lost the horse I got in Hillsborough for they say in Richmond that he was taken by some officer who said he knew me, to bring to me, but I cannot find him. It will be a bad loss now. I hope brother Robert's visit is not to take Anna from Salem. If I can see brother Robert I think I shall be able to make him more sensible about her.

Now my precious wife, as to writing to you to "come on at once" that is out of the question for we know not one day where we may be the next. But rest assured my dear wife no effort of mine shall prevent our seeing each other this winter, but we must wait until active operations are over. I send you some vaccine matter which you must use at least twice unless it takes at first. You all had better use it for smallpox is rife in the country. I was vaccinated last spring and it will not take now. I must close. God in His infinite goodness protect you all. Kiss Pamela and tell her I shall not forget to play my part in her future prospects. She is a dear girl and I love her very much.

Your loving Husband

⚜

Summit Point, Va., Oct. 29th, 1862

My dear Wife

It has now been several days since I wrote you, but as you write but once a week, you will hardly complain. We reached this place this morning—about 10 miles from Bunkerhill on the R.R. from Winchester to Harpers Ferry, seven miles from Charleston. I give you the points so you can, if you choose, locate us.

It is much finer looking country than when we left and I think will be pleasant to judge from the beginning, (to dine at a fine house and with three young ladies). If they should happen to be good looking I do not know how far I may go, it has been so long since I have spoken to a lady. One thing is certain, I shall get a good dinner if I am to judge of the preparations that have been reported to me as going on. Everything looks promising particularly as I have just received an order that no furloughs will for the present be granted except on surgeon's certificate. I know you will not blame me for trying to so make my time pass as agreeable as possible.

To judge from the Northern papers McClellan has not commenced any more. They will not come this way you may rest assured of it. We are only staying here to eat out the country and when we leave a place it might be said to have been accomplished to perfection. Since we came from Md. I never lived better and thanks to Maj. [H. L.] Biscoe [Brigade Commissary], just as sugar gave out he got a cow that gives enough milk for breakfast and supper.

As rheumatism is not dangerous and very good to get a furlough on, you will not be sorry to learn that for three days I have something very much like it. Just about the time I thought I might afford to apply on my other complaint—diarrhea—it is getting well so I shall have to fall back on rheumatism.

Jake received Pamela's letter of the 19th and I fear she was indiscreet in telling him that brother Robert thought Willie the best looking of the family for he takes it to heart, however he remarked by way of consolation that she bragged upon the good looks of his picture—did you notice mustachios were dyed? None of you need fear that Jake will not be able to take care of himself. He did what in my travels I have never learned to do—get a servant for nothing . . . a precious rascal he got out of jail. His horse was really a good bargain.

Darling, you need not trouble about boots for me for I have made arragements to get two pr. and my old ones will last me some time to come. I did the other day what I used to think I should never do, put on woolen drawers and shirts—like your father's—and I find them very pleasant. I ought to keep warm, two woolen and one silk shirt and woolen drawers and lined pants. Maj. [N. E.] Scales is to bring me a thick overcoat from Raleigh. I intend to take better care of myself this winter than I used to. By the way, I am out of socks, or next thing to it. I wrote to Mamma to have me some woolen ones knit for I knew you could not knit always pulling the thread so hard to get it so tight that you could not work the needles. I wrote in my last that I sent you some vaccine matter but could not get it. I will try to send some in this which you must certainly use. Small Pox is in the whole land or will be, unless great precaution is taken. It took on me last spring, but I had it tried twice recently without effect.

Now my own darling I have written about all the nonsense I can and news we have none. I am getting to be about the most home sick man you ever saw. Any pretext for a leave would be taken advantage of. I do want to see you so much. It seems to me more than I ever did. My dear wife if you knew how often I resolve the various ways of getting a leave in my mind and how much I think about it, you would not for one moment suspect me of missing any chance to see you. I was glad to learn through Pamela that the shoes such as they were reached you. It was the best I could do.

Good bye, my dearest and best wife and rest assured that if my love is all that you require to make you happy, you shall be so. My love to all.

Your devoted Husband

My dearest Wife

...I have not had much chance to write anything. Honey, consider your plan for housekeeping well and then do as you please and I shall be satisfied for I have always found your judgement good.

...The 6th N.C. stands up nobly. They had 104 killed and wounded at Manassas and 105 at Sharpsburg and still have about 400 for duty. Maj. Webb got a slight wound and made straight for home. Cols. Avery and Ruffin are both anxious to get under me.

Now my own dear wife, I must close. I should like very much to see Frank and Helen before they leave if they have not gone. Give them both my love. Tell Pamela I am glad to hear she had a pleasant time and give her a thousand kisses for me. I was very uneasy about Dorsey and you can imagine my relief to hear that he was well again. My dear, do not trouble yourself about with fears of having no more children. You are young yet. God bless you darling and the dear boys.

Your devoted Husband

Have you plenty of money such as it is for your country?

◈

In November Pender spent a furlough with Fanny in North Carolina. Upon returning via Richmond to his brigade he learned that Lincoln had replaced McClellan with Ambrose Burnside who aggresively moved his three "Grand Divisions" toward Fredericksburg. From the Confederate capital Pender wrote Fanny as follows:

◈

Richmond, Va., Nov. 22nd, 1862

My dear Wife

I reached here last night having to lay over yesterday in Petersburg. No one can tell me where I can find Jackson, and Gen. Cooper advises me to remain until I can learn something. I telegraphed to Jackson's A.A.G. I have been very busy all day and have not yet seen the Sec. of War, Mr. Seddon.

I got my money today for Blucher [Pender's horse]. They allowed me $600 but stopped $75 on an old account, but the Government owes me more than that, which I intend to get soon. I sent David $450 which will reduce my acct. with him to $996. Tell Ham I send his clothes to him by express.

Gen. Lee is at Fredericksburg and I have no doubt will be around Richmond in less than ten days. There is no doubt in my mind but that Burnside is going to try Richmond by way of Suffolk or at least by the south side of the [James] river. So you need not be surprised if we are cut off for a few days from N.C. My word for it, he will attack by way of the south side of the river. Everything is dull here and no one knows anything of our army movements anywhere. I am very well thus far.

Capt. Moffit says I can and ought to get pay for the horse I lost.

Tell Ham that the only surprise I felt in learning that he had gone home was that he a well man would leave the army now.

Col. Stephen Lee has been promoted and sent to Van Dorn to take command it is supposed of Vicksburg.

My love to all. I will probably write you again tomorrow.

I saw Mr. Stuart today. He has been in Md. running the Blockade. God bless you my dear wife.

Your devoted Husband

I will send you some money in a week or so.
I am not promoted.
I bought you some silk.
I was joking about Ham.

❧

Camp near Fredericksburg, Va., Dec. 3rd, 1862

My dear Wife

This command after a long and fine march has at last come to anchor for awhile unless the Yankees cross the [Rappahannock] river, which I do not think they will attempt, altho they pretend to be making preparations for it. If they were afraid to advance from Warrenton it would look like nonsense to attempt it here. One cannot imagine the degree of confidence and high spirits displayed by our men. I am truly glad to get once more where we can get our mail and the papers. Here we can get both very easily.

I believe about everybody have moved from the town which will cause great suffering. They are scattered all through the country. A temporary depot post by us today had any quantity of furniture lying around with several old gentlemen shivering in the cold, apparently watching it.

Gen. Lee is very anxiously waiting for a fight. He told me today that he believed he would be willing to fall back and let them cross for the sake of a fight. All accounts are to the effect that they will not fight, and their numbers are not as terrible as might be supposed.

As A. P. Hill has been recommended by Gen. Lee for Lt. General, I hope he will be promoted which would be a means of both getting us out of Jackson's command and myself a Division. General rumor and general feeling both have pointed me out to be Gen. Hill's successor. He told me the other night that he hoped I would soon be a Major General. I had no idea that I was a man of reputation in the army until I got back. This is not to be repeated even in joke, for I do not like to have it thought that I might have my head turned, etc., etc. My people were glad to see me and they all said that they knew I would be back before the fight came off. The men seem to think that I am fond of fighting. They say I give them "hell" out of the fight and the Yankees the same in it.

Jake goes to Richmond tomorrow to attend to some little matters for the mess and himself. If we have nothing special I shall let him go home to spend his Christmas. I told him if he would not drink or smoke any between this and then, he might go. He makes a fine caterer and has improved generally. I think, since I left. Do not say I am disposed to underrate him and "wish that he had not joined me" etc.

I have finally settled upon an A.A. General. What would you say to the husband of that agreeable lady that called on you in Raleigh, Maj. [Joseph A.] Englehard. He is going resign his position as Brigade Quartermaster in [James H.] Lane's Brigade [late Branch's]. You must not judge him by his wife for he would be done much injustice as I would be honored to be esteemed by your goodness and good qualities generally. Honey, when I look around I feel more and more how thankful I ought to be for such a wife, and I do feel thankful. I feel, Honey, that I owe you a great deal for I know I should not be what I am if I had not married you.

Tell Pamela I saw a few days ago her brave Capt. [W. A.] Fry. He will do tolerably well to be shot at but not so remarkable to flirt with. He says he is going to Mr. William's soon and of course will call on Pamela. She must not let his wound work too powerfully in his favor. Tell Ham it is time for him to return. Honey, I hope things will so turn up that I shall have you with me soon, but as long as we remain fronting the enemy as we do, it will be impossible. The Yankee papers do not seem so loath to have their troops go into winter quarters as they did. I must now close. My love to all and a kiss for Pamela and the boys. Tell her she must not give up Stephen Lee. How do you like the hoops. I rather pride myself upon having thought of them. The belts I fear were poor and not appropriate.

I suppose you know by this time how things will be for the next *nine months*. God bless you and the children. Please let me know as soon as you have settled the thing in your mind. Good bye.

Your devoted Husband

ᴄᴠ🐝ᴧ

Near Fredericksburg, Va., Dec. 5th, 1862

My dear Wife

You may be assured I am getting very impatient to hear from you, as I have not had that pleasure since I left. The omnibus driver caused me to leave ¾ of [an] hour sooner than necessary that day. I have not ceased to regret leaving you when I did, but I know you do not blame me.

Since getting here I have not changed my opinion as to having no fight at this place and I am inclined in Va. Last night we had snow and today it is melting which will make the roads worse than they were, which the Yankees complain very much of. Scarcely a shot has been fired even between the pickets. They throw up their works and we throw up ours.... You see however in the papers about all that can be said. Nothing new. Our Army is increasing every day and theirs from all accounts decreases.

I bought me a horse yesterday. Paid two hundred dollars for a very good horse five years old. In one month I shall be able to sell her for at [least] $300 if not more, and what is better I have enough money to pay for her. I am very anxious to sell Fan for she is no use in the world to me and it would cost too much to send her home. Do you think it would be wrong under the circumstances to sell her? Please write exactly what you think about it. I came near losing her while on the march down the Valley, she getting so lame as being barely able to travel.

My dear did I write you that I had reduced my debt from $1416 to $856 since leaving home. I hope the end of this month will find it less. Fan would bring about $300.

How glad I should be to hear that you had again escaped. You have no idea nor would believe from my past conduct, how much I think about it. And it all arises from the great grief it gives me to see or know that you have to suffer so much. How pleasant it would be if you can come to see me this winter with both your boys running around and you as well as when I went home.

Jake has not yet returned from Richmond and therefore cannot give you the news from that place. I had a very serious notion of appointing Henry Robison on my staff, but thought I would try a little more to get a N.C. man, and now I know of two or three.

Tell Pamela I am going to write to Stephen [D. Lee] today asking him to place himself matrimonially in my hand.

How will Joe Williams get off from going with the state Army for the Bill especially mentions Justices of the Peace as fit to be taken.

What do you say to selling out negro property to old Abe and quitting the war? He seems to be getting tired of it, and I only hope the old villain will get more tired before he gets through with it.

My dear I hope you have not been worrying yourself this time over my leaving and absence. There are no ladies to trouble you this time. I had a pressing invitation yesterday to dine where there were several pretty young ladies but did not go. You do not believe me when I tell you how much I love you and how much I think of you. Indeed, Darling, I love you more dearly every day and think more about you than I once thought it possible.

Dec. 11th, 1862

My dear Wife

No letter from you yet, but as we get no mail I could not expect otherwise. I expect one today as we have some hope of getting a mail. I really have nothing to write you about except the enemy are shelling the Town [Fredericksburg]—commenced about 6 A.M. [and] are still at it 11 A.M. The barbarity of the thing is unheard of, for I do not believe they even want to cross there. To shell an unfortified town is against usage. However, they make laws for nations to suit their own convenience.

I went to a negro concert last night that was really very good, and I enjoyed myself much better than if I had stayed at home smoking myself over a green wood fire. They had eight or ten ladies present, who seemed to like it as much as myself. I am tired of waiting for the coming fight and shall be glad when it is over, for then we may hope for some quiet for a month or two, and if we are to judge by report I shall not be impatient much longer.

Honey, you must excuse the shortness of this note, but the mail man is waiting and will not more than have time to get back by night. May God bless us and protect us, allowing to go down to a good old age in health of spirit as well as body. Recollect Honey that you have a loving husband, one whose principle and almost desire has been to please and make his wife happy. If I have failed it has not been for lack of love or the desire. My love to all. Kiss the children and sister.

Your loving Husband

✦

Two days later Burnside refuted Pender's forecast that there would be no engagement at Fredericksburg by attacking Lee's strongly entrenched veterans south of the town. During the furious seesaw battle on Jackson's front Pender's brigade, posted on the left, met and repulsed a determined enemy assault by Major General John Gibbon's Second Division.

In the melee Pender was shot in the left arm. As he rode by the Thirteenth North Carolina, formerly the Third N.C. Volunteers with whom he had served as colonel, Colonel Alfred M. Scales bounded across the churned up snow shouting, "General, I see you are wounded," to which Pender replied, "Oh, that is a trifle, no bone is broken. I want you to send at least two companies down to the railroad and drive those scoundrels out." Then bowing to entreaties that he receive medical aid, Pender let the doctors dress his wound after which he rejoined his men.[60]

When twilight curtained the one-day battle of Fredericksburg, the Confederates had inflicted over 12,000 casualties on Burn-

60. *O.R.* 21, 648; *N.C. Regts.*, I, 665; *N.C. Regts.*, II, 687.

side's army which subsequently withdrew across the Rappahan-
nock. Lee incurred less than half this toll, but among them was
Lieutenant "Jake" Shepperd, Pender's brother-in-law who served
as his aide.

While the dispirited Federals went into winter quarters at
Falmouth, Pender's veterans built huts on a large timbered tract
four miles south of the Rappahannock at Camp Gregg. Here
Pender received a call from a fellow officer from North Carolina,
W. G. Lewis, who later recounted: "I called on him at his head-
quarters and though I was much inferior in rank, he then being
Brigadier General, he received me most cordially and courteously,
and I had a very pleasant visit, and one of profit to me, as I saw
plainly in his camps the results of true military discipline and
careful attention from Headquarters. His camp was a model of
cleanliness, regularity and good order; his sentinels and guard
saluted, in strict military style, all officers wore the badges of their
rank. I was particularly impressed with this, as it was not by far,
universal in the Army of Northern Virginia."[61]

From his new winter quarters Pender resumed his correspon-
dence the last day of the year.

~❦~

Dec. 31st, 1862

My dear Wife

Your telegram of the 26th and letters of the 23rd and 28th
inst. all came today. You must rest assured of the pleasure your
letters gave me, but it makes me feel sad to have you write in such
a sad and despondent tone. I will not reason with you on the subject for you will at once say that it is my want of feeling. Do you
know Honey, your letter of the 28th when I first read it over gave
me the impression that under existing circumstances you did not
wish to come on, and it was some time before I came to the conclusion that I have, to send after you. You never forget or forgive.
There are some words that I have spoken that you will bring up to
me a hundred years hence if we should live that long. Honey,
the more I think of you and your letters the more sad I am. I
feel like shedding tears.

I will tell you of the arrangements I have been able to make
here for you in case we shall be here when you come on. I have
engaged a small attic room—with fireplace—to stay in and will

61. Letter of W. G. Lewis to D. Gilliam, October 21, 1893.

have to send your meals to you from camp half a mile off. Washing can be done in small quantities, no place for servants. You can judge as to bringing one of the children. Joe could take care of Turner. Rather than not see you I would say bring both, but if you could be satisfied to leave them it would be better for there is no telling how long before or when we may move. Turner would not be so much trouble to travel with as Dorsey. It might be possible to leave Turner in Edgecombe. But finally do as you please. We can get along with Turner very well. But whatever you do come quick. You may find it necessary when you get to Richmond to remain there a few days—in case we should be moving—in which case Mr. Young will look up Dr. Brewer—brother of the Colonel and husband of Miss Maria Cook you saw in Washington—who will find a place for you.

I am very sorry your father should feel hurt at my not writing. I did not have much time at first and you know—want of feeling —that I dislike sad subjects. I will send Jake's horse home by the first good chance. I could not send it by Mr. Young because it would take too long; going as he does after you. In the meantime I shall let Capt. [L. H.] Hunt, who is Act. Inspector Gen'l on my staff use her. He will have better care taken of her than I could with those other horses. Mr. Young, I forgot to tell you, is my volunteer aide and a very gallant young man. He was near me when I was hit the other day.

Honey, Pamela's affection for me is not misplaced for indeed I believe next to you and the children I love her better than any else—and of course excepting my good old Mother. I have felt more for her in this your trouble than anyone else because she loved him [Jake] better than she did anyone else.

Honey, I fear my last letter was but poor comfort to you, but honey I was in a terrible state and you must excuse me. Indeed I love you well enough never to wound you by word or act, if it were not for my bad nature. . . . As for peace, it depends a great deal upon the impending battles in the West. Come quick Honey and use your good judgement. God bless you, My love to all. Kiss dear Pamela.

Your fond Husband

Bring sheets and chambers. We get the room, bedstead, mattress and chairs only. I have blankets.

There is a gap in Pender's letters from December 31 until the latter part of February during which Fanny was with the General at Camp Gregg. On her return journey Pender accompanied Fanny as far as Richmond where he milled around for a few days after her departure.

∾᪣᪶

Richmond, Feb. 25th, 1863

My dearest Wife

A duller place I never saw and I am heartily tired of it, and if I can be pardoned for this offense I think I will never come to Richmond again without business. I shall leave day after tomorrow. Everyone has treated me very kindly. I went to call on Mrs. Walker—the bride—last night and she is a beautiful little woman. I do not wonder at Walker's being caught by her. I took particular note of her dress—she had just been to dine out and of course was doing her best—so I could write you what her style was. She had on a very pretty dress and accompaniments. I went out today to get you some belts but could not find any. I shall try again tomorrow.

My promotion hangs as it did and really I do not expect it for months if at all. Gen. Jackson is in my way having recommended another man. I never will vote for his being President. Everyone here seems to think that our prospects are still bright[en]ing, that the Yankee conscription Bill if it passes the House will only serve to make matters with them worse. I hope so.

There is really no news here at all. It is reported that they have commenced firing at Vicksburg with one of their Batteries. Honey, I will try to search down the river when I get back to get you some things, if I find they can be had at reduced prices. I think however before summer is gone things will be cheaper.

How did you find the boys. Honey, you wrote that you had deferred writing while here so you could let me know if you had escaped again, but did not say. Darling, in looking around I do not find any ladies who to my eye that [are] any prettier than my wife. Mrs. Walker is considered a great beauty, but I was comparing you last night while there and I came to the conclusion that you were the prettiest, and by far more intelligent than any lady I met. God bless you—how I do want to see you and the children. I wish I could buy something for you altho' my money is about out.

Honey, I will write you a long letter when I get back to camp. You know how difficult it is to write in all the confusion one is in for the first day or two in a city. I am going to dine with my old Captain, now Gen. [Arnold] Elzey, today.

My love to everybody.

Your loving Husband

ᴧ✿ᴗ

Camp Gregg, Va., Feb. 28th, 1863

My dearest Wife

I received yesterday your letter from home and today your letter by Willie. He came day before yesterday, but I had not returned. I went down there today. They move to Hamilton's Crossing Monday. Darling I was grieved to hear that you had such a hard time and it is well that I did not hear it until after receiving your letter from home, which altho' you did not say it, I should judge that you had not suffered any more than the temporary discomfort.

Fanny, indeed you ought not to write me as you do about Dorsey. You know that I would be happy to hear and want to hear all about him. One would suppose that you take my jokes in earnest about his not being my boy. If you want no difference made by one between them, let me advise you for the future not to draw these distinctions when you write.

But I will not write you a mean letter. I sat down in a loving mood to write you a long and pleasant letter. I was glad enough to get back, but now I do not know what to do with myself. You may well believe that I have wished you back and I will confess that if you were here I do not think I should send you off soon. But it was my fault and I can blame no one but myself, still I do not want you to blame me. Willie will probably be courier for Gen'l Hoke.

... Cousin Robert seems to think that no N. Carolinian will stand in the way of my promotion, but that it will be between Gen'l [R. E.] Rhodes and myself. Maj. Englehard left yesterday on a ten days leave. Your arrangement with the money was perfectly in accordance with the way I wish you to act. Honey, I wish I could keep [a] list also, but I cannot. I hope the time may soon come when we can keep it together. In your prayers Honey you will always think of me and feel that they avail much for me. I am truly anxious to do right.

Col. Scales is going to marry a Miss Henderson near the Depot by that name. My love to all and kiss the children and Pamela. I have written you four or five times since you left. I hope we will soon be able to form some favorable conclusions as to the probable close of the war. God bless you my darling. Write me often and tell me all about the children. Tell Turner I am glad to hear that he is such a sweet boy.

Your loving Husband

～✤～

Camp Gregg, Va., March 4th, 1863

My dearest

We have been badly out of order up this way lately, the bridge over the South Anna between this and Ashland having washed away—but it is now all right. I think the mail arrangements got so disarranged that I am to be cut out of my letters for a longer period than is pleasant.

My dear did that wetting do you any damage? Altho' you wrote as if you were well, still I cannot but feel some uneasiness about you, supposing you to be in a condition that might give you some trouble provided you took cold. Your letter of the 24th ultimo contained the latest news I have of you. I am glad you met with no more serious accident on your route for it is said that if one escapes being run off the track in the N.C. road he may consider himself to be lucky.

Indeed, Darling, I feel lonely and wish I could be with you. If you were here I could give you such a nice treat in the way of apples. Sutler Edwards still continues to send me nice ones. I got a dozen today from him and ½ doz. the other day, but as I am doing penance today I have not tried the last batch. I let my tongue fly [a] little loosely last night so I refused myself my eggs this morning and my apples today. I have really been ashamed of myself and sorry for the way I talked. I hope I shall do so no more. I have also stopped taking that occasional toddy. I made the resolution about the toddy the day I went to Richmond and altho' very much pressed since, [I] have kept to it. When I make up my mind not to use spirits I find no difficulty in sticking to it. These are small matters now but may lead to good results in the future. I always want to be not only a Christian—which I cannot— but a husband whose habits his wife may approve of.

Honey, don't you think I try to please you in trying to do

what you think right. Do you not always find me reasonable so far as taking your advice. Bless my little wife! She has been to me a wife indeed, and a good angel. Fanny, if I should show myself insensible to so much love and goodness, I ought to be hung. Surely no man has such a wife. So much devotion, so much good sense, and last but not the least, in quantity, so much good looks. Honey, you always pretend to think that I am joking when I talk about your good looks. Indeed, Darling, to me you are very pretty and sweet, and I know you have quite a reputation for beauty. Honey, I feel in a loving mood and if you were here I would hold you in my lap and kiss and kiss you to your hearts content.

Honey, I got my cloth in Richmond but really I will not pay such outrageous prices for making as they ask. Just to think of giving $110 for the making of a coat. I will wear sacks first. I think I will have the pants and sack cut out and sent to you to have made by some of your seamstresses. I prefer a sack anyhow for they are so much more comfortable.

Willie has taken my bay mare. I let him have her for what I gave, $200. I shall sell Fan also, for she has gotten so that she eats off the tails of every horse she can get to. . . . I sent my Capt. Sammy to the extreme western part of the state for a horse. I also wrote to brother Robert. Two good horses are all I want and by selling two and buying one I shall probably make one or two hundred dollars to send home. You have no idea how I am eschewing to get out of debt. I intend to be as close as a miser. I spent only about $50 while gone to Richmond, including the $20 for my cloth. . . . Honey, I have clothes and cloth enough without that [which] you bought in Hillsborough. Suppose you sell that. Now do not get worried and say it is because you bought it. I shall not be able to use all I have for a long time and we [had] better have money than surplus cloth. There is no hurry about it however. In Richmond it would bring at least $12 per yd. I shall want my drawers after awhile, and you might put it in a box with them and send to Sgt. [A. D.] Montgomery [aide-de-camp] by any good chance to keep for me some few of my socks and those old rags of undershirts. He is on Wall St. above Maine about half a block in a house marked on the door "Billiard Room." If you have no good chance they can be sent after awhile by express. I will get him to sell the cloth unless you can get a good price for it. I will write again about this matter. The cloth I got in Richmond is very nice.

If Maj. [H. L.] Biscoe and Capt. [J. O.] Simon fill the orders I gave them you will be fixed out nicely for the summer. I am determined you shall have some more skirts, come what may. I wrote Mag Cox yesterday [and] having a good chance I asked her to write me back. I took it for granted she would like to hear from her relations on this side.

Honey, do write me about the children alike. Tell me how much Dorsey can talk, etc., etc. Darling, did you think about yesterday being the anniversary of our marriage? Four years, how short they seem. . . . We are more violently in love by far than the sweethearts. The Lord grant many returns and as happy as the past have been and we cannot complain. Now I will close. I wrote to your father a few days since. Does Turner talk any about me? Did you notice that Stephen Lee has been placed in command of the Batteries at Vicksburg and how he was complimented upon the improvement he was working. Kiss the children and Sis, and my love to Mary and father. Good night.

Your loving Husband

March 5th, 1863

My own Dear

Will you grant me one request? Indeed I do not make it lightly, but in all earnestness and sincerity, hoping that you will grant it. Will you take back that resolution and say you will let me know if you should get very sick? Darling, I ask this with tears in my eyes. Do this Honey and then I will feel that you have forgiven me. Honey, I could not but fear that you were sick, ever since I heard that you had to walk through the rain.

Honey, if I had got your letter sooner, you should have had the black goods, but today is Thursday and Maj. Biscoe left Monday and is by this time, if nothing has happened to him, on the other side of the river. If I get all the things sent for, you and Pamela will be set up. I put her in for lots of things, supposing she would want them. Ham sent for Mary. I sent to Baltimore for a doz. prs. kid gloves [and] a doz. handkerchiefs. If they come and you do not need them all, it will be very easy to dispose of them. I sent for nos. 6 and 6½, unfortunately no 6¼.

My dear pet I sent you the medicine given me by Dr. Powell. Dr. Holt is not here and as Powell brought Mrs. Hill through so well, I thought I would try him. Tell Father that his letter containing the invitation came today dated Jan. 29th.

Fanny, my dear child, do you know I felt very sorry when I

got to that portion of your letter where you said that I had punished you severely enough. My dear wife, God knows that if there is one human being in this world that I desire to make happy and at the same time do my duty by, it is you. Believe me, Fanny, when I say it, that I love you as a husband should love his wife. O child if you knew how hard I try to be worthy of my Angel wife, you would think better of me. Honey, if an evil thought gets in my mind I drive it away, feeling that I am doing you an injury. May our Blessed Father protect you and make me to be as I should.

I cannot help but think that Napoleon [III] means to interfere in this war, but my wife I have about made up my mind to a year or two more of it. If it comes sooner, so much the better. But we cannot well have such another year as the last. They may get men, but they will never fight as they have. As to my promotion, I received a letter from cousin Robert today. He had an interview with the Sec. [of War] and seems to be pretty sure of my promotion, provided the Sec. has anything to do with it. I have heard since I came back that Jackson did recommend me, still I am prepared for either result.

I shall try to send this by hand as far as High Point so you will get it without delay. I am very glad to hear that the children are doing so well and I should like to see them very much. You mistake very much Honey as to the pleasure of my visit to Richmond. As it is past 11 O clock I must close. My love to all. I got a letter from brother Robert today, he writes that they are all well. They expected you to give them a call. I will write to them why you did not. May God bless us and forgive us to each other in this world and to our Saviour in the next. Kiss the children and tell Turner I will write him soon. Good night.

Your loving Husband

Darling, I send the pills for you in a small box which I hope will reach you in time to be of use.

Camp Gregg, Va., March 10th, 1863

My dear little Wife

I received your letter of the 6th today, and I can assure you its contents gave me anything but pleasure. Indeed I did sincerely hope that you had escaped this time, but darling it must be the positive and direct will of God that it should be so, for would you not have supposed that it were next thing to an impossibility? I know it would look like mockery for me to say try to bear it as cheerful as possible. I who have none of the pains or troubles, but indeed my solicitude for you is next thing to the actual condition itself. The Lord be kind to you and bring you through it with as much comfort as under the circumstances could be expected.

Honey you cannot give me credit for the sorrow I felt today when I read your letter. But let me hope it is not so. If you are not positively certain, would it not be well to use Dr. Powell's prescription, for if you only use three of the pills and take the baths three days, there could be no harm done if you are as you write. It comes in a season of the year when you would like to be able to enjoy yourself, and when I hoped that you would be able to go from home somewhere and have a nice time. God bless you and he only knows what I would do for you if the doing of it would do you any good. I am very anxious to go to see you more by a great deal than ever. Would a few days visit to you do you good? I am almost tempted to ask for a leave, but I do not think it would be granted. O, that miserable five days I went to Richmond in.

My dear wife, indeed if I know my motives, you wrong me in saying that I sent you off to show people or you that I would have my own way. I really think I could rise above such conduct as that. Your letter was a very doleful one honey. Yet I do not blame you, for in your place I no doubt would write much more so. I have written you at least upon an average every other day, the last week nearer every day, and I hope that you will get them after awhile at least. Capt. [G. M.] Clark, who took me home, was four days behind time, which puts me in a very disagreeable position, since I have commenced arresting officers for staying over, altho' his is not as bad a case as the others. Still if I do not get after him, they will say it is because he took you home. If I do he no doubt will think he got bad pay for his kindness. I shall sleep on it tonight.

You can keep the money until you get a good excuse to send it down. I only wanted it out of my hands to keep from spending it. Honey dear, if you supposed that [the next] increase should be a little Fanny, would it not be a little consolation to you? If so, make up your mind it will be and get that much comfort.

My Brigade is still increasing. I have now 2150 and will have one or two hundred more. As to the war, I have not been able to help thinking that Lincoln does not expect to use the conscripts.

That they will try with what soldiers they now have in the field, and if they fail then, to have the conscript law to frighten us into the best terms they can, for if it is not so, why should they put off three months after the old men go out before they commence raising the new men when they could have commenced at once just as well. If they fail in their first spring effort—which I think they will—they cannot renew the thing again.... Our army is large and in fine condition. We have never had such an army before as this.

I will write you very often and I hope you will do the same to me. My love to all. May Heaven bless my dear wife.

Your loving Husband

❧

Camp Gregg, Va., March 13th, '63

My dear Wife

Your letter of the 8th and 9th was received yesterday and a real pleasure it was. I was so glad to have you write in so much better spirits. You have no idea how much I want to see you and how blue I was before it came. I got so I could not stand it, so I went to Gen'l Hill to ask him of the propriety of my applying for a leave. He gave me no satisfaction but said he would approve it although thought the chances were it would not go through. I slept on it and came to the conclusion that it would not do for me to apply so soon after having a leave.

So that miserable visit to Richmond comes back upon me. If I had not gone to Richmond I should have had no difficulty. It cannot be helped and I have been in low spirits more than I usually allow myself. As to your coming to see me, that has entered my mind several times and I was almost tempted to write to you to come on, but that my own darling would be very imprudent this late in the season. I might have kept you a month longer if I had known it, but my dearest wife don't blame me. It was done as much for your sake surely as anything else. I cannot bear the idea of your having to go round as some ladies do by themselves and in such crowds, not darling that I do not think you are able to take [care of] yourself, but honey you know I like to protect you from the necessity of having to receive the assistance of anyone, whoever he may be, in traveling about. Honey you know how particular I am where you are concerned. Honey it is all my love for you; that I feel that you are so much better than other people. If I could help it I would never have you dependent upon any but myself for the slightest attention in the way of service. I want you admired but at a distance. O, darling indeed I love you and appreciate you as no man would have done. And how much I have wanted to get you. Indeed, I say the truth when I say more than when you came on. You have some idea how much it was when with my notions about leaves, etc., I went to Gen. Hill merely to get the slightest encouragement.

I am so glad you got the medicine and I only hope it will get you all right. I saw Ham and Willie yesterday, they were both well. We have nothing new, unless it be a rumor I heard this morning that our Division was to move to Hamilton's Crossing tomorrow, but as it is now nearly 9 o'clock and no order, it must be untrue. I hope so, for unless we are to move some distance I had rather not move; we are very comfortable here. I should not be surprised to hear of something of interest from the eastern part of the state at any day. It may be a great thing for us if what I surmise turns out to be true.

Did Pamela get any letter? I wrote her a long one.

I really begin to have some fears from all you write, that the poor people in the west may really suffer. I wish the railroads were better conducted and more honestly. They complain that the Government takes all the transportation, but speculators who can afford to pay high freight get the precedence [over] the Government. Everybody has gone crazy on the subject of money making. I believe I should get to trying my hand if I had a chance, at least I am glad I am not subject to the temptation.

Your accounts of the children are very gratifying, but one thing would please me better than seeing them are the closing [of] the war and the other, seeing you. But do not force Turner's mind or let Dorsey get spoiled. My dear, if your worst fear should be realized, try and bear it as well as you can and that is as well as any one could do, and honey the amount of suffering you have borne since we have been married and so uncomplaining too, I could not bear it, I am sure.

I am now reading "What will he do with it." I have read since you left "Bleak House," but the last few days were gone and I could not but worry about it altho' I knew it when I commenced the book. It is a fine book, much better than I thought, for I did like it much the first time I read it. Dr. Holt has not returned yet. He is, I feel, still in Richmond trying to get a hospital. If he does I wish him joy before he gets through with it. I have not the slightest confidence in his principles. I never did have much, but it has been decreasing for some months.

Now my own darling I must stop. Write me often, not only once in six days. May God bless you and the boys and may [we] be preserved at least through a long, Christian and happy life. My love to all. Kiss the dear boys.

Your loving Husband

ᘏᘏᘏ

Camp Gregg, Va., March 15th, 1863

My own dear Wife

Your letter of the 11th has just reached me. While it gives me great pain to hear that you are still suffering, still it is a great pleasure to hear from you. Yes darling, write me regularly if only a line. I will not ask you, nor do I expect you, while suffering so much in body and mind, to write long letters. Let me but hear from you and I will be satisfied on that score. My precious wife, you have no idea how terribly anxious I am to see you and nothing but the strongest conviction that I could not be spared now, and a fear that my application would be refused prevents me from trying to get to you.

... Darling, so far as any fears you might have had about my sentiment for the lady that was Mary Sumner are entirely groundless. Indeed, I tell the whole truth when I say that I never had a regret about the matter in my life, except in having allowed my vanity to have carried me so far. I never loved her nor did my judgement ever sanction any connections with the family; and I can say truthfully that I always regarded it as a most lucky escape.

For Miss Adams I had more admiration and a higher opinion, but no more desire that she should be my very wife. Fanny indeed you may rest assured of the truth of what I have so often told you, that I never saw but two women who I would in a cool moment and in which my judgement would have allowed me to [be] married. One I never loved and the other I married, and do love with all my heart and soul. O my wife, my wife if there ever was a husband who adored his wife and thought her so near perfection as flesh can attain, it is yours. I know my treatment of you when together belies this profession, but if you knew how immeasurably beyond every one else you are in the influence you wield over me, how hard I tried to obtain to excellence in this world to please you and how much better I am, bad as I am, than when you took me for "better or for worse" you would believe. Honey, try to believe me, and have that much happiness.

May God bless you for the goodness you have shown me. I did want to see Mrs. Long but not to test myself, not to see if I had, as you may think, conquered any feeling for I had no old love to conquer, but more in curiosity to see how a girl of sixteen looked at twenty-four and because she was one of several who had made my time pass pleasantly. I made love to Mary Sumner to spite her mother who slighted me. Let this matter pass away from you for the future so far as any trouble it might give you. Honey, I addressed you because I wanted you for my wife. My judgement sustained me, a decision reached in 1854 and maintained up to this moment, and I fear not that it will ever be shaken.

We have rumors of an early engagement here, but I cannot believe it, for in the first place the roads are still much too heavy for an army to move, and in the second place I cannot but believe that [Major General Joseph] Hooker [who superseded Burnside] will stave it off as long as possible. We are as ready for it as we can be, but to speak for myself, I hope it may never be.

I went over to hear Mr. Williams preach today and heard a very good sermon. He asked me to particularly express to you his regrets that he did not see more of you. Soon after he called, Col. McRedy was hurt and he nursed him night and day. He really seemed sorry that he had not seen more of you. I have today made up my mind to try and observe Lent for the rest of the forty days. I hope I may succeed. I am today reading "Lenten Feast" by Bishop Kipp. I fear I shall fall through, but I cannot try too soon. I restrain my appetites too little at all times and surely risk my professions. I ought to restrain them for a few days.

Tell Pamela she is a dear little sister for being so kind to you and that I am already under too much obligation to ever forget them. Tell Turner he must answer my letter or I shall set him down as a lazy boy who does not love his papa. My love to every-body and kisses for the children. O darling, may you be active by the time you get this.

I have been consulting Dr. Powell and he says two or three days before your monthly period arrives to commence using the foot and hip bath, and take the pills. Continuing this from say about three nights before the time, until two or three nights after, making about a week in all. As the prescription was used before, after the period had passed, it did not have nature to assist it. It is upon the baths that you must rely principally as the pills are more to get your bowels in condition (use them however). If they all fail that, you can use the pills as occasion may require as a laxative. Do not allow yourself to get costive.

He says if his remedy fails this time your trouble will be so developed by the next time that there will be no doubt, but seemed to indicate that if any doubt should remain you might try it again. He seems rather to desire that you should not push it too much at any one time as trouble might arise. I will not give up yet that it is the worst.

. . . As weak as you are getting, you had better not fast, but eat whenever you can. Do you not think so honey?

WDP

༺ৡৡ༻

Camp Gregg, Va., March 19th, 1863

My dear Wife

Your letters come so very regularly now and you do not know how gratifying it is to hear from you so often. Your letter of the 15th inst. came today. Darling, I did not want an excuse for myself, but one that would have carried my application [for a leave] through. I made up my mind to apply but Gen'l Hill said he did not believe Gen'l Jackson would approve it. So my dearest wife rest assured that I want to see you bad enough to have you if I could have done so. I never felt such a longing to see you as since you left me. I got tonight from Richmond a gutta percha syringe for you and in a few days will send it to you, when honey, you must give Dr. Powell's prescription a faithful trial. You will be weak enough without that wasting disease too.

I wish if you have any good opportunity you would send my drawers and undershirts to me, to Sgt. Montgomery, Wall St. just above "Main" marked on the door post "Billiard Room." Also a few prs. socks.

I wrote you two days [ago] of Major Biscoe's failure to get anything for you, but he sent my order to Phila. and seems confident that the articles will come. My time is pretty well taken up. For the last four days I have been on a Board to examine some officers reported for incompetency and tomorrow I go upon a Gen'l Court Martial. As Maj. [George] Gordon [of the Thirty-fourth N.C.] would say, it is a regular swell court—being composed of three Majors and four Brigadier Generals. We are to try a Brigadier and tis said for cowardice. A few days since things looked as if Hooker might soon be up to something, but Stuart's fight and the snow that is now falling may stop him awhile longer. I do not care if it does. It is too early to commence the campaign for comfort.

I got a letter from Ham tonight and I fear my writing that he rode a horse that was a disgrace to the family made him a little angry. You know I was joking. Do not let Mary think anything of it. Did I write you that Col. Scales married a girl only seventeen. Best evidence in the world that he is getting old. Maj. Englehard says he must be Court Martialed for going off without letting anyone know it and get married in that way. Poor thing, she does not know what is in store for her, or she would not have been in such a hurry to get married.

I did hope when you left me that you had escaped, but we poor mortals know so little of the future. Surely we never need make any calculations again. But darling you were disappointed before in the name you had to give, probably it will be more in accordance with your wishes this time and there would be some little consolation to you would it not. Do not forget that I want F in it.

My heart and dearest of wives, why should you feel mortified at my praise. Do you know in a single particular where you do not try to do everything you should and if you knew how successful you are, you would see that you ought to think that you got no more than your dues. Yes, my own little angel, you are the best and sweetest little wife in the world. I see none so intelligent, so pretty, or half so good. No not one. And I always feel as if I ought to be doing something. Oh, if I were rich what luxury you should live in. May Heaven bless you my guardian Angel.

Tell Pamela I am too selfish to have written her a long letter for any pleasure it might possibly afford her, but the pleasure I hoped to reap by an answer and that she must not let all my labor be in vain. I am getting Stephen [Lee] all right. I am dying to hear something of the bride and bridegroom. She must write all the news about them.

Dr. Holt when he got back got a bottle of his hospital brandy and presented me, leading me to infer that he had brought it as a present from N.C. but I am too old to [be] got around in that way. He is trying an arrest awhile. He had the impudence to [tell] Dr. Powell that he thought I did not expect him back at the end of his furlough.

Honey dear, as soon as you are able you must take exercize and you increase in the amount as your ability increases. You will want all the health you can get. Do not try to keep Lent any longer for whenever you can you ought to eat. Recollect your comfort depends so much upon your strength. The stronger you get, the less nervous you will be.

Now my own dear wife, good night and I say with a Christian feeling, God bless you. I think of you all the time. Kiss the dear boys and my love to all the family. What is the matter with your eyes honey. I take it, it is a part of your case or I should be very uneasy. I have tried to write large so you could read it.

Your loving Husband

∾✤∾

Camp Gregg, Va., March 21st, 1863

My dear Wife

I feel that this letter will be but little comfort to you and I should therefore make it short. I have felt quite uneasy this evening, Darling, as your letter has not reached me. I have been receiving them so regularly lately that the failure tonight and the state you were in when you wrote last, necessarily make me have fears that you are worse.

I am very well but find my time hanging on me as heavy as a millstone. I feel blue tonight which must excuse the tone of my letter. It has been snowing for two nights and a day and now it is raining. The roads will be as bad as ever. We have no news at all since Stuart's fight.

It is well that Gen. D. H. Hill accomplished all he intends and says so, for one would not have judged so from the meagre accounts we saw in the papers, unless he intended to accomplish but little.[62]

I wrote a letter today to the widow of Col. [R. H.] Gray.[63] Poor woman, she has lost her husband and without even the satisfaction that his death accomplished anything except to show how soon one can kill themselves with whisky. He was a fine soldier, and a nice gentleman. If his officers had let me know of his condition I could have stopped his drinking in time probably to have saved him.

Major Englehard, poor fellow, has bad luck in his family. The last news he has, is to [the] effect that his wife and two of his children are sick. His wife had been quite sick, but better and

62. On March 13-15, 1863, D. H. Hill made an unsuccessful attempt to overwhelm General J. G. Foster's 14,000 raiding Federals who were menacing the eastern coast of North Carolina.

63. Colonel R. H. Gray of the Twenty-second North Carolina died on March 16, 1862, following a siege of delicate health.

judging from one of her symptoms—convulsions—I should take it that you are not alone in your misery, or that I am not the only husband whose prospects for an increased family are brightening.

Now I have sold my horses I fear I shall not be able to buy any more. The accounts brother Robert writes me are not at all flattering. He is going back to Tarboro as soon as he can get him an overseer. I do not blame him. All are well at Town Creek.

Now my own dear wife, accept of my entire love. Gen'l [A. P.] Hill wishes me to give you his regards. My love to all the family and kiss the children. God bless you my dear wife.

Your loving Husband

∽✿∾

Camp Gregg, Va., March 26th, 1863

My dearest Wife

Your letter of the 22nd came today and I was very sorry to hear that you were no better, for in your last I thought you must be improving. You do not say anything about taking the tonic prescription I sent you, for that old wracking disease. I hope nevertheless that you are trying it, and that you will find it of use, for you could not need it more than now. I start a box for you tomorrow containing some nice note paper, a few envelopes and 45 lbs. nice brown sugar. It will go from Richmond by express and I hope you will get it, for the sugar is very nice. Altho' I feel that in doing as plenty others have done, and claiming that it is right, still I [would] rather it should not be known generally for those who cannot do the same might make occasion to talk about it. You will be surprised to see what nice sugar can be bought for 3½ cts. per lb.

Tomorrow we have [a] fast day and may the Lord grant us the grace that will enable us all to so importune Him that he will grant our prayers. Gen. Lee has published an order exhorting all to do as we should on such a solemn day. I shall go over to hear Mr. Williams in the morning and try to get him to preach to my Brigade in the evening. Gen. Lee, I should judge, is determined to strike home and so effectually as to close the war, if possible, soon. We all feel confident of our success so far as this Army is concerned.

You will be very much surprised to hear that Gen. [A. P.] Hill preferred charges against me last Sunday, but in this wise. I wrote what I intended to be a semi-official letter to, as I supposed, my friend [E. A.] Palfrey[64] in Richmond and through him I suppose it got to the Sec. of War, and as it is against orders to communicate with him except through intermediate commanders, it was returned to Gen. Lee, calling his attention to the order and he ordered Gen. Hill to prefer charges. Gen. Hill sent them up, but disapproved them, stating that the letter was only semi-official, so Gen. Lee sent them back authorizing Gen. Hill to withdraw them. Gen. Hill acted most kindly and delicately, taking the paper out of the general packet so it would not be made public. I cannot feel too kindly towards him, for altho' no court would have done anything to me, still it would have injured me with the public if I had been brought before a court martial. If Palfrey did send the paper to the Sec. of War, it was a mean act and he can keep clear of me in [the] future. I wrote asking him if he did it.

I am going to break up my mess as soon as we move, taking Maj. Englehard and Capts. Kirkland and Hunt with me. We have too many now.

Honey, I was sorry to have to dampen all your hopes about seeing me, but I saw it was merely allowing you to hope for what could not take place. Let us hope that the next time we meet it will not be to separate again soon.

Col. [W. W.] Kirkland has been elected Colonel of the 21st N.C. and altho' they have no right to elect, it will secure his appointment no doubt. It is generally thought that our staff will be increased, giving a Brigadier an Inspector General [with the] rank of Major and another Aide-de-Camp. If so, I shall try to keep Capt. Hunt.

We hear bad reports from N.C. of late, but I for one hope our campaign may be brilliant enough to silence all such treasonable proceedings.[65] [The remainder of the letter has been lost.]

Camp Gregg, Va., March 28th, 1863

My Dearest Wife

I have but little to write about, except to tell you for the thousandth time of my love and desire to see you. I did not get any letter today as I hoped, but knowing how little you can feel like writing, I cannot complain. I write you every other day be-

64. A. P. Hill's Assistant Adjutant General.
65. Pender is alluding to the peace movement in North Carolina instigated by William W. Holden, editor of the Raleigh Standard.

cause I hope it may be of some pleasure to you, to hear. Yesterday I think was more truly observed than any fast day I ever saw. I heard two very capital sermons from Mr. Williams.

The news we got yesterday was truly encouraging. I cannot but feel that this war is near its close. More fighting we must have of course, but not as severe or as much. How I do long for peace and quiet enjoyment with you.

Today our Court Martial met and commenced work. It is going to be a tedious job indeed. Some of them wanted to sit tomorrow [Sunday] but I got Gen'l. Hill on my side and we carried it against such a wish. But altho' tiresome it is a relief to the dull monotony of camp. Anything to be employed. I cannot bear to be idle; less now than ever. I heard today indirectly from Stephen Lee [that] he expects to be promoted to Maj. General. I think if claims were considered I should be promoted too, but I have given up that idea. If the war can come to an early end I shall be content to get through with it. You will think me just as much a hero as if I were a full General and love me just as much and what more need I care for, and then I know I stand high with those who know me.

I shall send tomorrow a letter of W. B. Reed's of Phila. to father cut out of the *Sentinel*. I think he will enjoy it. Maj. Morgan is going to leave the General [A. P. Hill]. He is going to his brother John to get a Regt. I think the General will be very glad to get rid of him. He sees what weak men he has around him and regrets it too. I expect he will keep Maj. [W. H.] Palmer [Chief of Staff]. Col. Scales is the most homesick man I ever saw. I got after him about marrying such a young girl, but he says she is 18 and not 17 years old, and that as she possessed those qualities he wanted, he did not think youth ought to have a counter-balancing effect.

I have been looking very impatiently for Pamela's letter, hoping she would give me some of the local news, but have about given her up.

I know you will be glad to hear that my Brigade is increasing very rapidly. They are sending me conscripts now. I have nearly 2,500 present, and they are coming in every day. I shall have more men than I ever did. The more the better, if I can get them drilled any. We have had nothing but rain lately, except yesterday, which was a most beautiful day. It rained nearly all night and today, and you may rest assured that the country is nothing but a quagmire. No movement for sometime.

Now my dear, let me write about you a little. I wrote asking you to send me word of all your symptoms, but I suppose you did not comply because you felt that there was no longer any doubt. I was reading in the Bible the other night where it stated that children were such blessings and given as an evidence of favor in God's sight. Ought we to complain so at·what is evidently His direct will, for did we not try to oppose it? and with what effect? Let us look upon the bright side of it and be cheerful. I do wish you could go through with it without being so sick. You will not, poor thing, be able to enjoy this spring and summer any. My love to all. Tell Turner never mind if none of them write to papa for him, that he can spell them some of these days. My dearest little wife, accept of my entire devotion and believe that you are ever in my heart. May God bless you.

Your devoted and fond Husband

ᴧᵛᶻᴧ

Camp Gregg, Va., March 29th, 1863

My dear little Wife

After I wrote you by today's mail I cannot refrain from writing you tonight. Your letter of the 25th which came today gave me so much pleasure that I must let you have a little benefit from it. Yes, honey, it was the most delightful letter, you wrote in such good spirits and you are evidently trying to take your troubles in such an agreeable and resigned way. Continue darling in the same spirits. I hope I have not complained in my letters nor have I wanted to do so, but you have no idea how happy I have felt since getting your letter today. O, you are the best creature in the world. And do you know honey that instead of my laughing at what you say about being the mother of another one of my children, it makes me feel so proud to have such a woman to feel that way about him. May our Father in his infinite goodness bless you. Yes indeed darling, I pray night and morning that we may be spared to each other to a good old age.

Honey, I try very hard to be a Christian and I do have hopes of the future, and I hope it is not too presumptuous, but I cannot but hope that my honest efforts will not go unrewarded by such a loving and merciful Saviour, not for the good I may do, but for the gratitude and love I try to bear him. I think the observance of Lent has been of some use to me, and I find what I thought would be almost impossible, very easy. I want to be a Christian to have "Faith, Hope, and Charity, but above all Charity," and I think I am getting to be less hard-hearted toward my neighbor than I used to be.

How I wish you had three apples I found in my trunk this morning, but Dr. Holt is going to write tonight, to a gentleman near High Point to get some and send you. I shall want to borrow enough money from you to pay for them. I shall write Mr. Sullivan to pay for them, and forward to you and you can send the money to him. I got a letter from David today saying he had started the horse to me. . . .

Honey, I think of trying to get Mr. Williams as Brigade Chaplain, in which case he will stay with me. Everyone seems delighted with him. Even Col. Scales—a strong Presbyterian—was delighted with him. Honey, your coming on will be out of the question as we are expecting orders to move at any time. So soon as the roads get dry enough there is but little doubt that we will commence operations.

ᘓᕉᕽᕽ

Camp Gregg, Va., April 1st, 1863

My dearest Wife

Your letter of March 28th came yesterday and altho' it was my night to write I put it off because I felt blue and did not want to write a low spirited letter. Your letter was a very charming one and by no means tended to make me low. Your letter gave me great pleasure. You do not [know] how low spirited I felt when you were only able to write me short notes. Tell Sis that I am very sorry to hear that she is in bad health and still more so that I cannot go to see her.

The horse David sent me is a very handsome one and quite a good saddle horse. I sent him some money today to send you, or to give you an order for it on some one in Salem. Capt. Kirkland returned yesterday very much improved but not fully restored. I was very glad to see him back.

Gen. Lee has been quite sick but is better. I do not know what we should do if he were taken from us. There is but little doubt but that Hooker will attempt to cross again as soon as he can, and we all think still less doubt but that he will get well whipped for his pains when he does. I have just twice as many muskets now as at Fredericksburg. It is a very remarkable fact that all the complaining and disaffection at home does not produce any bad effects upon our soldiers. I heard yesterday through an officer of Gen.

Rodes staff who had returned the day before from amongst the Yankees on the other side, that thirty seven of their Regts. go out May 2nd and that their Governors had sent on men for the especial purpose of trying to get them to remain, but that they declared their intention of going, and moreover that according to the general interpretation of their Conscript Law, they could not retain them. If they do go, it will take about 20,000 men from the army which will make a big hole in an army none too large now for the work expected of it.

Col. [James] Connor [Twenty-second N.C.] who has just returned seems very confident of our ability at Charleston to maintain our position. In the army the impression prevails that in six months the war will be virtually over. You say you dreamt that you were riding in a hearse and that it was a bad sign. I thought dreams were interpreted by contraries; that hearses indicated a wedding or something of that sort. We are now eating nice shad. I wish you had some. I got a dozen shad, a doz. herring and two rolls this evening. Capt. Hunt still manages to feed us well.

Our court is still in session and will be for a week longer I suppose. I am getting quite tired of it. We had quite a snow night before last but it all left yesterday leaving the ground still more soggy if possible.

As soon honey as you can, you must walk regularly as you did last year, and darling try to cure your piles as well as your other trouble. Make it a rule to attend to those matters and it will give you something to do besides stitch and think all the time. Honey just reflect that either one of them might result in a disease that might subject you to a most painful and disagreeable operation. Write to me and say you will do it and then I shall feel certain that you will do it for you always keep your promises, especially when I am absent. I told you in my last about a box I had sent you and about some apples I had ordered to be sent you.

Honey do you ever see any husbands who are more devoted to their wives than I am. You often say I do not love you as I should, but do you see any who show more signs of affection than I do? You certainly see none who try harder to please their wives than I do. You know honey in your heart you feel that Joe Williams never was glad that you did not have him. Now he is married I do not care anything about him either way. Do you think Mrs. Williams [is] satisfied with her daughter? She visited you to impress you with the belief that she was.

Tell Pamela I give her up and that I will not trouble her

again with reading my nonsense. She shows she does not want me as a correspondent. My own dear girl, good night and may the Lord keep watch over you.

Your devoted and loving Husband

~✻~

Camp Gregg, Va., April 3rd, '63

My dearest Wife

I write you tonight because it is my regular night. I went to see Ham and Willie today. They are both well, altho' Willie has been suffering somewhat with his leg. I was glad to learn that Gen. Lee is better and able to be up. The loss of his services would be irreparable to us just now.

I have not heard a single item of news lately. The box of sugar is still in Richmond, the express company refusing to carry boxes weighing over 40 lbs. I will send it on in a few days by a man. I hope you will send my clothes as soon as possible by express to Sgt. A. D. Montgomery, Richmond.

Today I should liked to have gone to church but did not know until too late of any services. Mr. Williams will be back for Easter. I hope we will get through with our court Tuesday. If the Staff Bill passes Congress, I shall try to get Ham with me as ordnance officer and make Mr. Basm one of my aides, as I could turn him off now and besides he is a very nice young man.

Did you ever see the papers so barren of news in your life. I expect it will be changed in three weeks, for by that time we shall in all probability be on the move. I hope by that time you will be restored to strength and be comparatively free from trouble. I learn that D. H. Hill brought out immense quantities of bacon and corn when he went to New Bern—that that was his object in going down, merely to drive in their outpost so as to get at it.

Have you heard from Frank and Helen lately? You must not fail to send me a memorandum of what articles you want for yourself, children present, and the one expected.

Capt. Hunt has just sent me in two large pieces of cake and this morning I got a dozen nice apples. How I always wish you present to help me eat when I get anything nice. I sent down by Mr. Williams to get me if he could "The Prince of the House of David."

Honey, I wish you would send me the children's likenesses with my clothes soon if they cannot be taken as well as you would like them, and also provided Pamela is willing that of her and Miss Conally, or if she has one of herself alone taken within the last year or so that she would be willing to let me have.

I find it intolerably dull here and begin to want to be on the move. I think the sooner the campaign opens the better both for the army and the country. Our people always get gloomy when they have no excitement and there is too much disposition to desert from the army....

Holden's treasonable articles [advocating that North Carolina sue for peace] are doing their work and unless we can have a successful and early campaign there is no telling where it will stop. The Conservative party [organized and spearheaded by W. W. Holden] will bring disgrace upon the State yet, I fear....

... Let me ever get a home in which we are together and I will show you what a good husband is. My love to all. May God bless my ever dearest wife.

Your loving Husband

❧

Camp Gregg, Va., April 5th, 1863

My dear Wife

Your letter of the 30th ultimo came yesterday much to my great pleasure. My dear girl I had no idea that you had not been down stairs for so long. How I have wished to see you since you have been sick. I have never before since the war commenced been so anxious to go home and if I could only have seen ahead for a few weeks I should have made the attempt. I fear I shall not be able to get you any calf skin, but send me in your memorandum the sizes you will want for the children and for yourself and Laura. I expect to have a chance before the summer is over at Yankee assortments. Capt. Kirkland says his father got some very nice white domestic (unbleached) at Fayetteville for 35 cts. a yard a month or so ago. Would you like to have some. They have mills there and altho it has probably gone up, still it may be cheap. I can write to my cousin Henry Marover who could send it to you by stage.

I went to Communion today. Mr. Williams officiated. He desired to be remembered to you. I think of getting him for Brigade Chaplain.

The snow fell last night to the depth of at least four inches. It was preceded by a most terrible storm in the midst of which I heard several wish most earnestly that it would sink the blockading squadrons.

Honey, your charge that I love you better when absent has something in it—there is no doubting, to be based upon; I always make more professions of love when you are away, but let me ever be able to trouble you with my presence again and I will show you a different state of affairs. O you dear girl how I should like to have you with me in that big arm chair we spent so many happy moments in this last winter.

Don't you think honey that you had better starve Dorsey a little, and not let him get so fat and Penderish. I had rather he would not get fat and coarse for you will think that he is not of good blood. Turner is of the gentleman pattern, is he not? However, Dorsey may be trimmed down a little after we find he will not be on the small style like ourselves. Six feet add wonderfully in this world to a man's career.

Lent is over and I have not but felt that I passed the latter part of it a little better than I ever did before and I hope I have become a better man. I have broken myself honey of using any thing like profanity even in telling what someone else might have said, and I very seldom say anything that I would not say in any company. I am trying very hard to break myself of anything like filthy speaking, so common amongst men. Honey, I believe fully in Christ and that he will save those who do His will and I try very hard to do so. . . . I have some hope and I try very hard to be charitable, particularly in not judging anyone lightly. It seems to me that I would be willing cheerfully to undergo anything for a certainty of future salvation. Honey, pray continually that my life may be spared this war.

We have nothing at all new. Bread, alias plundering, riots are becoming common. Some of the rioters in Richmond will probably get sick of it before they get through with it. My love to all. God bless you my dear wife.

Your loving Husband

จะ

Camp Gregg, Va., April 8th, 1863

My dear Wife

Your letter of the 4th came today and the cheerful spirit in which you write is very gratifying. Dr. Powell is not here, but will be back in a few days, when I will ask him about the prescription.

I do not care to ask Dr. Holt. Honey, I am very sorry that you keep so weak and sick at your stomach. One of my cousins starts home tomorrow and he will take the sugar to High Point, so you will be pretty sure to get it. I only wish I had something else to send you.

I suppose there ought to be eight button holes on each side of my sack. If there should not be buttons enough, don't bring any for I have plenty here. Please get it done as soon as possible and sent on so I shall get them. We may be off beyond the reach of boxes most any day. Do not forget the address. I cannot get along without my drawers. It matters but little how many buttons, or how put on, the coat has.

We hear rumors of a fight at Charleston [S.C.]. It is a very important point and vastly important to hold it. They would crow over the fall of that place more than Richmond. Our preparations are on the largest scale and if we do not succeed in holding it, we may give up all idea of holding any place that can be got at by their Iron Clads.

A deserter came over last night, and he confirms the report about 37 of Hooker's Regts. being determined to go out of service about the 1st of May. We are all getting anxious to be at them, not because we want to fight, but to try and close the war before they can drill their conscripts. I think it very likely we will attack them in several places, here, at Suffolk, and in N.C.

Honey, I sent you the *Sentinel* because it is the best edited paper in Richmond and so much more cheerful in its tune. . . . Six of my rascally conscripts have deserted but as I did not count on more than half of them being any use, I am not much put out. I have more than twice as many muskets as I had at Fredericksburg.

I like your enthusiasm for Gen'l [A. P.] Hill and I hope I shall not forget the many kindnesses he has done me. Gen'l [Harry] Heth . . . is in our Division and a very nice gentleman he is too.

You will get some money through David which will enable you to pay for Maj. Englehard's cloth. We get through our Court tomorrow much to my relief. My dear wife, I wish so much that you were well as when you came on to see me. I should feel so much more at ease. Bless my dear wife, she is so prejudiced when judging her husband. Your praise, darling, is very gratifying to me, and makes me the more anxious to do, to make myself worthy of it. You asked me how we have been living. Very well indeed, Capt. Hunt being the best caterer we have yet had.

What has become of Willie's horse he left at home. I think it foolishness in his keeping a horse there to eat corn these hard times. Ham told me the other day that Pamela was sick. Is it so? How long will 45 lbs. sugar last you all. Let me know for I may be able some of these days to send you some more.

Capt. Lemon is considerably behind time and Gen. [J. J.] Archer begins to fear that they have caught him, so that order of mine is likely to bring nothing, but we are all making grand plans as to what we shall get when we get into Md. again, if we ever get there. I am inclined to think that will be the move we will make, march for Md. turning the Yankee Army and force them to fall back upon Washington. I am now in favor of going straight through Md. into Penna. and I believe we can do it. Gen. Lee undoubtedly has some bold plan upon foot. Unfortunately, he has not yet recovered.[66]

I understand Gen. Jackson has been making some inquiries about me and said he was sorry he did not know more of me personally—the old humbug—this was when Gen. Hill sent up his last recommendation. He [Jackson] asked an officer of his staff in whom he has great confidence, the other day who was the best Brigadier in the Corps and I think he told him that I was. All of this, however, gives me but little hope of promotion.

You would be surprised to find what a good boy Joe has been since you were here. I pressed him a little which seemed to do him a great deal of good.

Now my dear wife, as I have said nothing worth reading and have nothing more half as entertaining, I will stop. My love to all. Kiss the children and Sis. Does Pamela really care anything for me. Since she will not write me I have really commenced to have some doubts. She is a dear girl and I love her dearly. God bless you my dearest and best of wives and may you soon be well. Let me know if you got the apples I wrote about.

Good night my sweet wife.

Your loving Husband

ᘐᘏᘐ

Camp Gregg, Va., April 11th, 1863

My dear Wife

Your letter of the 5th came day before yesterday. I get all your letters, but some come in four days and others in seven or eight.

66. General Lee had contracted a serious throat infection which developed into a pericarditis that gave him sharp pains suggestive of angina. Douglas S. Freeman, *Robert E. Lee* (New York: Charles Scribner's Sons, 1935), II, 502.

I got up this morning before 7 o'clock—early for me—to write this. I was very glad honey to hear that you were able to go to church. The next time I hear I hope you will be entirely well.

The news we got from Charleston was very good was it not?[67] We are expecting to be on the move soon. A pontoon bridge was brought up the other day, so I understand, and I hear troops have gone up towards Gordonsville. We hear nothing of the Yanks except that 37 Regts. are going home the first of May.

Col. Scales is trying to get on foot a general petition from the officers of our N.C. Regts. here that I be promoted, but I have no idea it will succeed. I do not believe Gen. Jackson will have me promoted because I have been recommended by Gen. [A. P.] Hill. He wants someone in the place who will feel under obligations to him.

Indeed I do wish I could see Dorsey and all of you. I have wanted to go home very badly, but felt that I should be refused. Gen. Hill refused to let Gen. [Samuel] McGowan go altho' he said he would approve my leave, but that he thought it would not go through.

You said Dorsey is like me. I always imagined that I could see in Turner a very good likeness to myself. He, poor little fellow, is laying up many whippings for himself. Those who laugh at him little think what it may cost him in after years. I have always thought that he would give us more trouble than Dorsey. I should like very much to have a daughter, and a blonde. There are too many dark skins in the family.

Let me know when the paper I sent commences to reach you. I wrote to subscribe for the balance of the year. I suppose you will soon be having strawberries and other nice things. The impression seems to prevail that we shall have a fine crop of fruit this summer. I hope that Dutchman did not preach you a Union sermon on Easter. Did the Salemites keep a fast day and what was the tone of their sermons. I have not one particle of faith in those rascals. I learned last night that young Wheeler is one of the three surgeons to examine conscripts in your district. Was there ever such a lanky fellow in the world, and it is said he is the best of the three. Tom Settle follows the Board around to get off the conscripts. He asks them to place their cases in his hands and then gets money for it. He is killing himself dead and getting to be looked upon as a very dirty fellow.

I had Brigade drill yesterday and it came off beautifully. I

67. On April 7, 1863, Federal ironclads attacked Fort Sumter, South Carolina, but were repulsed with the loss of one monitor which sank.

am getting a splendid Brigade. Good size, fine drill, and discipline. My men say I am hard on them but that I treat all alike. It would worry me very much if I had a reputation for injustice. I try to be impartial. Now my dear, I must close.

Yesterday was the last of our mess. Today I have only Maj. Englehard and Capts. Hunt and Kirkland with me. I have gotten so that I cannot bear Dr. Holt about me. He is getting rather odious to all the mess. He showed so much selfishness. He brought some butter from home with him and after helping to eat what Capt. Hunt had brought and all we could buy (and he eats a pretty big share) refused to let us have any of his because the mess was to be broken up in two or three weeks from that time. After showing his manners by refusing, he sent it to the Captain and I am glad to say it was all eaten up several days ago.

Darling, I know you would use the Dr.'s prescription which I am sending. How is it Honey that you take medicine so much better in my absence? Is it because when I am present you like to have me cornering you to take it, and in order to get me to do so you have to be careless about it? If you did not fret about my absenting myself and not staying with you all day when we are together, I should feel that something was going wrong. I like it, and I like the little touches of jealousy you show sometimes, but Darling you carried it a little too far to be very pleasant about Suffolk matters. Bless my dear little wife if she did not abuse me a little occasionally I should think she did not love me so much as she used to. Do not try to change in those respects. I don't wish it.

Honey, do you do anything for the piles now? If not you ought to. Get to be a strong healthy woman, for if I should get wounded I should want you to nurse me, which I would not let you do unless you should be strong enough.

Your loving Husband

∾❦∽

Camp Gregg, Va., April 17th, 1863

My dearest Wife

Your letter of the 12th came yesterday and I was very sorry to hear that you were not as well as you have been lately. I will send the syringe if [it is] to be had in Richmond. I send my trunk off tomorrow. I do not know that I should have sent it but Capt. Kirkland and Maj. Englehard made so much fuss about them that

I did it principally to set them an example. I have been rather disgusted with them both.

Col. [W. W.] Kirkland stayed with us two or three days. I like him very much. He seems to be a very correct and good man. He says his wife took a great fancy to you. He seems very much devoted to his wife.

We have nothing in the world new, and you may be assured I am lonely and tired of doing nothing. I have been having Brigade drills to pass off time, but those are becoming tiresome. You have no idea how sorry I was to hear that your peaches were killed. As for myself, I did not expect any, but you would enjoy them and expected them. I suppose you have heard that brother Robert has moved to the vicinity of Town [Creek]. Upon reflection I fear I could not live out of the Army or a city. The country would be rather lonely I fear.

It is reported by those who come from the other side the river that Hooker draws rations for 90,000 people. If that be true his army is not so large by many thousands as it was supposed to be and that number will be reduced by the going out of thirty old Regts. He cannot do much against this army.

You say you do not want me to go into Md. Honey, I feel nothing [is] left us but to go. If we do not, our Army will be on short rations and discontented, and we accomplish next to nothing. If we go we may do a great deal and I believe we will. This is a very different Army from the one we marched into Md. last year, and they have not as good a one to meet us. I am for going, but I have no idea what Gen. Lee will do, but one thing I feel certain of and that is we will not be idle much longer.

Honey, as fast as I save any money I shall send it to brother Robert to invest for me. You are no more anxious than I am to get ahead. I hope if I get through this war to get enough rank in the regular army to enable us to live well and save money. If I ever save any during the war I think I shall invest it in bonds—C.S.

Honey, you write me very sweet letters and they are very delightful to read. You are so loving and good, honey, how could anyone help being fond of you. I do not understand how anyone could help liking you, and there are but few I will venture to say that do not. As for me, I have enemies everywhere. I wish I could hold my miserable tongue. I can to a certain extent control my actions but that unruly little member is always saying something that had better be not said and for which I am very sorry. It has always been my greatest weakness. My love to all. Do you intend to let Turner wear britches this summer? Tell him if he can give [no] more than dried apples to see me, he cannot do it. God bless you my dearest wife.

Your loving Husband

∽✤∾

Camp Gregg, Va., April 19th, 1863

My dear Wife

Your letter of the 15th came today and I was very sorry to see that you continue so unwell. I do not feel alarmed, darling, but I feel so sorry for you and sympathise with you deeply in your sufferings. I think I wrote you to take a teaspoonful of the medicine three times a day, but I should have said a tablespoonful instead. Dr. Powell says it will discolor your teeth for the time, but that it will not be permanent. I think you had better continue taking it. I sent an order yesterday to Richmond for a syringe and some toilet soap for you. They will probably be sent by express.

Willie came down to see me today. He seems to be perfectly well. I will write to Fayetteville for a bolt of that cloth for you, provided it can be had reasonably. You may be able to have it bleached.

Have you received the *Sentinel* yet? Everything seems as quiet here as ever, the only stir being the passage of [a] great many wagons up the river above Fredericksburg yesterday and today, but as they paraded them so boldly it probably does not mean anything.

Have the peaches all been killed at Good Spring? I could and would have sent you some apples from Richmond, but Dr. Holt seemed to be certain that they could be had near High Point. Now I fear it would hardly be possible to get them in Richmond.

Honey, are you in earnest when you say you are proud to bear the name of Pender and that you want your children to be Penders in all respects? I am much more sensitive about the name than might be supposed. I have no particular fancy for it, but I do all in my power to make it respected and one not to be ashamed of, and if I can help it you never shall regret bearing my name in particular. It stands well in the Army I am happy to feel. I believe that I have more reputation than any Brigadier in this Army. I do not care much for myself. I am happy to be able to cause your husband to be one that you can claim with some pride officially speaking. Excuse this egotism, honey, but you touched a very sensitive point of my nature and made me feel very happy.

If I get the chance, and I have no doubt I shall, you shall have the things you wrote for and [a] great many more. Mr. Williams preached for us this evening, but I did not think he was so happy in his sermon as usual. He has [a] little too much sectarianism for the crowd he preached to, especially as he will join us soon and ought to come amongst us without having any prejudice against him if he could help it. He had a tremendous crowd.

Darling, you are not any more anxious to see me than I am you.

You say you hope we will not go into Md. I hope we will pass through it into Penn. and I believe the large majority of the Army would like to. Our people have suffered from the depradations of the Yankees, but if we ever get into their country they will find out what it is to have an invading army amongst them. Our officers—not Gen. Lee—have made up their minds not to protect them and some of our chaplains are telling the men they must spoil and kill. Our endurance has almost worn out. Sometimes when I think of their rascality I get furious. To think that the cowardly rascals will not let our women and children leave Washington, or in other words, to place them between themselves and Gen. Hill. Hill is going to burn the town down and he is right provided he will not take any prisoners. They have gone systematically to work to starve us out and destroy all we have, to make the country a desert. I say let us play at the same game if we get the chance. God bless you my own dear wife. Kiss the boys. Love to all.

Your fond Husband

∽✤∾

Camp Gregg, Va., April 21st, 1863

My precious Wife

Your letter of the 17th came yesterday, and a sweet letter it is. You have no idea how much pleasure it gave me. I could very easily imagine how my dear child felt and carried on, when fixing up my old rags and how happy she was to be doing something for me. Of course they will suit me for if such love as you carried into the operation could not do what was pleasing, what could?

Oh you dear little woman how happy I am in the possession of you and how much I want to see you. I often think darling that when we get together again that I will not be cross and look mad and refuse to talk as I used to do. I know you won't believe me, and I do not blame you, for I shall act just as mean as ever. It is in me and I cannot help it.

I am sorry you sent the butter for I fear you put yourself to inconvenience or possibly deprived yourself and you know we deserve no such kindness or self-denial. I have the stars on hand for the coat and it will not be long before I shall need it as my old sack is getting rather seedy. I am a thousand times obliged to Pamela and shall appreciate her present as it deserves. Kiss the dear pretty little Sis for me.

The paper was not subscribed for till the 14th, but if it has not reached you yet, let me know and I will write about it. I subscribed to 1st Jan., '64.

We are living horribly now and I am anxious for the month to pass away so I can install a new caterer. Maj. Englehard holds the office at present and justice requires me to say that I never saw one fill it worse and but one—Brewer—as badly.

I am very much worried of late about desertions. Our N.C. soldiers are deserting very rapidly. I have had about 30 in the last 20 days, and all due to those arch traitors Holden and Pearson[68] and Co. Poor old N.C., she will disgrace herself just when the worst is over, and after two years faithful service. I cannot bear to think about those rascaly "conservatives" as they term themselves. Next to a Yankee a "conservative" is the most loathsome sight.

I think the papers contain very strong indications of a letting down on the part of Lincoln, but we have refreshed ourselves so often upon false hopes that I will only say that this war as anything, must have an end and that each day brings that desirable result nearer to us. I cannot make out why Lincoln does not carry out his Conscript Law. There must be something wrong for it is all gammon about his having men enough. They have not enough now, much less will they next month.

Gen. Lee is about again attending to business much to the

68. Chief Justice R. M. Pearson of North Carolina exasperated the military by releasing deserters and conscripts from the custody of enrolling officers. On April 23, 1863, Pender protested to Army Headquarters "that at least 200 men have deserted from the Twenty Fourth North Carolina Regiment in this corps within the last thirty days.... In my humble opinion, the whole trouble lies in the fact that they believe when they get into North Carolina they will not be molested, and their belief is based upon the dictum of Judge Pearson . . . that the conscript law was unconstitutional.... Unless something is done, and quickly, serious will be the result. Our regiments will waste away more rapidly than they ever have by battle." *O.R.* 25, pt. 2, 746-47.

gratification of all. There is no special indication of a move, but we hold ourselves in readiness to move at any time.

I will see Dr. Powell and ask him if something cannot be done to help you retain your food on your stomach. I feel very anxious that you should get well, for it is hard enough upon you without having to contend against sickness and then I always feel that I am to blame for it.

... The next time I send any money home I will write David to buy you some N.C. money. It is only about 7 per cent and that would be a saving to you amongst those Yankee Dutch. I wish I had thought of it before for by the time I pay for the horse that Capt. [D. F.] Sumney bought for me, it will be two or three months before I can send any to you. Can you get along for two months longer upon what you have? Do not stint yourself by any means for by the end of May I shall be a hundred dollars or so ahead.

I wrote a letter to brother Robert but did not send it, for after thinking about the matter, it looked so absurd for me to be trying to buy a farm that I did not have the face to send it. I know you each laughed at me enough by this time about it. Bless you my dear wife it is all for your sake, for I know how much you would like to have a home where we could live quietly together. I fear I began to feel that there is no alternative for us but the army for life. If I can get a good position, it will be better than anything else I could do, probably. It will certainly be a gentlemanly position.

I went this morning to Fayetteville for a bolt of cloth and if you should not want it all, it will not be difficult to get rid of. Can you not get a straw hat made for Turner, and if not why not let him wear a bonnet. Anything these times. My love to all. God bless you my dear good wife, in all things.

Your fond and loving Husband

ᘛᘒᘚ

Camp Gregg, Va., April 23rd, 1863

My dear Wife
... We have had a terrible rain today and the 13th was out in it all, having started off this morning to be stationed up near Gordonsville to try to catch deserters as they make their way homeward.

I went up to Gen. Lee's yesterday and I was told while there that [Edward] Johnson and [W. H. C.] Whiting had both been nominated for promotion. Johnson was my competitor so you see my hope is gone. Not much disappointment as I have expected it some time. I have two drawbacks and heavy ones too: I am a N. Carolinian and a friend of Gen. [A. P.] Hill. The first will work against me with Mr. Davis, and the latter with Gen'l Jackson. But I say I am not cast down, for I am what I am altho' from N.C.

I am glad you like the *Sentinel*. I think it the best paper in Richmond. It is hopeful without being foolishly sanguine.

Honey I am very sorry you are so unpleasantly situated, but you need not refrain from writing me about it, for I have known it long ago. I wish I had a pleasant place amongst my relatives for you to go to, but it would be imprudent to go to my country in the summer. Suggest some means by which you can get rid of the annoyances any place you would like to go and I will cheerfully do all I can to make the arrangement. I am now able to have you, for my expenses will not be much over $100 per month and I would prefer your being contented and well situated to anything else.

Maj. Englehard wants his cloth sent to his wife. I see D. H. Hill left Washington and I expect any day to hear that Longstreet has left Suffolk. It seems they were intended only as large foraging parties, and in this respect have succeeded finely. I have no idea what we shall do or when we shall commence, as there seems to be no hurry on either side. I have no doubt we will remain quiet if Hooker will, until in May when their two years and nine months men will have gone out. Gen. [A. P.] Hill is of the belief that we cannot have as much fighting as last year, and I sincerely hope it may be so.

Honey, what would you like to do to get rid of staying at your father's. I know I could not stand it and I would not blame you to leave him. Write me about any place you may have thought of.

I hope I shall never be as cross as our fathers, but as my mood is not always of the sweetest even now, I had better not talk, but try to be amiable. I do not see why we should grow so cross and peevish as to be disagreeable both to ourselves and those around us. I pity Pamela for she has not even the consolation of feeling that she could go if she would. I wish she had some nice fellow for a husband. If Stephen Lee had not gone west I should have it fixed by this time.

Capt. Kirkland got 20 lbs. butter yesterday and Columbus

came back, and we are doing much better than we did. Tell Turner I was very glad to hear that he behaved so nicely at church, and he must continue to be a good boy and papa will get him some pretty things this summer. Bless you my dear baby, of course you shall have some confectionary when I can get [it]. I was just the other day thinking how much you would be pleased to get some nice French candy.

Does Turner ever swear any now a days? He and Dorse must have a great time playing. I used [to] think about the time when they would be large enough to run about and play together. My love to all. And may God bless you my ever dear smart wife.

Your loving Husband

~⚜~

Camp Gregg, Va., April 26, 1863

My precious Wife

Your sweet letter of the 22nd came today, and of course it was a great treat. You do not know what an influence your letters have on me; if they are cheerful so am I, and if the contrary, so it is with me. . . .

I have just received a bill from Richmond for a syringe and 5 cakes of soap. They will be sent by express.

David wrote me that Ruth's husband had been sent to Richmond and sold. He ran away and his mistress promised brother Robert that she would sell him to him—for me—but as soon as he came in, he was sent off to Richmond, and they will not tell him to whom he was sold. I have advertised to find out where he is. I do not care so much to own him, but Beck is dear to me, and I hate to see her husband whom she seems to love, torn from her in that way. This separating man and wife is a most cruel thing and almost enough to make one an abolitionist. I know you will approve my trying to buy him. David also wrote, "My family is well with *family prospects* brightening," and adds that the same thing that elated him makes us rather down hearted.

I approve your sending the bill to brother Robert. It will either make him ashamed of himself, which it ought to, or it will furnish him with information that he desires. It may teach him a little lesson, namely to forget sometimes that he is a business man, bringing every transaction down to cents. If he is my brother I must say it was a very small thing in him. He is though, a purely business man and brings every transaction down to it. He has been generous in his way to me.

I suppose I hope that [D. H.] Hill and Longstreet were never intended to take the places they surrounded. I hear that the latter is getting a large quantity of stores around Suffolk. The loss of Stricklands' Battery was a very ugly thing and does but little credit to the General responsible in the matter. The idea of sending a Battery two miles from any support.

I went to Communion this morning and altho' I did not feel that I was prepared I thought it would be more excusable in me partaking, and trying the harder afterwards, particularly as I may not have an opportunity again soon. I hope my feeling of utter worthlessness and shame at being caught as it were, will have a good effect. I went this afternoon to hear Mr. Patterson and I was very much pleased. He is a little queer, but preached a good sound sermon, one that would be likely to strike home to every hearer. Mr. Williams is about the best preacher I know. His sermons are always good and I sincerely hope to get him.

I am sorry to have raised, if I did, any hopes in you of a future home, for the idea of my buying a farm looked so ridiculous that I did not have the face to send my letter to brother Robert. But we will try to save and buy one, some of these days. I do not despair for I am learning the value of money. I hold tight to it and a few more lessons will make me pretty proficient, at least in keeping what I get.

... Honey let us hope that the next [offspring] will be such as you wish. We have more grounds to expect it than the contrary, for it scarcely happens that all are boys. I am very glad you have become so well reconciled to your condition. You will not be worse off than many others....

I cannot bear the idea of your becoming broken and old look-ing, not my own dear that I shall love you any the less, for my love does not depend upon your looks, but I love you for your love, and goodness.

... My love to all and may God bless you my precious darling.

Your loving Husband

◈

Camp Gregg, Va., April 28th, 1863

My dear Wife

Your letter of the 24th came yesterday. I hear from you very regularly and often now. I am so glad that you are improving and hope you will continue to do so. Do not fail to take [a] good deal of exercise, so you will get strong. . . . We are feasting now on fish, and I wish so much that you all had some. Maj. Biscoe sent up yesterday about 600 lbs. and today brought about 2000 lbs. for the men. I hope now to give them fish every day unless the Yankees break up our fisheries. The Major brought me a rock fish today weighing 28½ lbs, besides shad, herring, and pork. How you all would enjoy them. Ham came to see me yesterday, on his way after fish for his Regt.

We have nothing new, and seem to be as far from a move as any time in the last few weeks; but as something must be done, it will commence after awhile. But for the monotony of camp life I should be content to remain here and if the war could be brought to a close by this inactivity I should much prefer it to the slightest skirmish. There is no doubt but that the 38 Yankee Regts. have determined to go home, but whether they let them or not is another question, altho' they have promised in a General Order published by Hooker. If they keep them it will be an element of weakness instead of strength. This spring will be our time to strike them and may we pay them for some of their devilish acts. I almost get beside myself sometimes, when I get to thinking about the way they treat our people in their lines. I could keep cool last year, but now I get very excited when the subject comes up. How shall we get even with them, unless we strove to be devils incarnate like themselves, which I hope may not be the case. Surely the just God will punish them. Granting that we were wrong morally and politically, it could not have justified such treatment as they have been guilty of. . . . They are merely giving us a taste of what we might expect if they should conquer us.

Honey, I want you to write whenever you think of anything you want that I might possibly get, for if I can, so much the better, and if I cannot, no harm will be done by writing. I have not the slightest doubt but we shall at least make the attempt to penetrate their country. This has been my belief, based merely upon what I have thought ought to be done. We shall certainly never have such another chance and may God grant that we may succeed.

Darling, you cannot be any better satisfied with me than I am with you; nor any prouder. In my estimation there is no such woman as my dear sweet wife. None so smart, good or lovely, nor do I see any as pretty. You will pretend to think that this is all talk, but I assure you honey that I do not know anyone who to me is as pretty as you are. I pray we may yet live to be together and never be parted. Let us think honey that we shall have a little girl whose name shall be Fanny. You named the boys and I shall claim the privilege the next time.

Did you ever see a fellow who is so much carried away as David? Did Mary escape while here? If so she is a lucky woman. My love to all and kiss Pamela for me.... God bless you my precious wife.

Your loving Husband

જ⁂ૐ

Near Fredericksburg, April 30th, 1863

My dearest Wife

Your letter of the 26th came a few moments ago. You no doubt will have heard before you get this that the enemy have crossed here again. The impression prevails that we will not fight here for they commenced crossing night before last and have but few men on this side and seem by no means anxious to do anything. They have crossed [the Rappahannock] above and if you hear that we have fallen back you must not be uneasy for we are all right. We are concentrated and can fight where we please and whip them too. Some of their Regts. have gone out and others go day after tomorrow. After they crossed our men commenced to fire at them, when they asked us not to fire, that they did not want to hurt us and that as they had only three days to serve, they did not want to be hurt. Ham and Willie were to see me today. Do not feel alarmed as to the result of any battle we may have with Hooker. If we should fall back the fight will not come off for several days at least.

I am very glad that you are getting so well again. My box is in Richmond in the care of Sgt. Montgomery, so you may feel easy as to its getting to me. How long do you expect to stay in Edgecombe? You had better not stay later than the middle of July for you might get chills and fever.

My love to all and tell Pamela that I will write her after this affair blows over. Our people here are in fine spirits. God bless you, my dear wife.

Your loving Husband

Do not think that I do not want you to go to Edgecombe, for I do and I think the change will be beneficial. You must [not] carry the children. I have a strong notion of sending Joe home.

∾⚜∾

The next morning Pender's brigade struck its tents and marched westward with the main army toward the hamlet of Chancellorsville to confront Hooker's powerful flanking columns which were moving against Lee. After skirmishing with the Federals on the first day of May, Lee, on May 2, sent Jackson's corps far around Hooker's right to deliver a surprise onslaught which stunned and reeled back the Federal right. The attack which began late in the afternoon was halted by darkness. In his haste to resume the assault and annihilate Hooker, Jackson rode ahead of his line, manned by Pender's and Lane's brigades, to reconnoiter. On returning to his troops, "Stonewall" was mistaken for an enemy officer and fired upon by Lane's men. As the mortally wounded Confederate commander was assisted to the rear he encountered Pender who stated solicitously: "Ah, General, I am sorry to see you have been wounded. The lines here are so much broken that I fear we will have to fall back." The mere mention of withdrawal roused Jackson to vehemently issue his last order: "You must hold your ground, General Pender, you must hold your ground, sir!"[69]

During the night "Jeb" Stuart assumed command of Jackson's corps and ordered the attack renewed at daybreak. In the ensuing attack on the strongly fortified Federal lines, Pender spurred his men on by grabbing a regimental color and leading his followers "up to and into the Federal intrenchments." The North Carolinians responded in a manner which drew the following proud comments from their brigadier in his official report: "I can truly say that my brigade fought May 3d with unsurpassed courage and determination. I never knew them to act universally so well. I noticed no skulking, and they never showed any hesitation in following their colors."[70]

After the brilliant victory at Chancellorsville, the Army of Northern Virginia returned to its camps around Fredericksburg where Pender wrote a description of the battle to Fanny.

∾⚜∾

69. R. L. Dabney, *Life and Campaigns of Lieut.-Gen. Thomas J. Jackson* (New York: Blelock, 1866), p. 690.

70. *O.R.* 25, pt. 2, 840; *O.R.* 25, pt. 1, 935; *N.C. Regts.*, II, 689; Montgomery, "Life and Character of Major-General W. D. Pender," pp. 17-18.

Camp Gregg, Va., May 7th, 1863

My dear Wife
We are back again at the same old camp after eight memorable days. The enemy are all once more on the other side of the river and may God grant that they may go still further. We have had a terrible time of it and surely I have enough to make one grateful to Almighty God for.

We had the most terrible battle of the war, not because they fought better but because they had such terrible odds and held such a strong position and so well fortified. Hooker thought he had us but Lee is too much for him, and while he was waiting for us in his front we fell upon his right flank and but for night coming we would have cut him to pieces Saturday night. Saturday night he had time to change front and fortify but to no purpose only to make it harder upon us. After five terrible hours commencing 5 A.M. Sunday, 3rd, we drove him from his position. I was in the front line to start at them and went through to the last. Fought my Brigade until the final repulse and then took command of other troops as they came up.

If not before, I won promotion last Sunday and if it can be done I think I shall get it. Our N.C. troops behaved most nobly. [J. Dodson] Ramseur covered himself and [his] Brigade with glory. My Brigade behaved magnificently and got cut up terribly. Six out of ten field officers [were] hit. Two are dead, [C. C.] Cole and [Laban] Odell. Cols. [A. M.] Scales and [J. S.] McElroy, Lt. Col. [S. N.] Stowe and Maj. [M.] McLaughlin [were] wounded. Four out of the seven Generals of our Division were hit but none seriously. Hill, Heth, Pender, and McGowan. I was hit the next day while standing behind entrenchments in a miserable skirmish, but it is only a very slight bruise by a spent ball which killed a fine young officer standing in front of me. It is on the right arm near the shoulder.

We took over 6,000 prisoners and between 15 and 20 pieces [of] cannon and lots of small arms. I will write you more of the fight in my next [letter] for I am very tired and sleepy now. We only got to camp this afternoon. Gen. Hill is in command of the Corps and I of [James] Archer's, [Samuel] McGowan's, [James] Lane's and my own Brigades. This last is temporary. Stuart commanded the Corps in the Sunday fight, Gen. Hill being unable to ride horseback and right noble did Stuart do. He is now going after [Major General George] Stoneman's cavalry.

We may have some rest now, at least for a week or so. We had about 30,000 in the fight, and they not less than 65,000. This is Chancellorsville. Near Fredericksburg Sunday afternoon Gen. Lee had about 22,000 and [Major General John] Sedgwick about 30,000. You will have to read closely to understand for our Army had three or four fights, all of which were completely and wholly successful.

Our papers in Richmond made themselves disgustingly ridiculous. Honey, thank our Gracious Father for his great protection to me. My love to you all. I will write again tomorrow or next day. I saw Ham and Willie today. God bless you my dear.

Your loving Husband

❧

Camp Gregg, Va., May 9th, 1863

My dearest Wife

I had promised myself to write you a long letter tonight but fear I shall not as my shoulder is a little stiff. I have been a little under the weather yesterday and today, but feel better tonight since the medicine I took operated. . . .

I hear that Gen'l Jackson is thought to be in a very serious condition. He has pneumonia contracted by wrapping himself in wet towels after he was wounded. He will be a great loss to the country and it is devoutly to be hoped that he may be spared to the country. Some think in his absence Stuart will be made Lt. General, but I hope not. Rhodes it is said has been promoted. The Yankee loss is much greater than I expected. We will probably get from the battlefields at [least] 25,000 muskets, 10,000 of which probably belonged to our men that were killed, wounded and straggled.

I got today 1 doz. white hankerchiefs brought from Baltimore. . . . I . . . was very sorry to hear that Pamela was sick. I hope she is better. I am so glad that your health is much improved. Honey, excuse this short letter. God bless you my dear wife. . . . My love to all.

Your loving Husband

❧

My dear Wife

Your letter of the 10th came today, and I was much gratified to hear that you continue so well and that Pamela has completely recovered. Honey, I do not laugh at you as much as you seem to think, and be assured that your appearance would have no influence in preventing me from writing for you [to come]. I am not accustomed to tease my wife in that condition.... You should come on the first time it is safe. I was very much tempted to write for you as soon as I got back here, but the great uncertainty of our movements prevented.

My health darling is very excellent, and I take as good care of myself as possible. Rest assured that I value my life too highly to throw it away uselessly. Honey it looks little probable that I should outlive you to see your wishes carried out, but if such should be the case, no one could be mentioned who I should prefer to take charge of our children, but you know Pamela may be expected to marry some of these days, and some one else's wishes would have to be consulted. Tell Pamela that I am surprised that she should prove so false to poor browbeaten little Turner. That now she has placed her affections upon Dorsey and deserted Turner, I do not know what the dear ... will do, for you never thought as much of him as of Dorsey. Poor little fellow, all seem to be deserting him.... I love him as dearly as a father ever did his child, not that I do not love Dorsey as I should for I think a great deal of him, and always think of them together and not Turner alone as you sometimes seem to think.

The Yankee papers are beginning to confess a great defeat, and some of them say it will be some long time before they can try it over. Do not believe all you see about the last words of Jackson, for some designing person is trying to injure Gen. Hill by saying that he frequently said that he wanted Ewell to have his Corps. After it became apparent that he would die, he was delirious most if not all of the time. It is strange what a jealousy exists towards A. P. Hill and this Division, and for what cause I cannot see, unless it is because he and it have been so successful. I hope to stick to him for he sticks to me.

The next move will probably be here and on Richmond, from the White House simultaneously. The White House is on the Pamunkey just above its entrance in the bay that runs up by Yorktown.

I have sent for my box and will probably get it Saturday. . . .
[Letter trails off incompletely]

❧

Camp Gregg, Va., May 18th, 1863

My dear Wife
The box has finally been received and everything is so nice.
My clothes fit beautifully. Without exaggeration the cake was the
best I ever ate. Everyone who tasted it made the same remark.
And tell Sis I am a thousand times obliged for the cravat. The
buff cloth came the day after the box. I sent Ham some of the
butter.

We have nothing in the world new, but all feel that something
is brewing and that Gen. Lee is not going to wait all the time for
them to come to him. They have finally admitted that they were
terribly whipped, and if the truth was known I have no doubt
that it was worse than we thought.

Honey, do as you please with your time this summer and enjoy
yourself. You may go anywhere you please but to Nick Williams
and that I cannot consent to. Honey, you must excuse this short
note. I will make up for it tonight or tomorrow morning. My
love to all and may God bless you and protect us.

Your loving Husband

❧

Camp Gregg, Va., May 23rd, '63

My dearest Wife
Your sweet letter of the 20th came today much to my great
gratification. I wish my letters could go to you as quickly as yours
come to me. The longer we stay here the more I wish I had sent
for you, but as Turner and Dorsey were both so sick it would have
given you great uneasiness, if you had come with me. I am so
glad that they are both better and hope soon to hear that they
are both well.

Honey, I like your summer. I shall send tomorrow to David
$150 to help defray your expenses at the springs [near Raleigh].
Do try to get Pamela to go with you. She would enjoy it and you
both would be better pleased. But if she does go, make her understand that the thousand and one human beings in Confederate

uniforms she will meet there are skulkers from duty. Most of them who will be getting sympathy upon the pretext of wounds will be well enough to be with their commands. I judge by what it was last year. Go to Edgecombe and from there to the springs, but under whose care are you going?

[Brigadier General Junius] Daniel and his Brigade came up a few days ago and [A. H.] Colquitt's Brigade went from here to N.C. We got a large Brigade for a small force. Everything looks quiet this way. Stuart has 12,000 cavalry now and it is said is up to some big raid. It is to be wagered that he will do better than Stoneman.

Honey, I thought I told you about my arm. I certainly intended doing so. It is getting on very well, but last Sunday it was very painful. It has turned out to be a little deeper than it appeared at first but still it is but trifling.

I should like very much to help you eat some of your strawberries, but I do not expect any such delicacies this season. You have no idea how anxious I am to go home and shall take any reasonable pretext to take a little furlough. I find but few so conscientious about leaving as myself.

It is rumored that Stuart has tendered his resignation because they will not give him this Corps, but I cannot think him so foolish. I heard this evening that Gen. Hill had gotten it. The same state of affairs as you relate about deserters exists in [a] great many places in western N.C. We have lost [a] great many men by desertion since the fight, most from N.C. Regts. Vance has published a Proclamation which will have a good effect. Gen. Hays' sword was presented me and I sent it to Vance to be kept at Raleigh with a very patriotic letter.[71] That is the way to make glory tell. Did you see a little notice in the *Journal* of your husband, but I am getting to care very little for newspaper compliments; I feel that they [are] worth but little compared to the good opinion of my superiors.

We have Communion tomorrow. Mr. Williams is a nice man and good chaplain. I wrote a few days ago to brother Robert to get you some N.C. money and about Anna's going back to Salem and think he cannot withstand my appeals in her favor.

Take Pamela to Edgecombe and Kittrells[72] by all means. God

71. Brigadier General William Hays, commander of the Second Brigade of French's Third Division in Couch's II Corps, was captured by Company E of Alfred M. Scales's Thirteenth North Carolina Regiment during Pender's attack on the morning of May 3. *O.R.* 25, pt. 1, 891, 935, 936.
72. A town about 40 miles north of Raleigh.

bless you my dearest wife and kiss the dear boys. I was joking about loving Dorsey best. Love to all. If you find you will want more money than I have sent, please call on David for it.

Your loving Husband

∾❧౿

Camp Gregg, Va., May 27th, 1863

My dearest Wife

I feel very sad this evening for I have been refused a leave to go to Richmond and have written a telegram to send to [Sergeant] Montgomery to send you. Gen. Lee says from information he has received, it would be preferable for me to go to Richmond some other time, as my command may be needed very soon. I judge that he anticipates another fight. The damper to my hopes of seeing you is very grievous to bear, but I know it will be more so to you. I almost hope you may have left home before you get my dispatch not to come. I have not much doubt but that a fight is on hand. If it is to come all right. [Major General J. B.] Hood and [Major General George] Pickett are both within striking distance and also Pettigrew's Brigade, making us 10 or 15,000 stronger than before. I have no idea that if Hooker should cross again, that his men will fight as well even as they did at Chancellorsville which was bad enough. They had more than 3 to 1.

Honey I am anxious that you should go to Kittrells and will write to secure you a room. I would like to know who will be with you. Tell David I say he must take Mary and go with you unless you have plenty of good company already.

You wanted to know about the silk shirt; it fits very well indeed, and answers finely.

You are suffering only what is too common, for reports come to us from many parts of the state of the disgraceful conduct of deserters. Such men as Judge Pearson, Nick Williams, etc. are to blame. You seem to maintain your good opinion of Mr. Joe Williams under all circumstances. You will yet come to the conclusion that he really is without principle. No man could be as deficient of patriotism as he is, and be honest.

Capt. Kirkland has sent in his resignation on account of his suffering which renders him unfit for service. If I knew for certain that Henry Robinson was in Richmond I would get him, but not knowing it, expect to offer it to Lt. Rosborough of the 6th

N.C. I am glad that Ham will not be thrown out by the new Law about Commissions.

Honey, I do not expect you will get this so I will close and write again soon. Our mailman has been robbing the mail and throwing the letters away.

I sincerely hope the children are well. My own dear, try to bear up under all disappointments. God bless you. My love to all.

Your loving Husband

᷅ঞৣ

In the weeks following "Stonewall" Jackson's death on May 10th, General Lee formulated plans for reorganizing his army. In place of the two corps previously commanded by Jackson and Longstreet, Lee recommended to Davis that the army be divided into three corps under Lieutenant Generals Longstreet, Ewell, and A. P. Hill. For A. P. Hill's successor to head the famed Light Division [now consisting of the brigades of Lane, McGowan, Scales, and Thomas], Lee chose twenty-nine-year-old William Dorsey Pender, who thereby became the youngest Major General in the Army of Northern Virginia.

In recommending Pender for promotion, Lee wrote the President: "Pender is an excellent officer, attentive, industrious and brave; has been conspicuous in every battle, and I believe wounded in almost all of them."[73] Prior to Chancellorsville Lee had considered transferring Pender to bolster the cavalry about which he was concerned. However, he was deterred by the difficulty in obtaining an officer to replace him as an infantry brigadier.[74]

On May 30th the announcement in Lee's Special Orders No. 146 of Pender's appointment to command the Light Division in A. P. Hill's Third Corps, was greeted enthusiastically throughout the army. A. P. Hill had urged the selection of Pender on the grounds that he "has the best drilled and disciplined Brigade in the Division, and more than all, possesses the unbounded confidence of the Division."[75] A surgeon in the Light Division characterized Pender as "a very superior little man though a strict disciplinarian. . . . He was as brave as a lion and seemed to love

73. Douglas S. Freeman, *Lee's Dispatches to Jefferson Davis, 1862-1865* (New York: G. P. Putnam's Sons, 1915), p. 93.
74. Lee to Davis, April 27, 1863.
75. A. P. Hill to R. E. Lee, May 24, 1863.

danger."[76] *Lt. Col. W. G. Lewis of the Forty-third North Carolina wrote that "It was reported and generally believed throughout the Army of Northern Virginia that General Lee had said that General Pender was the only officer in the army that could completely fill the place of 'Stonewall' Jackson."*[77]

Fanny and the boys fortuitously were visiting Pender at the time of his long-cherished promotion. But this last visit was cut short as General Lee prepared to start the army northward to invade Pennsylvania. After Fanny and his two sons left, Pender wrote a letter from Hamilton's Crossing near Fredericksburg.

∽✲✐

Hamilton's Crossing, Va., June 7th, 1863

My dear Wife

I should have written you before but we were ordered here Friday night and I was so sleepy and tired yesterday that I could not write. The enemy crossed here Friday afternoon so you see you did not get off much too soon this time. I have no idea that we shall have any fight for I do not believe the enemy have any force to speak of, at least they do not show it. We may have a little skirmishing.

Mrs. Hill did not go until yesterday and I know you are too good a wife to have given me as much anxiety and trouble as she gave the General.

We have been in line of battle since night before last. I have no idea what Hooker is up to, but suppose he is holding us here with a small force when he moves the larger part to meet Gen. Lee up above.

I find that the horse David gave me will be of no use for one hard ride uses him up and he is always sick. David wrote at first to sell him if he would not suit and the other day he said send him home if he broke down, so he could be fattened up. He will sell for as much here as at home and then it would cost $50 to get him there besides the trouble. What shall I do?

The campaign has commenced at last and now we may expect sharp work. I have no fears but that we shall whip Hooker, but then general straggling and deserters will worry us a great deal.

I hope you reached Tarboro safely and in good spirits. Keep

76. Spencer Glasgow Welch, *A Confederate Surgeon's Letters to His Wife* (New York: Neale Publishing Company, 1911), pp. 72-73.
77. Letter of W. G. Lewis to D. Gilliam, October 21, 1893.

cheerful, Darling, and trust in God for kind protection to your husband.

Mr. Williams got back Friday and brought you a basket of cherries. You must go to Shocco[78] if you can get a room. I wrote to Pamela to beg her to go with you. I am trying to [get] Ham as Assistant Commissary in my Division. Early's commissary and [Brigadier General R. F.] Hoke's are both trying to do the same, so between us he will certainly be retained.

I will write as often as I can. Give my love to all and tell Sister Mary when you see her I will write and that she shall have the paper.

God bless you my dear wife.

Your loving Husband

Direct your letters to A. P. Hill's Corps, Richmond and they will be forwarded.

~✿~

Hamilton's Crossing, Va., June 9th, 1863

My dearest Wife

Your note from Richmond and letter from Tarboro have both reached me. My dear wife you need not have made so many excuses for yourself for you did nothing that required it. You hated to leave and thought I was hurrying you off and very naturally expressed yourself, but I knew that in your heart you did not blame me for doing what you knew I thought was best. You were not out of the way much too soon, although I do not believe we shall have any fight at this point, we expect however at any moment to move up the river to Longstreet's assistance.

My dear, you do not seem to like Ransom. Do you not think you may in a measure do him injustice? He has some good qualities I know.

Your description of [Gabriel] Rains is very characteristic of him. What a blessing it was that so few of those old fellows came over from the old service. They would all have claimed high positions and been able to do nothing to help the cause.

Darling, if you had stayed much longer I fear you would have gotten [so] weak that you could not get home. It seems to be fated that I am always to cause you to get worse if sick and sick if well. I shall feel easy about you when I hear that you and the

78. Shocco Springs, a resort village about 45 miles northeast of Raleigh.

children are at Shocco. Let me beg you not to get any economical notion in your head and imagine you must go home. If you enjoy yourself, and you ought to, stay until you get tired or your stock of money gives out and then if you want more send to David.

In a *New York Herald* of the 5th, Bennett says there was never such a meeting on the continent as the Peace Convention of the 3rd. If we are to believe him we may hope for something good to come of it. If Vicksburg holds out, and there is no reason why it should not, public sentiment in the North must and will do us good.

As the mail is about to close, I must. Be assured, Darling, that I was not mad nor did I think that you did not love me as you should, for I know it was that very love that made you dislike so much to leave. Give my love to them all at home. I shall write to Shocco as my letters will meet you there by the 16th. Good bye and God bless you.

Your loving Husband

❧

Hamilton's Crossing, Va., June 10th, 1863

My dear Wife

I wrote you yesterday but had to close abruptly and I know my letter was very unsatisfactory. We have been lying here in the trenches since daylight Friday morning and to all appearances are as far from a fight as ever. They have but few men on this side and everything indicates that they are merely holding us here while Hooker gets after Gen. Lee above. I think for once we will be out of the fight, for unless we start soon they must meet up about Culpeper before we get there.

Would you believe it, John Conally called on me ... to ask a favor. To get him out of his Brigade, and when I told him it could not be done he said Gen. Lee must do it and talked about letting Zeb Vance know of it, etc. In fact, he made himself very ridiculous. He is a most conceited fellow and talked as if he thought that if we were not promoted soon he would be most outrageously treated and said that if any Junior Colonel was promoted over him he would resign, etc. It was a source of great pleasure to me to have him ask a favor of me. He left with the determination to try to get his Brigade in my Division in which I will try to help him and then try to teach him his place.

... I fear my promotion has caused [Brigadier General J. J.]

Archer to be cool towards me. His manner the last time we met was not as cordial as heretofore, and he seemed very much embittered and rather down on Gen. Hill and I suppose because I will not join him in the latter he will grow cool towards me. I am sorry for it but know I have done nothing to forefeit his good opinion or will.

I wrote to sister Mary today and told her to keep William at school and send the bills to me.

I think things look very well for us out West, but the worst is not over I fear, but still I do not fear the worst. Each side is evidently reenforcing as heavily as possible and there will undoubtedly be a great battle in the rear of Vicksburg. We have this advantage that their troops will mostly be demoralized by the regulars at Vicksburg.

In Gen. Lee's army we shall whip [Hooker], I feel confident. If Gen. Lee should not be completely victorious at the first brush, recollect that more than a third of his army will probably be absent at the time. My love to all. God bless you my dearest and best wife. I hope you soon get over your fatigue.

Your loving Husband

ฉะ

Hamilton's Crossing, June 12th, 1863

My dear Wife

I am again disappointed in not getting a letter from you by today's mail. I have not heard from you since the first note you wrote after getting to Tarboro. I hope you are not sick, but will have reached Shocco by the time this gets there. Mrs. Englehard writes the Major that she had taken a very nice room for you, with a fireplace. She had to engage it from the 8th which I am glad she did. I can only see one objection to it so far as you are concerned, and that is its proximity to Mrs. Rains and family. I hope you will find it pleasant enough to tempt you to stay all the summer, for then you will not be subject to your father's ravings and unpleasant forebodings. Do not let the expense prevent you from staying, for now we have commenced the campaign my expenses will not be as much as they were during the winter, and I can well afford to board you two or three months in two years. Once [and] for all, if you find it more pleasant than Good Spring, stay the season out and call upon David for money when you want it. I shall either not draw my pay or send David drafts on Richmond.

I fear I did Mrs. Englehard injustice in my last, for I have no doubt but that she is a very kind hearted lady, but her husband acts the fool when he writes her to have a good time with the young men. I want my wife to enjoy herself as much as anyone, but I know she will do it as a sensible young married woman ought to do.

We are occupying the same position we took last Saturday morning. The only change I can see is some heavy earthworks thrown up by the Enemy on this bank of the river, which looks to me as if they did not intend to fight here, but hold us here to watch them, while Hooker operates above. I am getting tired of it and shall be glad to move up. We are in a very unsettled state, neither one thing nor the other. I have no doubt we have more troops in the vicinity of Fredericksburg than they, which we cannot afford. The Cavalry affair in Culpeper [i.e. Brandy Station] was a sad one and our loss was very serious. Stuart lost some of his best officers.

Poor Sol Williams and just married. I pity his desolate young widow. A strong argument against marrying while the war last[s]. It would be much better if she were Miss Pagonne instead of Mrs. Williams. I suppose it is all right that Stuart should get all the blame, for when anything handsome is done he gets all the credit. A bad rule either way. He however retrieved the surprise by whipping them in the end.[79]

Honey, by some means I kept your Bible, did you get mine? If you want my trunk write to Montgomery and direct him to send it to you. You will find that it holds about as much as the one you have and will be much more convenient. If we get North I shall get me one, and if we do not I shall not send it. I would prefer your having it. It has no key, the lock being broken, but it locks by the hasp and to unlock it put your finger on the top of the hasp, push down toward the floor and pull it out at the bottom. Write to Mr. A. D. Montgomery, Box 1453, Richmond.

I hope you made it all right with brother Robert about sending Anna to school. Did they not make a big fuss about your staying so short a time in Edgecombe?

I tease Mr. Williams a good deal about wanting to go home to spend his wedding anniversary with his wife, giving him to under-

79. Pender refers here to the cavalry engagement at Brandy Station on June 9, 1863, in which Pleasanton surprised Stuart.

stand that no such excuse will do. I had a funny dream the other night. I thought I had been married to a young lady without ever seeing or hearing of her before. I was very bashful and had a hard time to keep jealousy from arising in the first of my two wives. It was a hard time I had in my experience of two wives, showing that one is better. She was nothing like as pretty as you. This was a very prominent part of the dream. It was a very strange dream for I had had no such thought beforehand. The next night I dreamed that Mr. Williams had got his leave and snapped his fingers in my face. I see occasionally late Northern papers and they are all full of the dissension in the North and complain—some of them—about the apathy in carrying out their Conscript Law.

Mrs. Englehard writes that she [never] saw so many children as at Shocco. I feel convinced that Turner will be the brightest of his age there. I suppose you of course let them go barefooted during the warm weather. May you have good weather for yourself as much as possible under the circumstances. Present my compliments to Mrs. Englehard and thank her for me for her kindness about the room. God bless you my ever dearest wife. Kiss the boys.

Your loving Husband

ᘛ⃰ᘚ

Hamilton's Crossing, June 15th, 1863

My dear Wife

Tomorrow morning we start as I suppose for Penna., the enemy having left the vicinity of Frederick[sburg] last night apparently in great haste and fright. We march for Culpeper direct, going by our last glorious battle field of Chancellorsville. I will write you from Culpeper where we shall be Thursday evening if nothing interferes with our march. All have left here but my Division. I went over to Falmouth this afternoon to see the mother of Col. Green who was with me at Cold Harbor and who was killed there. They have been amongst the Yankees all the winter. I really feel sad in leaving this part of the country altho' my anticipations are of the most sanguine. Thus far Gen. Lee's plans have worked admirably, so says Gen. Hill who I suppose knows them. I do not, but can see far enough to look into Md. May God in his goodness be more gracious than in our last trial. We certainly may be allowed to hope as our mission is one of peace altho' through blood. The enemy seem to think we have 90,000 men which will scare them so badly that they will be half whipped before they commence the fight. I do not anticipate any fight this side of the Potomac.

Honey, you must thank Mrs. Englehard for me for her kindness in getting you a room. Try and enjoy your stay there and make it last as long as pleasant. I shall feel much better satisfied if I know you are enjoying yourself. Do not think of the expense for mine will be much reduced now. Honey, be as cheerful as possible, hoping for the best. Continue to pray earnestly for me and let us have faith in our Merciful Father's kindness. I suppose you will hear from our advance before you get this, but if not I will tell you that Gen. Ewell's Corps was within 20 miles of Winchester last Friday, and probably by this time is ready to cross the Potomac. Gen. Lee has gotten fully one week ahead of Hooker, who has been slumbering here in front of one third of our force. If things turn out well in the west we may expect good results by Fall.

Darling, rest in the confidence of undying love for my dearest and best "little wife" in the world. I hope you found Pamela with the children and ready to stay with you at Shocco. I will try to send you some nice things by the first chance. God bless you and those dear to us. Write me as often as you feel like it. As soon as I see Gen. Lee I will ask him to let me have my letters addressed to his care which will insure my getting them more expeditiously. My love to all.

Your loving Husband

~☙~

Stephensburg, Va., June 17th, 1863

My dear Wife

According to promise I write you but one day earlier than I expected. This place is about six miles from Culpeper, so we go beyond tomorrow. We have a grand race on hand between Lee and Hooker. We have the inside track, Hooker going by Washington and we by Winchester. Gen. [J. A.] Early stormed the latter place the 15th instant and took all [Major General R. H.] Milroy's cannon. They are evidently much scared about Washington, but I think Gen. Lee is making for the nearest point of Penn. and Ewell's Corps is undoubtedly across the Potomac by this time.

Everything this far has worked admirably and if the campaign goes on as it has commenced it will be a telling one. Two deserters came and delivered themselves up today and they say that the estimate of numbers in Hooker's army does not come over 90,000, which if true makes him but little more than we have. They told me that 37 two years Regts. from N.Y. had gone out besides the nine months men from the state. A proportional number go out from other states.

I feel in much [better] spirits than when I started but not so well in point of rest. I have slept but little for two nights and I feel very sleepy. Responsibility is a load that is anything but pleasant. I bring up the rear of the Army and have been somewhat expecting a raid on my rear but now I feel secure as there is no doubt but Hooker is going for Washington in too much hurry to think of me.

Honey, I feel that I ought to write you a long letter for it may be some time before you get another one from me. I can send you one from Winchester five or six days hence. I am very anxious to hear from you as your last told me that you were in bed, but as you announced your intention of leaving in a few days thereafter for the [Shocco] Springs I have felt easy about you.

Honey, I know you will take this miserable letter for what it is intended to be and not for what it really is. May we meet again is my constant prayer. I do not think we shall have much severe fighting this summer. We will get North for a few months but we shall have to come back by September or Oct. for their force will be increasing while ours will be decreasing, but by that time we shall probably give them such a taste of war that they may be willing to say quit. My love to all. Kiss the boys. God bless you my dearest wife.

Your loving Husband

June 21st, 1863

My dear Wife

Since I wrote you I have had some hard marching and some grumbling, but the boys are now in fine plight and spirits. We shall get to Berryville tomorrow where Gen. Lee is. We have all sorts of rumors but all that I feel any surety of being true is that Early captured 4700 prisoners, 300 wagons, 29 cannon, small arms, ammunition, animals, etc. Rodes is just across the

Potomac and Early and [Edward] Johnson are ready to go to him at any moment. [Brigadier General Micah] Jenkins' cavalry has been to Chambersburg, Penna. Our cavalry are fighting [a] good deal on the east side of the mountain and getting the best of it.

Everything thus far has worked admirably. I would not be surprised if we went into Penna. so that we shall have no communication with you rebels, so if you do not hear from me do not be uneasy. You send about one letter in every 10 or 15 days to me addressed to the care of Gen. S. Cooper, A[djutant] and I[nspector] Genl., Richmond. and he may forward it for me. I will try to write occasionally if it comes to that and get Gen'l Lee to send it for me.

Darling, however much I want to write you, I find my thoughts so distracted by all I have to think of, and the fatigue of body together, render it almost impossible for me to write intelligibly. I am in fine health, living well and have high hopes of the future. I often think of you at Shocco and hope you are comfortably situated and well pleased with it. I feel that you are having a nice holiday and I feel much easier about you.

Tell Mrs. Englehard that the Major is enjoying himself finely, and that she need not fear his being led off by the young ladies, that I set him a good example, hardly ever noticing them; that he will not have the face to do anything to make her jealous.

I will write you from Berryville probably tomorrow night. We hear nothing from our rear. You have no idea how much out of the world this Valley seems, and although one of the finest countrys I ever saw, I do not like it. My love to all at home and may God ever bless and protect my dear little wife. Keep in good spirits, honey, and hope that this summer's work will tend to shorten the war.

Your loving Husband

৵৶৵

Camp near Berryville, Va., June 23rd, 1863

My dear Wife

I was delighted last night by again hearing from you. Your letter from Goldsboro and one of the 14th from Shocco and also one from Pamela came. I do not wonder that you did not like your quarters at Shocco, and think very likely you will be much better satisfied at home [in Salem]. I want you to go where you like best.

I wrote you a few days since that you might not be able to hear from me this summer, which Gen. Lee says was wrong, so I shall be able to communicate with you. The General seemed yesterday in fine spirits, but said he was going to shoot us if we did not keep our men from straggling. They marched finely coming up here. I told him if he gave us authority to shoot those under us he might take the same privilege with us.

I think our prospects here are very fine. Gen. Lee has completely outgeneraled Hooker thus far and then our numbers are more equal than they have been. It is stated on all sides that Hooker has a small army and that very much demoralized. The General says he wants to meet him as soon as possible and crush him and then if Vicksburg and Port Hudson do their part, our prospects for peace are very fine.

Gen. Ewell's Corps is in Md. and ours has started. I will move this evening or tomorrow morning, but will be three days before crossing. Our army is in splendid condition and everyone seems hopeful and cheerful. Cheer up my dear little girl and hope for good things ahead. Ewell captured 31 cannon and 4700 prisoners, but still Milroy claims a complete victory figuring it out that he lost only 300 men and no cannon or arms.

Col. Scales has been appointed Brigadier [in charge of Pender's former brigade]. I am anxiously looking for him every day for his presence is much needed. Col. [W. J.] Hoke [Thirty-ninth N.C.] is the greatest old granny and had the impudence this morning to ask me to recommend him for promotion which I did not promise to do, nor shall I.

We are living here on fine mutton, milk, butter, etc. I have two fine [wagon] trains at my headquarters, and you may rest assured that they will have to haul a goodly quantity of dry goods if we get a chance which I think we shall. I want to fit you out nicely by fall if not before.

... What do you think of Mrs. Englehard? I am getting so that I cannot bear Maj. Englehard, he is so presumptuous but I will take some good opportunity to set him down, which will, I think, improve him. I gave Dr. Holt a raking last night and now one for the A.A.G. will I think set things right for awhile. Capt. Hunt is my best man. Capt. Kirkland has been reappointed ... as I want a staff officer immediately.

Write to me about twice a week, honey, and I will probably hear from you occasionally. The children no doubt enjoyed themselves very much going down to meet you and repaid all the trouble. I will probably write you again before I cross the Potomac. Mr. Williams sends his regards.

My love to all and my own darling may God bless you and all that are dear to us.

Your loving Husband

∾⚜∽

Shepherdstown, [Va.], June 24th, 1863

My dearest Wife

Tomorrow I do what I know will cause you grief, and that is to cross the Potomac. The advance of our column is at Chambersburg, Penna. tonight. May the Lord prosper this expedition and bring an early peace out of it. I feel that we are taking a very important step, but see no reason why we should not be successful. We have a large Army that is in splendid condition and spirit and the best Generals of the South. Our troops are sending [a] good deal of stock out of Penna. and Gen. Lee has issued [an] order which altho' [it] prevents plundering, at the same [time] makes arrangements for the bountiful supplying of our people.

The inhabitants of this part of the country are very enthusiastic in our favor. We hear all sorts of reports of rebellions in Baltimore, etc. but how true they are of course [we] cannot know. One thing is certain, however, and that is that the General commanding the Federals is much scared and asking for reinforcements. No one seems to know where Hooker is, only [that] he is between us and Washington. I hope the conflict will soon come off, for I feel that the first battle is to settle the campaign, at least until they are able to get forces from the West. I was sorry to hear tonight that Burnside had taken Knoxville, Tenn., but I hope if he has not left—which I hear also—that he soon will.

Hope and pray for the best. This is a momentous time but at the same time we are in better condition to meet it than we have ever been.

We will get many a horse before we come back. We have the authority and everyone seems determined to have all mounts and transportation well fixed up. I have written very regularly up to this time but of course after this my letters will be exceedingly irregular. I have been very handsomely entertained today by a fine family.

Darling, rest in a certainty of my great love for you and try to be as cheerful as possible at our distant separation. My love to all and now my own darling may God in his infinite mercy watch over us.

Your loving Husband

࿇

On Sunday, June 28, the day that General Lee decided to concentrate his army east of Chambersburg in the direction of Gettysburg, Pender penned his final letter to Fanny.

࿇

Fayetteville, Penn., June 28th, 1863

My dearest Wife

Our mail came in today and the only thing I heard from you was that four letters had reached Shocco the day after you left. We are resting today after marching 157 miles since leaving Fredericksburg twelve days ago yesterday. If I had any surety that you would get this in a reasonable time, I should have [a] good deal to tell you.

Until we crossed the Md. line our men behaved as well as troops could, but here it will be hard to restrain them, for they have an idea that they are to indulge in unlicensed plunder. They have done nothing like the Yankees do in our country. They take poultry and hogs but in most cases pay our money for it. We take everything we want for government use. The people are frightened to death and will do anything we intimate to them. The rascals have been expecting us and have run off most of their stock and goods. I bought a few articles for you yesterday and will get you a nice lot before we leave. We pay about 200 percent.

I am tired of invasions for altho' they have made us suffer all that people can suffer, I cannot get my resentment to that point to make me feel indifferent to what you see here. But for the demoralizing effect plundering would have on our troops, they would feel war in all its horrors. I never saw people so badly scared. We have only to wish for a thing and it is done. I have made up my mind to enjoy no hospitality or kindness from any of them.

Everything seems to be going on finely. We might get to Phila. without a fight, I believe, if we should choose to go. Gen. Lee intimates to no one what he is up to, and we can only surmise. I hope we may be in Harrisburg in three days. What a fine commentary upon their 90 days crushing out [i.e., Lincoln's original call for 90-day volunteers to crush the Confederacy], if we should march to the Capital of one of their largest states without a blow. It seems to be the impression that Hooker will not leave Washington, but [will] leave the states to take care of themselves.[80]

We are in Adams Co., having marched through Franklin. If we do not succeed in accomplishing a great deal all of us will be surprised. Our men seem to be in the spirit and feel confident. They laugh at the idea of meeting the militia. This is a most magnificent country to look at, but the most miserable people. I have yet to see a nice looking lady. They are coarse and dirty, and the number of dirty looking children is perfectly astonishing. A great many of the women go barefooted and but a small fraction wear stockings. I hope we may never have such people. ... Nearly all of them seem to be tenants and at first I thought all the better people must have left. And such barns I never dreamt of. Their dwelling houses are large and comfortable, looking from the outside—have not been inside—but such coarse louts that live in them. I really did not believe that there was so much difference between our ladies and their females. I have seen no ladies. We passed through Hagerstown ... but saw little Southern feeling displayed. The fact is the people in N.W. Md. are as much of the Dutch Yankee as these, and I do not want them.

I hope you reached home safely and feel satisfied with me, and see that this time at least, you did not leave camp much too soon.

I never saw troops march as ours do; they will go 15 or 20 miles a day without leaving a straggler and hoop and yell on all occasions. Confidence and good spirits seem to possess everyone. I wish we could meet Hooker and have the matter settled at once. We got the Richmond papers of the 24th today and they bring us good news from Vicksburg. This campaign will do one of two things: viz—to cause a speedy peace or a more tremendous war than we have had, the former may God grant.

Joe enters into the invasion with much gusto and is quite active in looking up hidden property. In fact the negroes seem to have more feeling in the matter than the white men and have come to the conclusion that they will [im]press horses, etc., etc. to

80. On June 28, 1863, Lincoln appointed Major General George G. Meade to supersede Major General Joseph Hooker as commander of the Army of the Potomac.

any amount. Columbus is laying in a stock for his sweetheart and sisters. Gen. Hill thus far has managed the march of his Corps and I think will give as much satisfaction as Lt. Gen'l as he did [as] Maj. Gen'l.

My love to all and keep my folks in Edgecombe posted as to my well being. Write to me occasionally through S. Cooper, A. and I. Gen'l., Richmond.

Now darling, may our Good Father protect us and preserve us to each other to a good old age. Tell Turner I have a pretty pair of low patent leather shoes with heels for him.

Your loving Husband

AFTERWORD

AFTERWORD

᷈᷈ᴥ᷈

Three days after Pender wrote his last letter to Fanny he led
his division in the fierce assault which swept General Abener
Doubleday's bluecoats from their strong position west of Gettysburg through the town to the heights beyond. The next day, July
2, Lee planned for Longstreet's two divisions on the right to as-
sail the Federal flank while A. P. Hill threatened the center and
joined in the attack if the opportunity afforded. For this offensive Hill placed R. H. Anderson's division next to Longstreet's
troops while Pender's veterans anchored the left of Lee's line
along Seminary Ridge.

Late in the afternoon Longstreet unleashed Hood and McLaws
who were joined about dusk by Anderson's brigades which pene-
trated Meade's center. During his furious engagement Pender
rode to the left of his line with Major Joseph B. Englehard, his
divisional chief of staff. Meeting Pender's friend, Lieutenant
Colonel William G. Lewis of the Forty-third North Carolina, the
General suggested that they sit on a large granite boulder and
chat while awaiting orders.

According to Lewis the trio "were having a pleasant conversation when all of a sudden the enemy opened fire with 350
pieces of artillery . . . directly on our line on Seminary Ridge.
Immediately on the opening of their artillery fire General Pender
turned to Major Englehard and remarked: 'Major, this indicates
an assault, and we will ride down our line.' It was said with
perfect coolness, though the air was full of exploding shells and
the shell and solid shot were knocking the granite boulders into

small rocks and scattering them over us. Before they reached the center of the Division General Pender received a wound in the thigh, caused by a ragged piece of shell about two inches square."[81]

Unable to mount his horse the next day, Pender made plans to return to Good Spring and recuperate. Although the wound was serious no fears were felt that it would prove mortal. In his report written "Near Gettysburg, July 4, 1863," Lee wrote: "Generals Pender and Trimble are wounded in the leg."[82] And as Pender undertook his journey accompanied only by an amulance driver, he inquired solicitously of Major D. T. Carraway, his Commissary, about the condition and comfort of his men and the quantity of supplies on hand.[83]

By the time Pender reached Staunton his wound was healing nicely and it seemed that his remarkable record of recoveries would continue. However, the first night in Staunton the large artery in his thigh began hemorrhaging. With his customary quick presence of mind he staunched the flow by improvising a tourniquet out of a towel twisted around his leg with a hairbrush.[84]

Alarmed lest the General bleed to death, a chaplain inquired about the state of his soul. Pender calmly replied in his soft, low voice: "Tell my wife that I do not fear to die. I can confidently resign my soul to God, trusting in the atonement of Jesus Christ. My only regret is to leave her and our two children. I have always tried to do my duty in every sphere in which Providence has placed me."[85]

In the meantime a surgeon, together with Pender's favorite brother David, arrived. The surgeon attempted to mend the artery but again it broke, whereupon the physician decided to amputate the leg. Pender survived the operation on July 18 but a few hours. However, his mind was clear to the end as he listened attentively to an aide's account of the Army's return to Virginia soil, and he expressed profound regret on learning of the death of General Johnston Pettigrew, a fellow North Carolinian whose

81. Letter of W. G. Lewis to D. Gilliam, October 21, 1893; *O.R.* 27, pt. 2, 658.
82. *O.R.* 27, pt. 2, 298.
83. Letter of J. T. Rosborough to W. D. Pender, Jr., September 5, 1904; D. T. Carraway MS, n.d., p. 5; Letter of James G. Field to D. Gilliam, n.d., p. 3; *O.R.* 27, pt. 2, 665; Montgomery, "Life and Character of Major-General W. D. Pender," pp. 20-22.
84. Rosborough.
85. S. T. Pender's account.

brigade he inherited after the battle of Seven Pines.[86]

General Pender's body was taken to his native Tarboro and laid to rest in the serene pine-sheltered churchyard of Calvary Parish. The inscription on his recumbent headstone reads, "Patriot by nature, soldier by training, Christian by faith." And a stained glass window in the church memorializes the General with the succinct quotation from St. Paul, whom Pender greatly admired, "I have fought a good fight—I have kept the faith."

Pender's loss to the Army of Northern Virginia was inestimable. Lee considered Pender the most promising young officer among his lieutenants,[87] and in his official report he paid tribute to him as one who "served with this Army from the beginning of the war, and took a distinguished part in all its engagements. Wounded on several occasions, he never left his command in action until he received the injury that resulted in his death. His promise and usefulness as an officer were only equaled by the purity and excellence of his private life."[88] In a letter that fall to Secretary of War John Seddon, Lee referred to "the noble Pender" whose services "the casualties of battle, alas, deprived us."[89]

A. P. Hill mourned the "irreparable loss" of his favorite subaltern whom he considered the best officer of his grade he had ever known. In his report on Gettysburg, Hill wrote feelingly: "On this day the Confederacy lost the invaluable services of Maj. Gen. W. D. Pender, wounded by a shell and since dead. No man fell during the bloody battle of Gettysburg more regretted than he, nor around whose youthful brow were clustered brighter rays of glory."[90]

The men in the ranks also missed Pender "with all our hearts"[91] and credibly gave wide currency to the rumor "that General Lee had said that General Pender was the only officer in his army that could completely fill the place of 'Stonewall' Jackson."[92] Although such a statement was alien to Lee's nature and undoubtedly apocryphal, there is impressive documented evidence that the commanding General definitely felt that Pender's mortal wound had deprived the Army of victory at Gettysburg.

86. Rosborough.

87. Letter from G. C. Wharton to James M. Norfleet, September 5, 1893.

88. *O.R.* 27, pt. 2, 325.

89. Lee to J. S. Seddon, September 9, 1863.

90. *O.R.* 27, pt. 2, 608.

91. J. F. J. Caldwell, *The History of a Brigade of South Carolinians Known First as "Gregg's" and Subsequently as "McGowan's Brigade"* (Philadelphia: King and Baird, 1866), p. 102.

92. Letter of W. G. Lewis to D. Gilliam, October 21, 1893.

General G. C. Wharton[93] recorded a conversation at General Lee's headquarters south of the Potomac shortly after the Army had retired from Gettysburg. When the discussion turned to the recent campaign, Lee remarked sadly, "I ought not to have fought the battle at Gettysburg, it was a mistake." Then after a pause he continued, "But the stakes were so great I was compelled to play, for had we succeeded, Harrisburg, Baltimore or Washington was in our hands." Then, according to Wharton, Lee concluded his analysis by stating emphatically: "And we would have succeeded had General Pender lived." Similar testimony by General Harry Heth and Major Joseph Englehard corroborate the fact that Lee viewed Pender as the decisive factor in the outcome at Gettysburg.[94]

When the General died Fanny and her two boys were at Good Spring awaiting his return to convalesce. Upon receiving the news, the pregnant twenty-three-year old widow closeted herself in her bedroom for three days during which her hair reputedly turned white. That fall she gave birth to a son whom she named Stephen Lee in honor of her husband's West Point classmate and dear personal friend. Pender had hoped to arrange a match for Pamela with Stephen Lee, but without the General's catalytic influence the romance withered. Instead, Pamela married Colonel William S. Mallory in 1867 and later settled down in Charlotte where she died in 1913.

Fanny proved to be the strong and resourceful woman Pender had told her she was. Refusing outside help she independently supported her boys by running a school and working as postmistress of Tarboro. Despite her success in making a new life, she could never bring herself to discuss her husband. Nor did she ever remarry, and when she died in 1922 at the age of eighty-two, she was buried beside her beloved General.

Turner, the eldest son and father of W. C. Pender who uncovered the General's correspondence, became General Passenger Agent for the Carolina and Northwestern Railway; Dorsey studied law at the University of North Carolina after which he practiced in Norfolk; and Stephen, whom his father never saw, entered the cotton business. Fanny thus fulfilled her husband's wish that the children be educated to take their places as useful servants in the new South.

93. Letter of G. C. Wharton to James M. Norfleet, September 5, 1893; D. T. Carraway MS, n.d., p. 5.
94. Wharton to Norfleet; C. G. Elliott MS, Letter to D. Gilliam, January 8, 1894; Southern Historical Society Papers, IV, 154; V, 38; VIII, 519.

APPENDIX

*

INDEX

APPENDIX

~❦~

The Family

Fanny—wife of General W. Dorsey Pender.

Turner—Pender's eldest son, born November 28, 1859.

Dorsey—Pender's second son, born May 28, 1861.

Pamela—Fanny's young, unmarried sister, born 1844.

Jake—Fanny's younger brother, born 1845.

Brother Robert—Pender's oldest brother, born 1820.

David—Pender's older brother, born 1831.

Mary—David Pender's wife.

Patience—Pender's older sister, born 1828.

Ham—Fanny's older brother, born 1836.

Mary—Ham's wife.

Frank—Fanny's older brother, born 1834, who served
with the Confederate Navy.

Helen—Frank's wife.

Willie—Fanny's older brother, born 1830.

INDEX

༺⚜༻

Ellis, Governor John W., 15, 18, 54
Elzey, Arnold, 198
Englehard, J. A., 191, 209, 210, 212, 220, 223, 227, 229, 245, 250, 251, 256, 262
Ewell, Richard S., 157, 241, 248, 251

F

First North Carolina Regiment, 19, 34
Fisher, Charles F., 50
Fray, Col., 167
Frayser's Farm. *See* Seven Days' Battles
Frederick, Md. encampment, 172-74 *passim*
Fredericksburg campaign, 189-96 *passim*
Freeman, D. S., vii, viii
Fremont, J. C., 157
French, S. G., 97
Fry, W. A., 192

G

Gaines' Mill. *See* Seven Days' Battles
Garnett, R. S., 40, 49
Garysburg, N.C., 15, 21-24 *passim*, 28
Gettysburg campaign, 242-60 *passim*
Glendale. *See* Seven Days' Battles
Good Spring, N.C., 24, 38n, 141, 245, 260
Gordon, George, 208
Gordonsville, Va. encampment, 163-68 *passim*
Gray, R. H., 210
Greenhow, Rose, arrival at City Point, Va., 153

H

Halleck, H. W., 170
Hampton, Wade, 113, 121, 126
Harper's Ferry, 37, 39, 175, 179, 183, 185, 187
Harris (Pender's manservant), 99, 109, 117, 121, 122, 126, 137, 138, 151, 164, 167, 173
Hays, William, 239
Heth, Harry, 220, 235, 262
Hill, Ambrose P., praises Pender after Manassas, 170; recommends Pender for promotion, 184; recommended for promotion to Lt. Gen., 191; hopes Pender will be promoted, 191; prefers charges against Pender, 211-12; many kindnesses to Pender, 220; threatens to burn Washington, 226; commands Pender's loyalty, 237; posthumous praise of Pender, 261; mentioned, viii, ix, 150, 154, 161, 162, 163, 175, 176,

178, 179, 204, 205, 208, 213, 221, 222, 229, 235, 239, 241, 243, 245, 247, 255, 256

J

Jackson, Thomas J. ("Stonewall"), secretiveness of, 164; quickness of, 165; enhances reputation at Second Manassas, 171; inquires about Pender, 221; Pender's solicitude for, after Chancellorsville, 236; mentioned, ix, 3, 114, 133, 138, 154, 157, 158, 161, 163, 167, 168, 173, 174, 177, 189, 191, 197, 202, 208, 221, 222, 234, 236, 237, 241, 242, 261. *See also* W. D. Pender
Jenkins, Micah, 250
Joe (Pender's servant boy), 108, 109, 117, 177, 186, 196, 234, 253
Johns, Bishop John, confirms Pender, 146
Johnson, Edward, 229, 250
Johnston, A. S., 133
Johnston, Joseph E., praises Pender's regiment, 100; mentioned, 39, 47, 51, 59, 96, 97, 114, 131, 134, 139
Joyner's Depot, N.C., 119, 122

K

Kearny, Philip, death of, at Chantilly, 171-72
Kirkland, S. S., 163, 176, 177, 180, 212, 215, 218, 223, 229, 240, 251
Kirkland, W. W., 103, 212, 224
Kittrells, N.C., 239-40

L

Lane, James H., 19, 234, 241
Leach, J. M., 103
Lee, Custis, 40, 41, 74, 112, 145
Lee, Robert E., tributes to Pender, 3, 161-62; reputation of, 74, 158, 173, 215; at Antietam, 175; keeps own counsel, 185; eager for battle at Fredericksburg, 191; illness of, 215; mentioned, 41, 74, 127, 158, 160, 162-64, 167-68, 172, 174, 179, 191, 195, 211-12, 221, 224, 226-28, 234, 236, 238, 240-42, 244-45, 247-53 *passim*, 256, 260
Lee, Stephen D., classmate of Pender's, 4; mentioned, 63, 77, 81, 88, 129, 132, 143, 153, 186, 190-93, 201, 209, 213, 229, 262. *See also* W. D. Pender
Lewis, William G., 19, 30, 195, 242, 156
Light Division, reputation of, 176, 178, 237; mentioned, viii, 163, 241

268

C/